Japan's Winning Margins

Japan's Winning Margins

Management, Training, and Education

JOHN LORRIMAN
Management Consultant

and

TAKASHI KENJO
Professor of Electronic Engineering

Oxford   New York   Tokyo
OXFORD UNIVERSITY PRESS

Oxford University Press, Walton Street, Oxford OX2 6DP
Oxford   New York
Athens   Auckland   Bangkok   Bombay
Calcutta   Cape Town   Dar es Salaam   Delhi
Florence   Hong Kong   Istanbul   Karachi
Kuala Lumpur   Madras   Madrid   Melbourne
Mexico City   Nairobi   Paris   Singapore
Taipei   Tokyo   Toronto
and associated companies in
Berlin   Ibadan

Oxford is a trade mark of Oxford University Press

Published in the United States
by Oxford University Press Inc., New York

A catalogue record for this book is available from the British Library

Library of Congress Cataloging in Publication Data
Lorriman, John.
Japan's winning margins : management, training, and education
John Lorriman and Takashi Kenjo.
Includes index.
1. Management–Japan.   2. Vocational education–Japan.
3. Occupational training–Japan.   4. Education–Japan.
I. Kenjo, Takashi.   II. Title.
HD70.J3L67   1994   658'.00952–dc20   93-37586
ISBN 0 19 856373 6

Typeset by Palimpsest Book Production Limited,
Polmont, Stirlingshire

Printed in Great Britain by Biddles Ltd,
Guildford & King's Lynn

Foreword

by Sir Peter Parker
Chairman, Bardon Group plc; Mitsubishi Electric (UK) Ltd
Chairman of the Court of Governors, London School of Economics

I made my first visit to Japan as a soldier, part of the occupying forces which took over immediately after the end of the war in 1945. Tokyo was desolated, autumnal with ruin and rust; the country's economy was a crumpled zero, its people were baffled and outraged and ashamed. That memory is an eerie contrast to the new Japan which since then astonished the world with its triumphs in the global market-place. Inevitably, books galore have tried to explain their phenomenal success, but so often I find our Western analysis suffers from undertones, never quite explicit. Sometimes there is a sulky style which, while admitting the prowess of Japanese technology, ends up patronizing the people themselves. Sometimes there is the Jamesian (Clive) touch of witty exasperation, which is fun, but which ends up with those awful TV games, mad and maddening. Then there is the school which admires what the Japanese have achieved—but gives up trying to explain: and then we are treated to large helpings of guff about East is East and so on. Of course, there is already a reaction to this Sun-bathing. We are now being reminded that the sun also sets; the bubble has burst. *Schadenfreude,* alas, is the most natural of reflexes.

So, against this background I find this book is a great relief—for at least three reasons.

First, it goes directly to the heart of the Japanese achievement: its faith in education. From this the blessings flow: investment in the educational system and the fertilizing flow into the economy and society. Japan's ability to adapt, to change and compete is rooted in this faith. If there is any country which can respond winningly to the global turbulence which attends the birth of the new century, it will be this educated country.

Second, the authors recognize that the credit for the achievement of the new Japan goes primarily to Japanese management; not to economists, ideologists, or to politicians, but to managers. Again, with a straightforwardness which is as refreshing as it is rare, the authors define the qualities of the good manager: to develop the best in his or her working community so that they can do better for the customer. That is another article of faith at work in Japan: *Kaizen,* continuous improvement, the commitment to communications in the whole group.

Third, there is no dodging the difficult question about the lessons we can learn from the Japanese approach to management, education, and training. The home-truths are likely to jolt a few open-minded Western managements . . . 'Japan has not only much more broadly experienced managers and employees in general, but also a willingness to lead from the front, much in the style of the British armed forces officer.' Not like the home life of our own MBAs . . .

I hope this contribution to international management will encourage readiness to make comparisons and constructive self criticisms. Japan has its peculiar problems, has its weakness too—including a failure so far to make the most of about half its people, women. The authors keep a healthy sense of proportion: good management is not good simply because it is Japanese. Good management is evident all over the international scene, but their point is that the Japanese have concentrated on the qualities of good management to formidably profitable ends. In doing so we are all reminded of key elements in the process, in Japan and indeed anywhere.

Perhaps the secret of enjoying this encouraging book is in the balance of the authorship, Japanese and British: the authors have combined their own Eastern and Western experiences in a work, vivid and compelling in its detail and—what a relief—enjoyable reading.

Preface

John Lorriman

'With opportunities comes responsibility'
– Sir Winston Churchill

On 11 February 1981 I attended a prestige lecture entitled 'Marketing, management, and motivation' given to the Institution of Electrical Engineers by Akio Morita, Chairman of Sony. 'Peter Drucker', he said, 'recently wrote that he is unable to understand why Japanese industry is so successful. In particular, he seems puzzled by the fact that, in comparison with their North American and European equivalents, Japanese managers appear so unimpressive when you meet them. Peter Drucker's problem is this: he does not understand what management is about. In Japan a manager's role is very simple; it is to develop the skills of his staff so that they can find better ways of satisfying the customers.'

At that moment began my fascination with Japan. For many years I had been frustrated by the incompetent man-management in British industry. None of the many training courses I had attended seemed to provide any real solution. Here it seemed to me might be the beginnings of a set of answers. I started to read widely on Japan, and in 1985 had the great privilege of being awarded a Winston Churchill Travelling Fellowship, one of around a hundred provided each year to people in all walks of life in memory of that great man.

During that six-week first visit to Japan I received great help and much advice and friendship from the late Professor Keith Thurley, Professor of International Industrial Relations at the London School of Economics, and probably Britain's greatest expert on Japanese personnel management. That link led to an Anglo-Japanese comparative research project, and also to that feeling of 'Eureka'; I had found simple, and with hindsight obvious, lessons from Japan that are universally applicable.

As Sir Winston Churchill said, 'With opportunities comes responsibility.' My responsibility is to share my experience with you. The report I wrote for the Churchill Trust on my return in 1985 was featured in a half-page article in the *Daily Telegraph* (1 July 1986). This led to requests for over three hundred copies, and to many invitations to present my findings to groups such as the Department of Education and Science, the National Economic Development Office, The Engineering Council, the Institution of Electrical Engineers, and the Fellowship of Engineering. In addition, I was asked to present papers on this subject in China, Finland, Germany, Greece, Italy, Malaysia, the Soviet Union, Syria, and the United States.

One encouraging comment came from Dr Okio Yoshida, at the time the Corporate Research and Technology Representative for Toshiba in London, who wrote to me, 'I found this a very unique report to reveal the secrets of the strengths in Japanese companies and industries. Your insight, I think, is quite different from those reported so far.'

The lessons, on the whole, are relatively simple, and fully transferable to the West. They revolve around such simple principles as being systematic and paying attention to detail. One little story perhaps illustrates this very well.

I first met my friend and co-author in 1985 in Tokyo, after he was strongly recommended and introduced to me by a third party. He told me later that he recognized me immediately, although we had never met before. He realized afterwards that this was because he had read an article I had had published in the Institution of Electrical Engineers' *Proceedings* in September 1980, which included a photograph of me. It was my first-ever published article, entitled 'Can engineers develop themselves as managers?'; it was undistinguished; and it was in a relatively obscure journal. Despite all that, Takashi Kenjo had taken the trouble all those years before to search out and obtain such an article from an unknown author! To me this story illustrates the very great dedication to detail, study, and learning which underpins Japan's success. Later I discovered that Takashi, amongst his many achievements, had invented the word 'Mechatronics' in 1964 (and had had it refused by Oxford University Press until 1984 as an acceptable word for his technical books, of which they were the English-language publishers!); today the word is in common usage throughout the West.

In 1991 I fulfilled a long ambition to become a consultant. This had two important consequences. The first was that I immediately found very great interest and success as a consultant in training and management. The second was that I was at last able to find the time to write this book, with the expert assistance and advice of Takashi Kenjo and the enthusiastic support of Richard Lawrence, our editor at OUP.

Surprisingly, there appears to have been no previous attempt to write a book explaining Japan's approach to management, training, and education in terms readily transferable to other countries and other cultures. The hope is that this Anglo-Japanese collaboration will help to improve mutual understanding and friendship in both countries. On the whole the Japanese themselves, for a number of reasons, seem incapable of explaining their approach in terms that are understood by the West. It takes, I believe, Westerners who have considerable experience of Japan to provide the answers. One such is Walter Dean, now Head of the Japan Business Policy Unit at Warwick University, who was working in Tokyo in 1985, and provided my first real insight into how things really happen in Japan; though I suspect that my own more recent interpretation is now not entirely his, and Takashi and I accept full responsibility for our own views. Keith Thurley was particularly helpful in the last few weeks before his untimely death. John Hawkins, for many years a Managing Director with British Alcan, gave me invaluable information on the successes of the Japanese business he developed over several years; more importantly still he very kindly read the early versions of this manuscript, as did Susan and Melissa Lawrence, and this provided much useful feedback at a key stage of writing. Thanks are also due to Dave Phelps, our copy editor, who suggested a number of valuable changes to our manuscript. Tony Barnes, Director Human Resource Training at The Europe Japan Centre, provided a number of key insights. Another important mentor has been Dr Kaneichirō Imai, Vice-President of the Japan Society for Engineering Education and a past winner of the highly prestigious Deming Prize, who has provided unique insights at our meetings at various conferences around the world. I also owe a debt to Seiichi Mitani, Executive Director of The Mitsubishi Bank Foundation, which played a key role in funding the international research by Keith Thurley and myself, as well as three international conferences we organized in Japan, the USA, and Britain.

One of the Japanese philosophies is *Kaizen* – continuous improvement. The fascination of the subject of this book is that there is always much, much more to learn. I know that I have a long road yet to travel in understanding Japan, but in the meantime my hope is that this book will help many organizations and individuals to be much better at releasing their inherent talent and potential.

J.A.L.
Nuneaton, November 1993

This book is dedicated
to the Winston Churchill Memorial Trust
without which it would never have been written

Preface

Takashi Kenjo

'True friendship grows through a meeting when the fruit is sufficiently ripe.'
– Doppo Kunikida (1871–1908), novelist and poet

If the switchboard operator had connected the caller to the right person, instead of first to myself, when someone telephoned our university to arrange part of John Lorriman's visit for his Winston Churchill Travelling Fellowship in 1985, this volume would not have been produced. When we met I felt as if I already knew him, without knowing why. It was soon after his return to the UK that I remembered that I had in fact read his first paper, published in a 1980 IEE journal, which included his photograph. Several months later I received a copy of his Fellowship report, and was impressed by his insight into the Japanese approach to engineering training and management. I started thinking of our writing a collaborative book together like this one, since I too had become very interested in problems of this sort as a staff member at our university, which concentrates on the study of vocational/industrial education in Japan and the training of specialists in this field.

Previously our university had, as its first Principal, Professor Naruse, the discoverer of the principle for designing a one-tooth gear; he had been attracting students to his classes at Tohoku University, and I was one such student. He used to talk about the splendid technology of the West, where he had spent his younger days. We were inspired to work towards raising the standards of Japanese industry. As he often said that the staff in a German technical university had always had good industrial experience, after obtaining a Master's degree and completing a small project in physics I went into industry. After one year and a few months, in 1965, I accepted Professor Naruse's request to join his staff, and began my study of mechatronics, together with the training of students in that field.

In the year I came to Tokyo, the first Shinkansen train ran and the Tokyo Olympic Games were being held. The construction of the Shinkansen and the successful staging of the Tokyo Olympics were national goals for the Japanese people at that time. A colour TV broadcasting system was extended throughout the nation and highways in the capital were constructed in time for the biggest international event that Japan had ever hosted. After that, transistor technology progressed rapidly, and the growth of other industries, both light and heavy, followed. Engineers, businessmen, bankers, and bureaucrats were all absorbed in their efforts to raise Japan's economic level to that of the USA. Those activities and our success in them made life exciting.

However, 18 years later, when I was in the latest Shinkansen on my way to attend a twenty-years-on university reunion, we were already noticing that Japanese cars had become so cheap and reliable that they were being driven everywhere in the world. The standards set by Japanese industrial technology were leading the world in a wide variety of fields, with the exception of a few specialized areas. The goals which had been set when we were students had already been attained. Since technological progress had occurred more quickly than had been expected, diplomatic relations with the USA and European nations became very complicated. Understanding the real meaning of Japan's success and resolving the diplomatic issues it raised became our new problem.

My interest in the Japanese approach to the training of engineers is also reinforced by the international function of our university; we have English-media courses for people working in vocational training facilities in Commonwealth and other developing countries, and these have been strongly influenced by Western approaches. Through this I have become aware of some differences between Japanese and Occidental ideas in training and education.

However, my main role for this volume was to assist John to put across his interpretation and views, and I would like to acknowledge that this became possible through the friendship and support of several other people. Mr T. Kato produced some illustrations. Mr K. Izumiyama kindly read the draft and gave me valuable feedback. Mr W.Z. Sim, who was sent by the Government of Singapore to be trained in our university and undertook his final-year project under my supervision, as an unusual youngster educated in three languages – Chinese, English, and Japanese – provided me with many novel insights. My special thanks are extended to Mr K. Tanaka, who helped me collect statistical data on Japanese education and vocational training, and also to Mr T. Ohara, from whom I learnt about Japanese On-the-Job and Off-the-Job training relationships.

T.K.
Tokyo, November 1993

Contents

10.   Lessons for the West   189

A question of survival——The need for a vision——The importance
of a cohesive system——Maximizing internal expertise——A
structured approach to formal training——Towards the multi-skilled
employee

11.   Fifty years on from the Second World War——the implications for Japan   209

The rising yen——Some effects of the bursting Japanese bubble——
Opportunities are changing for women too!——Too much bureaucracy
in Japan——The story of Nidec – a world class company built on
learning faster than competition——The real competition to Japan
comes from South East Asia——Japan has yet to come to terms
with information technology——But there can be no complacency in
the West!

Index   239

List of figures

List of tables

1

Introduction

'If I have seen further it is by standing on the shoulders of giants.'
– Sir Isaac Newton

This is a tale of two cultures – Japan and the West. A century ago Japan faced the need for rapid industrialization and sought, and received, much valuable advice and assistance from other countries, mainly Britain and the United States. Japan used that assistance to develop one of the most technologically advanced economies in the world.

The irony of course is that it is now the rest of the world, particularly those two major nations which provided the original inspiration and support for her modernization, that has increasingly been turning to Japan for expertise and new technology. Indeed, it goes much further than that. Britain is increasingly relying on Japanese companies to restore its industrial base in such key areas as motor vehicles and electronics. In the United States there is even rising concern in the Pentagon at their increasing reliance on Japanese microchips.

Henry Dyer – the father of Japanese engineering

Interestingly enough, it was a British engineer, Henry Dyer from the University of Glasgow, who set up the first School of Engineering in Japan. That was in 1873, and it became part of the University of Tokyo, and so is now the Faculty of Engineering in the premier University in Japan. Henry Dyer was appointed Dean of the School at the age of 25, and formed it into six Departments, all headed by colleagues he invited from Britain.

The uncomfortable truth for us in the West is that the Japanese have proved themselves extremely adept at learning from others and in adapting others' ideas and technologies to suit their own environment. It is even more uncomfortable to realize that the West is pre-eminently bad at both. On his return to Britain in 1892 Henry Dyer was increasingly ridiculed and rejected for insisting that Britain had lessons to learn from Japan, and for saying that Japan would become the Great Britain of the East. It would have greatly saddened him if he had known that just under a hundred years later, in early 1991, a House of Lords Select Committee on Science and Technology would publish a report stating that it was 'conceivable that we will end up with no significant British-owned manufacturing industry in the UK'.

The importance of learning and adapting

Japan has been quite extraordinarily successful in both learning and adapting. Starting from a position in 1855 as a result of an almost total lack of modern armaments at that time, of having effectively had to concede their defeat by the United States and (very reluctantly) to open up their country to foreign influence, in 1905 Japan defeated one of the world's largest and most powerful navies, the Russian, at the battle of Tsushima. Many of the Japanese warships that achieved this astonishing victory were built in Britain on Tyneside (near the area where Nissan's 300 000-car- a-year factory is now sited at Washington, England), and the skills of her navy were learnt from British instructors.

By 1945 Japan's industries were all but destroyed, in a land with very little in the way of natural resources; and yet their subsequent economic growth has been astounding. By 1966 Japan had achieved a standard of living half that of Britain, and had overtaken Britain by 1980. In 1989 even the home of the BBC World Service, Bush House, was sold to the Japanese company Kato Kagaku for £130 million, as part of a property investment spree in Britain by Japanese companies that spent £1.4 billion in 1990 alone, £1.2 billion of it in the City of London. On the other side of the Atlantic, when Americans returned to Hawaii in December 1991 to commemorate the fiftieth anniversary of Pearl Harbor, they found that almost every hotel there was Japanese-owned – surely a supreme irony and humiliation.

Compared to an income per head in 1950 of $131, less than a tenth that

Table 1.1. Average manufacturing sector productivity growth rate (per cent) 1970–86

Japan	USA	W. Germany	France	UK
5.9	3.1	3.0	3.1	2.9

Source: Yasuhiko Inoue, *Key to Improving Productivity*, p. 1. Overseas Technical Cooperation Department, Japan Productivity Centre.

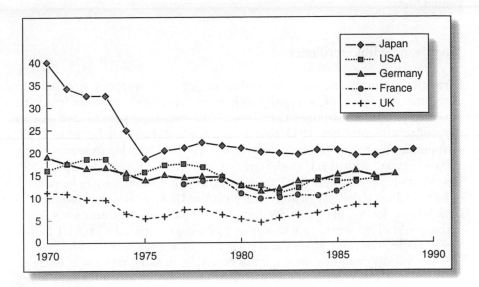

Fig. 1.1 International comparisons of gross rates of return (per cent) on capital employed in manufacturing. *Source*: OECD (1984, 1990). *National accounts*, Vol. 2: 1970–82, 1977–89. OECD, Paris.

of the USA, by 1987 the average Japanese had the highest annual income in the industrialized world (£13 400).[1] The average annual growth rate for manufacturing output in Japan between 1960 and 1987 was 8.8 per cent; comparative figures for the UK and the USA were 1.6 per cent and 2.5 per cent respectively. Japan has consistently produced higher gross rates of return on capital employed in manufacturing than other nations (Figure 1.1), as well as a higher increase in productivity (Table 1.1). One reason, without doubt, is that the average annual investment in fixed assets by Japanese companies between 1960 and 1985 was 27 per cent of gross profits; this was twice the 14 per cent of the USA, and considerably higher than the 20 per cent average figure in European companies.[2] In order to achieve this, it must be emphasized, Japanese companies had to have available the appropriate skilled manpower – a significant factor which far too many economists and industrialists in the West normally overlook!

Statistics on the average annual percentage changes in real domestic product per employed person again show Japan well in the lead (Table 1.2).

According to the Japanese Economic Planning Agency, Japan became the world's richest nation in assets at the end of 1987; it said Japan's national assets totalled \$43.7 trillion, compared with \$36.2 trillion owned by the United States.

Japan's incredible resilience

Particularly remarkable was the ability of Japanese industry not only to overcome the effect of a rapidly rising yen in world currency markets, but even to emerge stronger than before. An exchange rate of 242 yen to the dollar in September 1985 rose to a crippling 144 yen by June 1987, slashing the profits of Japanese companies. Yet by 1990 Japan was running a trade surplus with the United States of \$50 billion a year. In April 1991 Japan's trade surplus with the European Economic Community reached £1.5 billion, and exceeded Japan's surplus with the USA, which that month was £1.3 billion, for the first time. By July 1991 Japan's current account surplus with the rest of the world rose to almost £3 billion compared with £1.1 billion a year earlier. On trade alone the surplus rose by 62 per cent, to £5.1 billion. Finance Ministry officials were quoted as saying that the trend was likely to continue, and a worried senior official said 'There are factors in sight pointing to an expanding surplus. There's concern over its future.' This reflected the xenophobic attitude of much of the rest of the world to Japan's continuing economic success, which in September 1991 reached the longest and most powerful cycle of expansion in its history; the Economic Planning Agency said that economic growth was in its 58th month, exceeding the record 57-month boom that lasted from November 1965 to July 1970. Japan's current account accumulated surplus over the April to September 1991 period was \$38 billion, two-and-a-half times that a year earlier, while the unadjusted trade surplus, at \$51.2 billion, was up 66.4 per cent.

This economic boom was in stark contrast to the economic recession in other leading industrial nations, such as Britain and the USA. By 1992 Japan was in the middle of a so-called 'recession': the stock market had indeed collapsed, but, quite unlike its competitor nations, Japan experienced no unemployment – but instead a growing skills shortage.

Table 1.2. Average annual percentage changes in Real Domestic Product per employed person, 1960–86

Japan	West Germany	UK	USA
5.5	3.1	2.2	1.2

Source: *Productivity and the Economy Chartbook*, March 1988, p. 24, US Department of Labor, Washington DC.

A nation of perfectionists

The Japanese are fanatical about improving efficiency – a characteristic which stems from their perfectionism. They pay enormous attention to the structured skills development of their employees, and do so in the most cost-effective way.

An interesting question for European and North American readers is how Japanese companies are so successful when there are only four MBA courses in the whole of Japan, graduating about 100 students each year. Why is it that the rapid growth of MBA courses in Europe and North America (with the USA alone producing some 70 000 MBA graduates each year, and the UK turning out around 5000 annually) has been accompanied by an equally rapid decline in the competitiveness of industries in those countries compared with those in the Far East?

The vital importance of day-to-day learning

Japan, as this book will illustrate, puts great emphasis on OJT – On-the-Job Training – a concept which is ill-understood in the West, but which is critical to developing the highly competent, multi-skilled workforce that is at the core of the Japanese approach. In addition, great importance is attached to effective communications and the passing on of skills and knowledge. It was with principles as simple as these, rather than with the knowhow from MBAs, that Toyota were able to sell their Corolla car in the USA in the early 1980s for $2500 more than the price for which General Motors were able to sell their almost identical Chevrolet Nova; both cars were made in the same joint-venture factory, but by then Japanese vehicles had attracted a reputation and an image of quality which far surpassed that of their American equivalents.

Between 1981 and 1991 General Motors invested $90 billion in modernizing their factories, more than would have been required to *buy* their Japanese competitors such as Toyota. This sum included $77 billion in plant and equipment, of which $40 billion was spent on robotics alone. The payback was that in 1991 the company made a loss of $4.5 billion, the largest in American corporate history. Even this astounding figure was exceeded in February 1993, when GM reported a loss of $23.5 billion for the previous financial year, just a few days after Ford posted losses for the same period of $7.4 billion and IBM losses of $4.97 billion. Furthermore, GM still required 39 man-hours to produce a car as against half that number of hours for Toyota – and this in spite of having operated the NUMMI joint-venture factory with Toyota in Fremont, California for many years. General Motors had not learnt the simple lesson that investing in high technology is a waste of time unless there is also a systematic investment in people. Nissan Motor UK, for example, invested 14 per cent of their payroll in training employees in 1991, and did so in a highly cost-effective and structured manner; this Washington, England, factory is claimed to produce the best-quality cars of any Nissan factory in the world, with a management and workforce that is almost entirely British.

Is Japan unstoppable?

Japan's continuing success is both inevitable and inexorable unless her competitors learn the simple lessons explained in this book.

For example, Japanese cars accounted for just 0.25 per cent of car sales in the USA in 1960; by 1980 this had risen to 22 per cent. In October 1991, Lee Iacocca, Chairman of Chrysler, demanded legislation aimed at preventing the Japanese from dominating the domestic American market. He said the States is 'out of the electronics business, the video recorder business, and soon we will be out of the car business'.

In his keynote speech to Wescon85, an electronics conference in California at the end of 1985, Charles Sporck, President of National Semiconductor, urged the US Government to take steps to protect US semiconductor manufacturers from the threat of Japanese dominance in the semiconductor market. Elsewhere in the same speech, he admitted that 'We have been outmanufactured, outmarketed, and outmanoeuvred by foreign competition.'

Ceramics is another key Japanese success area. By 1981 Kyocera had achieved a world market share of 70 per cent in ceramic semiconductor housings, a technology pioneered by US companies. Kyocera's first sales office was opened in the States in 1968, followed by the purchase of the loss-making Fairchild Camera plant in 1971, with the acquisition of the Honeywell ceramics plant in San Diego soon after. By 1975 Du Pont had closed down its ceramic production, since it found itself unable to compete with Kyocera.[3]

In 1987 the Japanese government made the decision to turn Tokyo into a leading financial centre, and indeed succeeded in that endeavour. In 1988 Tokyo overtook London as the world's biggest banking centre, with a 21.0 per cent share of international banking business, compared to Britain's 20.9 per cent, according to figures from the Bank of England.

In July 1991 *American Banker* magazine showed that none of the top 20 banks in the world, as measured by assets at the end of 1990, was American – for the first time in fifty years. Seven of the largest ten were Japanese, led by Dai-ichi Kangyo Bank, with assets of £264 billion. The other three of the ten largest were French. Citicorp had fallen from its premier position in 1980 to 10th in 1989, and to 21st in 1990. The largest British bank was Barclays, at number 12, with National Westminster in 16th place.

It is difficult to see any limit to Japan's financial and commercial successes. In April 1990 the upmarket clothing retailer Aquascutum was bought by the Japanese garment manufacturer Renown for £74 million, while in August that year the Japanese Aeon Group took a 15 per cent stake in the well-known fabric and clothing chain Laura Ashley. This was followed in February 1991 by the Japanese clothing company Sankyo Seiko purchasing the British company Simpsons, manufacturer of the famous Daks trousers. Losing your shirt to the Japanese is one thing, but losing your trousers as well shows the extent of the British decline! Indeed, even in the field of whisky, the best selling brand in the world by 1984 was not a Scotch, but Suntory Old.

The pace of Japan's investment in its own infrastructure is such that almost 10 per cent of GDP is spent on construction, compared with between 6 and 7 per cent in Britain and the USA, and 7 to 8 per cent in most of Europe. As a result, 23 of the 48 major construction groups in the world are Japanese, compared with nine from America, six from France, and five from Britain. Interestingly, only one Japanese group, Kumagai Gumi, has significant turnover outside Japan, indicating the threat to other countries that is still to come.

Britain's exports as a share of world trade declined from 15 per cent in 1964 to 7 per cent by the mid-1980s. And yet Japan's Ministry of International Trade and Industry in 1984 concluded that of all the world's 'significant' inventions since the Second World War, Britain produced 55 per cent, far more than any other nation; only 22 per cent originated in America, and just 6 per cent in Japan.

Why has so little been learnt from Japan?

What is so extraordinary is that the West has made such little real effort to understand the reasons for Japan's success. In general either the argument is used that Japan is too different culturally for any real lessons to be transferable or, alternatively, superficial analyses lead to the unsophisticated (and usually ineffective) transfer of such techniques as Quality Circles and Just-in-Time. The fact that most Japanese companies do not use Quality Circles in their overseas subsidiaries, and indeed are very flexible and sophisticated in their approach to personnel management overseas, illustrates the folly of such an approach.

This book aims to give the West a much more balanced and realistic understanding of the key reasons for Japan's success. We intend that it will be of value to those intending to do business with Japanese companies, to those thinking of visiting Japan, and to those wishing to compete, or even just survive, against the nation which is generally recognized as being the world's most successful economic power. Perhaps it will be of use, as well, to those catering to the rapidly increasing numbers of Japanese visiting other countries, with ten million overseas journeys originating from Japan in 1990 and half a million going to Britain alone in 1991.

There are now some one million Japanese working and living outside Japan. In a number of instances some of Japan's élite have studied at Oxford and

Cambridge, for example. Amongst these have been the Emperor's two sons, Crown Prince Naruhito (also known as Hironomiya) and his brother Fumihito (Ayanomiya), who were educated at Oxford University, going up there in 1983 and 1988 respectively – a mark of the very high respect in which Britain is held in Japan, despite its economic failures. The Vice-Minister of Foreign Affairs, Japan's highest ranking professional diplomat, Hisashi Owada, studied at Cambridge to obtain a doctorate during his training period as a diplomat. Thirty years later his daughter Masako, after graduating from Harvard University, spent part of her diplomatic training studying international economics at Oxford, going up there for two years in 1988; in 1993 she became Naruhito's bride.

During a visit by European and American managers to Japan in 1979 the founder of Matsushita, Mr Kōnosuke Matsushita, told them:

Only by drawing on the combined brain power of all its employees can a firm face up to the turbulence and constraints of today's environment.

This is why our large companies give their employees three to four times more training than yours. This is why they foster within the firm such intensive exchange and communication. This is why they seek constantly everybody's suggestions and why they demand from the educational system increasing numbers of graduates as well as bright and well-educated generalists, because these people are the lifeblood of industry.

We are going to win and the industrial West is going to lose; there is nothing much you can do about it, because the reasons for your failure are within yourselves.

Research by The Europe–Japan Centre shows that the average time taken to induct a new employee in a Japanese company is eight months; in a British company it is one hour – a typical and fundamental error of management.

As Robert Heller, Editor-in-Chief of *Management Today* has written 'Just as the conceit of the West was part of its undoing, so the inferiority complex of the Japanese has been part of their strength. Certain that they had a lot to learn from the West, they proceeded to master the very Western methods whose neglect back home has become painfully evident.'[4]

Winning and losing are relative

There is considerable truth in the joke told about the American and the Japanese on a safari together in the African bush. Suddenly they are confronted by a man-eating lion. The American turns and starts running, but notices that his Japanese colleague instead bends down and takes a pair of running shoes from his knapsack and proceeds to put them on. 'You'll never outrun that lion', shouts the American. 'I don't have to', replies the Japanese, 'I only have to outrun you!'

The simple fact is that for a very long time now the Japanese have been outrunning most of the rest of us, initially gradually, but now at an increasing speed. What is more, in many ways the success of the Japanese is still only in its infancy. As the Japanese saying goes, 'Mada mada korekara da', which roughly translated means 'You ain't seen nothin' yet!'

References

1 'Japan in the World Economy', a two-year study conducted by Bela Belassa, a consultant to the World Bank, and Marcus Noland, a visiting assistant at Saitama University in Japan. It was sponsored by the Institute for International Economics, a group financed by the (West) German Marshall Fund, other foundations, and private companies.
2 Yasuhiko Inoue, *Key to improving productivity*, Japan Productivity Centre, Tokyo, 1991, p. 10.
3 Gene Bylinsky, 'The Japanese Score on a US Fumble', *Fortune*, June 1, 1981, pp. 68–72.
4 British Airways' *Business Life*, June/July 1987.

Some highlights and implications of Japanese history

'Wen gu zhi xin' (Reviewing the past one learns new things)
– Confucius (551–479 BC)

Introduction

In order to understand why Japanese education, training and management are as they are it is helpful and useful to understand just a few historical and contextual details.

Are the Japanese really so unique?

The Japanese themselves are convinced of both their uniqueness and their superiority. Without doubt these strong inner beliefs, which are constantly reinforced by their culture and successes, give them that extra sense of self-confidence which in turn leads them to ever greater pinnacles of achievement. They know that it is widely believed in the West that the Japanese are indeed culturally so different that there are only limited lessons to be learnt from them; this suits the Japanese admirably. What better way of maintaining a winning advantage over your commercial enemies than by encouraging the myth?

It is, however, in everyone's best interests for Japanese history and culture to be much better understood by other nations – and a very attractive history and culture it is. Many are the Westerners, like the British author, who visit Japan for the first time and quickly become greatly attracted and fascinated by most things Japanese. But many too are the Western businessmen who visit Japan without doing their homework, who see little more of the country and culture than Narita airport and their hotel – and who all too often depart without achieving anything.

What follows in this chapter (and the next on Japan's culture) is no more than an introduction. There are many excellent books available, and the Japanese themselves are highly professional and helpful in providing information on themselves for those who ask. (The fact that the Japanese both propagate the myth about the difficulty in emulating their success, and at the same time are so ready to be open with information, is simply an example of the plethora of contradictions in the Japanese as seen by Westerners.)

Japan's myth of its origins

Just as many Western countries have myths about their origins, so does Japan. Amongst these is that the Japanese Imperial family is claimed to be directly descended from Amaterasu's great-grandson, who became the first Emperor, Jimmu, in 660 BC. The present Emperor Akihito is the 125th of the line, of whom 14 were mythical or legendary. It is said that this belief in the mystical origins of the Imperial family was enshrined in the religion of Shinto by about AD 200. Shinto – 'The Way of the Gods' – believes that many things in nature, such as beautiful trees and mountains, possess 'kami', a type of holiness.

The unification of Japan

The scientific evidence is that a number of small states across the islands of Japan were gradually unified, so that by the 4th century AD they were ruled by a strong political authority established and centred on the present city of Nara, near Kyoto.

Between the 4th and 6th centuries Japan saw great developments in agriculture and the introduction of Chinese culture via the Korean peninsula – Buddhism, Confucianism, and Chinese script.

Prince Shōtoku, at the end of the 6th century, played an important role as Regent for his aunt, the Empress Suiko, in strengthening the unification of the state. To this end he issued a set of precepts known as the 'Seventeen Articles Constitution'. Hōryūji Temple, the world's oldest extant wooden building, and the Buddhist statues inside it were constructed in this period.

In the Heian Period (794–1192) the Chinese form of state organization was modified to fit Japan's needs, and the native culture developed rapidly in a number of areas. A sophisticated culture, centring around the royal court, was created. The invention of *kana* script, to complement the *kanji* script consisting of Chinese ideograms, helped to provide a basis for Japanese literature. The 'Tale of Genji', a story of less than successful love and Buddhist philosophy, is one of the world's oldest novels.

In the late eleventh century the Imperial family sought to restore its political power relative to that of the aristocratic Fujiwara clan. This became a cause of many confrontations and eventually armed clashes in the city of Kyoto. These wars served to strengthen the power of the warriors ('Samurai'). The two most prominent samurai clans were the Minamoto (also known as the Genji; there is no connection with the Genji of the 'Tale of Genji') and the Taira (also known as the Heike). The Taira clan captured political power first.

The rise of the Shogunate (Bakufu)

Table 2.1 gives an outline of the chronology of Japanese history. An important change occurred in 1192. Until then there had been temporary military rulers ('Shoguns') commissioned to wage war on the emperor's enemies. Following the defeat of the Taira clan by the Minamoto, Minamoto Yoritomo based his military administration in Kamakura and coerced the emperor (still based in Kyoto) to appoint him as the first permanent Shogun. Thus a two-capital system was started. The real power in Japan then rested in the hands of the Shoguns for almost seven centuries. This military form of government was known as the 'Bakufu'. As from 1336, the Muromachi Bakufu was based in Kyoto for some 240 years, but induced a hundred-year war between rival warlords (the daimyō) in struggles for land, and in particular for its rice. In 1603 Tokugawa Ieyasu, the final victor, established the Tokugawa Bakufu in Edo (modern-day Tokyo), again remote from Kyoto, which was to last until 1868 when the Meiji Emperor was restored to power. The 265 years before 1868 (known as either the Edo or the Tokugawa era) were ones of stability and peace, with the power of the Shoguns enforced by the samurai.

The roles of the Tokugawa Shoguns, the daimyōs, and the samurai need explaining. The Shoguns were in effect the military and political rulers of Japan, deriving their legitimacy, in theory at least, from the emperor. The samurai were the hereditary class of warrior (never forming more than about 7 per cent of the total population) who fought on behalf of the daimyōs. Indeed, from 1588 until 1876 only the samurai were permitted to carry swords – the long *katana* and the short *wakizashi*. Disarming the rest of the population was a highly effective way of maintaining order; but the consequent failure to develop modern firearms and cannon had devastating effects in 1853 when the Americans arrived, as we shall see.

There were four main classes of occupation during the Shogunate: samurai, farmers, artisans, and merchants, in descending order of status. In addition there were courtiers, doctors, and priests. Generally speaking, everyone remained in the class to which they were born.

A very strong sense of national identity

One reason for the enormously strong sense of national identity amongst the Japanese is that they were almost totally secluded from the outside world between 1639 and 1855.

The Shoguns perceived the growing success of Jesuit missionaries, including St Francis Xavier, to be a major threat to the cultural identity of Japan. The

Table 2.1. A chronology of Japanese history

Century	Significant events	
	In Japan	**In the rest of the world**
6th	538 Introduction of Buddhism Construction of Hōryūji-Temple (world's oldest wooden building)	
8th	701 Taihō code promulgated 794 Capital transferred from Nara to Kyoto	
11th	1000 *Tale of Genji* written early in this century	
12th	1100 Heian era 1192 Kamakura Bakufu established by Minamoto and Hōjō clans	
13th	1232 Codification of Jōei Shikimoku	1215 Magna Carta in England
14th	1336 Namboku-cho (Age of the Northern and Southern Courts) 1338 Muromachi Bakufu established by Ashikaga Takauji 1392 Unification of the rival Courts	
15th	1477 to Age of civil war. Continuing 1568 struggles between the daimyōs	1492 Discovery of the American continent
16th	1543 Arrival of the Portuguese and introduction of the matchlock gun 1549 Francisco Xavier arrives in Japan 1568 Oda Nobunaga enters Kyoto 1573 15th Shogun exiled by Nobunaga 1582 Toyotomi Hideyoshi (1537–82) gains control of Japan	1582 Roman Catholic boy to envoys sent to Spain 1590 and Rome by Christian daimyōs
17th	1600 William Adams's arrival in Japan 1603 Tokugawa Ieyasu (1542–1616) establishes the Tokugawa Bakufu	1564 to Shakespeare lived in 1616 Britain

Note: The word *Bakufu* means the same as 'Shogunate'.

Table 2.1. *(cont.)*

Century	Significant events		
	In Japan		**In the rest of the world**
	1641	National Isolation imposed by Shogun	1613 to 1620 T. Hasekura sent to Rome by Masamune
			1688 Glorious Revolution in England
18th	1716	*Hagakure* edited by Tsuramoto Tashiro	1776 Declaration of Independence in United States of America
			1789 French Revolution
19th	1853	Commodore Perry arrives off Tokyo	
	1854	End of Japan's isolation	
	1860	Katsu Kaishū and Yukichi Fukuzawa travel to the USA	
	1868	Meiji Restoration	
	1868	Keio Gijuku founded by Yukichi Fukuzawa	
	1882	Waseda School founded by Shigenobu Ōkuma	
	1886	Imperial University Edict: Foundation of University of Tokyo	
	1890	Keio University founded by Keio Gijuku	
	1894 to 1895	Sino-Japanese war, resulting in Japan's acquisition of Taiwan	
	1897	Kyoto Imperial University founded	
	1898	Inazō Nitobe writes *Bushido*	
20th	1902	Waseda University founded	
	1902	The Anglo-Japanese Alliance	
	1904	The Russo-Japanese War	
	1907	Tohoku Imperial University founded	
	1910 to 1945	Colonization of Korean Peninsula	

Table 2.1. *(cont.)*

Century	Significant events	
	In Japan	In the rest of the world
	1912 Emperor Meiji dies and Taishō era starts	1914 to 1918 First World War
	1926 Hirohito becomes Emperor – start of Shōwa era	
	1931 The Manchurian Incident	
	1941 Attack on Pearl Harbor	
	1945 to MacArthur in control as a Shogun 1951	
	1951 Treaty of Mutual Co-operation and Security between Japan and the USA	
	1988 Hirohito dies, and Heisei era starts	

first Portuguese had arrived in 1543 as a result of a shipwreck. Six years later the Spanish Francis Xavier landed at Kagoshima, a port next to an active volcano in the south-western island of Kyushu. Over the next fifty years the Jesuits converted as many as half a million Japanese in western Japan; indeed, the first Japanese had set foot in Rome in 1583, when four young nobles were despatched there by Christian daimyōs in Kyushu to visit Pope Gregory XII. The Shoguns were aware of the colonization and exploitation by the Spanish and Portuguese in South America, and began ruthlessly persecuting Christians and then sealing the country off from all foreign ideas, including politics and science.

Minimal trading links were maintained with the Dutch (on condition that they did not proselytize) through a small man-made island called Dejima, near Nagasaki at the western end of Japan. Otherwise the nation largely isolated itself, other than for Chinese and irregular Korean envoys, until 1855. Indeed, given the events of August 1945, it is a great irony that the major concentrations of the one million or so Christians in Japan today are in Hiroshima for the Protestants and in Nagasaki for the Catholics.

On the other hand some argue that the sense of national identity derives not from this period of isolation, when the country was divided into hundreds of domains, but from the period after the Meiji Restoration of 1868, when the state brought nationalism into the schoolroom.

Bushido – the code of the samurai

The culture and traditions of the samurai are critical to understanding present-day Japan.

The Hōjō clan from an early date played a dominant role within the Minamoto Shogunate; and in 1232 Yasutoki Hōjō codified the Jōei Code, which codified the legal practices and customs of the samurai. Historically it is thought that this provided for the independence of warrior law from the imperial code. This code was the fundamental law during the following Muromachi Shogunate era (1338–1573). In the Edo period (1603–1868) it was used as a textbook for children. The self-discipline and military tradition of the nation must have been influenced, for example, by the samurai right of *kirisutegomen*, which stated that, 'Common people who behave unbecomingly to members of the military class or who show want of respect to direct or indirect vassals may be cut down on the spot'.[1] This was in fact an example of *tatemae* (things the way they should be, in contrast to *honne*, the real truth). If the samurai failed in some way, or was killed, for example, it was considered shameful, and was claimed not to have happened.

More importantly, at the heart of the samurai system of values lies 'Bushido', the Way of the Warrior ('bushi' being a warrior). This pervades Japanese business life, and is a word which first appeared in the early Edo Period. This was a long era of peace, and many scholars attempted to modify the warriors' code of behaviour to adapt it to this change from constant warfare. The fundamental basis was the introduction into Bushido of Confucianism, to construct a Bushido supported by the ability to use reason.

In *Bushido – the soul of Japan*, a classic book written by Inazō Nitobe in 1898 to explain Japan to his American friends, the publisher's foreword describes it as follows: 'Bushido has been variously defined, but it would seem that the definition most generally accepted is that Bushido is the unwritten code of laws governing the lives and conduct of the nobles of Japan, equivalent in many ways to the European chivalry.'[2] And yet Bushido has had a far deeper influence on the Japanese way of life than has chivalry in the West; no doubt this was due to the very stable, structured, and important role performed by the samurai over so many hundreds of years, especially in the Tokugawa era, when peace played an important role in establishing Bushido. There is no comparison to this in the West. Bushido encompassed virtues such as rectitude, justice, courage, the spirit of daring, benevolence, politeness, veracity, sincerity, honour, loyalty and self-control, as well as institutionalized suicide and redress. Inazō Nitobe explains rectitude in the following way:

I speak of Gi-ri, literally the Right Reason, but which came in time to mean a vague sense of duty which public opinion expects an incumbent to fulfil. In its original and unalloyed sense, it meant duty, pure and simple – hence, we speak of the Giri we owe to parents, to superiors, to inferiors, to society at large and so forth. In these instances Giri is duty.[3]

It is Giri, for example, which causes present-day Japanese managers to devote perhaps 20 per cent to 30 per cent of their time to personally developing their staff. It is part of the Japanese ethos of mutual obligation. Managers and supervisors in Japan are chosen mainly because it is considered that they will be good at developing their staff; this is the basis on which they are trained, and the main basis on which they are rewarded and promoted. The height of achievement for a supervisor in Japan is the promotion of one of his staff to a more senior position than his own; a special ceremony takes place, at which the centre of attention and honour is not the individual promoted, but the supervisor whose skill and efforts made it possible.

Bushido and the samurai spirit is therefore far more than an aggressive militarism driving Japanese society. In many respects it encompasses concepts close to rules of Christian behaviour, despite the Confucian origins of Bushido. And yet there are undertones of self-sacrifice which are not often at the forefront of Western thinking.

These values, while differing in their expression from the West, are not fundamentally different from those which are admired in heroes and heroines around the world. What is fundamentally different about the Japanese is the degree to which these values of self-sacrifice still pervade their society, although this is changing to a certain degree in the 1990s – but not to such an extent that Japan's technical and commercial leadership will be eroded. How reluctant are the Japanese, for example, to mention – let alone complain about – the long hours they work, including the commuting time to and from work of up to two hours each way.

The value system of Japanese management

What is certainly not changing is the value system of Japanese management. Indeed, there are companies such as Nissan in the UK which have shown that these values of Bushido can be adapted and improved by non-Japanese. The prime requirement, however, is the commitment of employees to attention to detail, continuous self-improvement, and teamwork. Japanese companies are noted for being highly selective in their recruitment of new employees, and for demanding high standards of self-discipline.

The self-sacrifice of the samurai

Particularly prophetic were these words by Inazō Nitobe almost ninety years ago:

When Mr Henry Norman declared, after his study and observation of the Far East, that the only respect in which Japan differed from other oriental despotisms lay in 'the ruling influence among her people of the strictest, loftiest, and the most punctilious codes of honour that man has ever devised', he touched the mainspring which has made New Japan what she is, and which will make her what she is destined to be.[4]

Almost two centuries before Nitobe's immortal work, in 1716, *Hagakure* ('Hidden behind leaves') – the great classic of Bushido – had been edited by Turamoto Tashiro from the original by Tsunetomo Yamamoto, a samurai of the Nabejima clan in Kyushu. The famous opening phrase in it 'The way of the samurai is found in death', is said to differ from Nitobe's definition of Bushido. The latter's description is 'the path for the samurai to follow in his daily professional life'. In both cases, however, there is the intrinsic concept (readiness) or thought that the samurai must have in his 'belly'. Yamamoto insisted on the virtues of Intelligence (*Chi*), Virtue (*Jin*), and Courage (*Yū*). *Chi* is to listen to others, *Jin* is to do for the sake of others, and *Yū* is to be patient. He said that their root is one's dedication body and soul to one's lord; if told to commit *seppuku* (or 'harakiri', the ritual form of suicide for a samurai) by one's lord, then one should just be thankful.

It should be noted that Inazō's father was ordered by his lord to commit *seppuku* to take responsibility for a financial matter concerning the Nambu clan in the year before the collapse of the Tokugawa Bakufu in 1868. His family's honour was restored, however, in 1876 when the Emperor Meiji visited the house which Inazō's grandfather had used for the headquarters of a huge agricultural development project, and granted an audience to the Nitobe family. Inazō was very much impressed, and was inspired to devote himself to Japan's development project for entering the modern world. Inazō described in detail the scene of the *seppuku* which a young samurai was ordered to commit to take responsibility for a clash with foreign troops in Kobe.

In 1873 conscription was introduced for all classes of society and, in the year of the Emperor's visit to the Nitobes, sword-bearing was abolished other than for the military, and the traditional samurai pensions were commuted. Thus in an unexpected way was the opening phrase in *Hagakure* fulfilled; *seppuku* was no longer ordered by the government, and the traditional role of the samurai itself came to an end. But while that traditional way did indeed find a death, it was but the beginning to a new and far more glorious role for samurai virtues.

The influence of the needs of rice-growing in developing a spirit of mutual co-operation

Many aspects of Japan's industrial success can be ascribed to two key cultural factors – the value system and the self-discipline. The value system of her managers, teachers, politicians, and bureaucrats owes much to the tradition of *bushido*, whilst the reputation of her population as a whole for strong discipline, mutual co-operation, and respect for authority stems from the ethos of *mura* – the tradition of rice-farming. Geographically, some 67 per cent of Japan's land area is mountainous, with most of it covered by forest. Agricultural land accounts for 15 per cent, residential land just 3 per cent, and a mere 0.4 per cent is devoted to industrial purposes.[5] In many respects the history of Japan has been the story of the struggles to control the land producing the rice crops. At an interpersonal level it became essential for peasant farmers to learn to live in harmony. The planting and harvesting of the rice, together with the need to share the water for irrigation, encouraged the hamlets and villages to become tightly knit communities with strong family relationships. Any disagreements would have threatened the communal approach to the host of activities required for the survival and growth of each community. One result was the tradition of informal meetings evolved to resolve any difficulties in advance of the formal village gathering. This philosophy still applies in Japan today, where there is a strong abhorrence of public disagreements at any level in society; almost invariably formal decisions are preceded by informal discussions behind the scenes, known as *nemawashi*.

Some examples of the importance attached to harmony and the discouragement of individualism

An interesting example of the importance of harmony (*wa*) to the Japanese occurred in 1985. The then Prime Minister, Mr Yasuhiro Nakasone, announced the Government's intention of scrapping the 1 per cent of GNP limit on defence spending, to which the Socialist party expressed its strong opposition. In a Western democracy, no doubt a ruling party with an overwhelming majority, such as the Liberal Democrats had in Japan at that time, would simply have outvoted the Opposition; not so in Japan, where, rather than ride rough-shod over the Socialists, Mr Nakasone subsequently agreed to postpone a definite decision on the matter to allow consultations with the Opposition. The definite decision to scrap the limit was not announced until 18 months later.

Another example of the seeking of harmony lies in the unacceptability of moustaches in Japan. 'The nail that sticks out gets hammered down' is an old Japanese proverb. In 1980 a taxi driver went to court when he was disciplined by his firm for growing a moustache, and in 1986 two Tokyo railway workers claimed that, for the same 'offence', they had spent the previous few months cleaning lavatories. The main objection is apparently that men with facial hair stand out from their colleagues, and this is seen as detracting from discipline and efficiency in Japanese firms, where conformity is highly prized.

Traditionally, too, there was no place for individualism in Japanese society. If a crime was committed by an individual, then not only that person but also their whole village were held collectively responsible. This ensured that cultural habits of mutual responsibility and mutual assistance developed throughout Japanese society.

A sense of social responsibility for failure

Greater responsibility is taken by Japanese leaders for any failures in their organizations than is generally seen in the West. After the Recruit Company scandal in 1989, senior executives in NTT, which was heavily implicated, agreed to cut their salaries by up to 20 per cent. The Prime Minister, Noboru Takeshita, resigned in order to take 'political and ethical responsibility' for the scandal, in which many politicians and industrialists reaped large profits from shares sold cheaply by an information services conglomerate, the Recruit Company. A day later one of Mr Takeshita's key aides, Ihei Aoki, committed suicide by slashing his wrists and hanging himself; this was seen as following in the tradition of the samurai warriors, as a way of accepting the guilt himself and preserving the honour of the master he had served for over thirty years. One of many other examples was that of Taizō Hashida, who resigned as Chairman of Fuji Bank, one of Japan's largest banks, in October 1991, taking responsibility for a series of financial scandals; at the same time a number of other directors in the bank took salary cuts in recognition of their corporate responsibility.

From the samurai to a modern state

During the long peace of the Tokugawa era the only partially literate samurai military evolved into skilled civil administrators; the need for them was paramount during the period immediately after 1868, known as the Meiji Restoration, when the Emperor Meiji reassumed power on the resignation of the last shogun. Many samurai became businessmen, and played a key role in facilitating the transformation of Japan from a country which was basically feudal in 1870 to one which less than a century later had made enormous global commercial conquests. In addition, many other aspects of Japanese life, ranging from the teaching profession to most of the senior ranks of the civil service, police, and armed forces, became staffed by the samurai.

There is no apology for belabouring this point concerning the value system of the samurai. Unless other nations understand that Japan has consistently applied the same relatively united and single-minded approach to commerce and technology that united Britain politically and militarily during the Second World War, for example, then they will fail to comprehend a major reason for Japan's success. In his book *Getting the best for the least*, Masanori Moritani writes;

In Japanese industry, in its emphasis on the place of production, we can glimpse the spirit fostered by Japan's old samurai in leading men from the front. They did not hesitate to fight themselves, struggling and sweating alongside their men, nor do present-day managers, many of whom have likewise fought their way up from the production line, put the concerns of the workplace behind them.[6]

Waging commercial war on the West

Equally, it would be wrong to deny that Japan has consciously and systematically waged commercial war on the West. Soon after the Japanese surrendered in 1945, they decided that, where military means had failed, the same ends could be achieved by commercial warfare. Significantly, it was the Ministry of Munitions which changed its title to Ministry of Commerce and Industry, and in 1949 adopted the present name of Ministry of International Trade and Industry. Equally significantly, only a small proportion of senior officials were removed, with the rest of the Ministry in 1945 continuing to spearhead Japan's battle for world supremacy.

Many observers have also noted how military terminology pervades many aspects of Japanese business; partly this is because the officers of their armed forces transferred their value system to their new jobs in industry in 1945, more so than in any other country; partly because at that time Japan lay in ruins, and there was literally a need to fight commercially for survival; and partly because the samurai spirit runs so deep in Japanese society. These military values include reconnaissance, with Japanese market research being of the highest quality and very thorough. They rejoice in factual knowledge and, surprisingly, parade it much more openly than is traditionally done in the West. Look at any Japanese company report or promotional brochure and you will find they boldly publish facts about their business in great detail. Ask them for facts and they hesitate only to ensure scrupulous accuracy.

It is true, however, that the book *The Japanese conspiracy*[7] provides convincing evidence that MITI has consistently channelled secret funds to Japanese industry on a vast scale in return for co-ordination by large companies of their resources in 'attacking' key world markets such as machine tools and electronics. On the other hand, the author Marvin Wolf misses the point that it is not Second World War aggression, so much as the spirit and value system of samurai history, which drives Japan so successfully onwards. And even without MITI, Japanese industry would still beat the West, albeit maybe a bit more slowly. As Masanori Moritani said to the British author, 'MITI is just the jockey. Doesn't the West wish it had a horse like our industry in Japan?'

The Meiji restoration

So what caused the famous Meiji Restoration? The colonial powers became increasingly frustrated by Japan's refusal to trade and by its policy of executing foreign sailors shipwrecked on its coast. The Bakufu (the military government) had issued an 'Expulsion Edict' which required of all citizens that 'Whenever a foreign ship is sighted approaching any point on our coast, all persons on hand should fire on it and drive it off.' Therefore in 1853 the American President Millard Fillmore sent Commodore Matthew Perry on a mission to the Japanese government. Perry arrived off Edo with his four famous black gunships and demanded that Japan open up trade links with the West. The shogun requested further time to consider the matter, and furious debate ensued within the country. Basically Japan's problem stemmed from its failure to develop cannon; there had been no need in a country under firm and peaceful control. When Commodore Perry returned in 1854 with a fleet of eight warships, therefore, Japan had little alternative but to accede to his terms.

This forced concession of trade and cultural links with the outside world led to political turbulence culminating in 1868 in the restoration of Emperor Meiji to the throne in an executive capacity and the end of the shogunate. This was a time of great cultural shock for the Japanese, who had come to refer to Westerners as 'White Barbarians'. The rallying call of the time was 'Sonnō Jōi', meaning 'Restore the Emperor and expel the Barbarians'. On the other hand, the Japanese admire no one so much as a victor, particularly one who has triumphed over them (a fact discovered to their great surprise by the Allies when they occupied Japan in 1945), and so the Japanese decided to do everything possible to learn from the West.

The Westernization of Japan

Feudal institutions were swept away and Western ideas of democracy and parliamentary government were adopted. In 1870, for example, a £1 million loan was floated in London to finance the building of Japan's first railway from Tokyo to Yokohama. A national education system was introduced in 1872, and the following year a monetary land tax was established and foreign technical experts were brought in. Subsequently both Imperial and Private Universities were established, following on from a long tradition of emphasis on education, about which more will be said in Chapter 3.

In Britain, faced with such a national crisis in education, training, or technology, the standard government response for 150 years has been to set up a National Commission, or perhaps a House of Lords Select Committee, which publishes a report on which little, and maybe no, action is taken. Not so in Japan.

In December 1871 the samurai leaders, led by Tomomi Iwakura, Toshimichi Ōkubo, and Kōin Kido, left on a hundred-strong mission to visit the United States and Europe. The group included most of the outstanding government figures, and was away until mid-1873. They returned clearly deeply influenced by what they had seen, and took every possible step to enable Japan to catch up with the West – and, furthermore, determined to overtake it wherever possible.

The samurai lead Japan's modernization

In many ways it is remarkable how the samurai took over much of the worlds of commerce and industry at that time – spheres which had been dominated up to then by the merchant and artisan classes. It was not surprising that they should dominate the government bureaucracy, but the extension of their influence into those fields which were to be critical in their nation's emergence into competition with the technology of the West was historically very important. They assumed this role as a direct result of their superior education compared with the rest of the population, and they brought this key advantage into the value system of their nascent industry, together with those other samurai values which have served Japan so well.

By 1908 it was recorded in *Jinji Kōshinroku*, the Japanese equivalent of *Who's Who*, that 77 per cent of the 117 engineers in fields related to engineering and agriculture (working mainly for the government or nationalized enterprises) were from the old samurai class, as were 75 per cent of the 102 scholars specializing in engineering, science, medicine, and agriculture. So were 35 per cent of the 1659 people there termed businessmen (excluding directors of small companies and those with minor posts in large companies), 41 per cent of the 159 calling themselves politicians (Dietmen), and 77 per cent of the 279 administrators (bureaucrats) and statesmen.[8] Since they formed only some 6 per cent of the population, this was a remarkable set of achievements for the samurai class.

Hiring foreign advisers

The slogan of the ambitious young Meiji leaders was 'Fukoku kyōhei' (a wealthy and strongly-armed nation), and, in order to achieve this, they decided to hire foreign experts in science and technology. More than 130 foreign teachers and engineers were brought in each year from 1871 to 1879. The largest number employed was in 1874, with the new Ministry of Industry alone employing 255; most remained in Japan for only a few years, until Japanese had been trained and were able to continue their work.

This policy of obtaining commercial advantage by hiring foreigners ('oyatoi gaikokujin') was repeated in a different way after 1945 by Japan's very large import of foreign patents, which in turn in the 1980s was replaced by an enormous export of Japanese patents. A key strength of the Japanese has been their readiness to learn from wherever there have been ideas, technologies, or practices which can serve their purposes. In contrast the Americans, for example, paid little attention to Joseph Juran and Dr W. Edwards Deming at the time in the 1950s when the Japanese 'discovered' them and used their ideas to help transform the quality of Japanese products.

Japan's commitment to learning from foreigners in those early days of the Meiji era is well illustrated by the story of General Capron. At that time the northern island of Hokkaido was considered a colony, under the administration of a special government office called the Agency for the Development of Hokkaido ('Kaitakushi'). Its Vice-Minister, Kiyotaka Kuroda, asked the American President Ulysses S. Grant for advice on agricultural experts. Grant recommended his Secretary of Agriculture, Brigadier-General Horace Capron, who accepted a position as adviser to the Office for the Development of Hokkaido in 1871 at a yearly salary of $10 000, which was actually higher than the then Japanese Prime Minister's salary of 800 yen a month, with the exchange rate in the Meiji era set at one dollar per yen. Capron, together with his assistants, introduced the American system of large-scale farming, and also proposed the founding of an agricultural college. He returned to America in 1875, having also given important advice on the construction of Sapporo.

William Smith Clark (1826–86) was invited from America to run the Sapporo Agricultural College. Nitobe was one of his students. Clark stayed only nine months, but the spiritual influence he left at Hokkaido University was immense. His last words, 'Boys, be ambitious!', are well known to the Japanese. In fact, less well known is that the full exhortation he gave was: 'Boys be ambitious not for money or for self-aggrandizement, nor for that evanescent thing which men call Fame. Be ambitious for the attainment of all that a man ought to be.'

British experts devoted to Japan's modernization

One of the well-known contrasts between Britain and Japan is railways. In Britain the trains are all too often late (as was found to his cost by the Japanese author on one of his visits to the UK!) and prone to breakdown, while in Japan it is usually safe to assume that if your train is more than a minute late in leaving or arriving, then you are simply on the wrong train. It is therefore particularly interesting that the father of Japan's railway system was Edmund Morel, a British railway engineer who devoted himself to his work with such fervour that he died of tuberculosis at the age of 30. In 1870, on the advice of the British government, Japan began an ambitious project to construct a national railway system. Morel was hired in 1870 as the chief engineer to supervise the laying of tracks between Tokyo and Yokohama, the first stretch of the network. That same year employment contracts were exchanged with 19 foreigners. Later, as railway construction advanced, the employment of foreign experts increased rapidly, peaking at 119 in June 1874, after which the number gradually declined. The number recruited fell off drastically from 1881 onwards, with only 14 foreign experts hired in 1888. Altogether over 800 foreign engineers and teachers were employed by the Meiji government, and of those something over 200 are believed to have been concerned with the new railway system.

Most of those foreigners employed on the railway system were British. They filled posts as wide-ranging as Director, Engineer-in-Chief, and Locomotive Superintendent, as well as skilled manual jobs, such as mason, carpenter, blacksmith, engine-driver, fitter, and pointman. Meanwhile, the Meiji government proceeded with the systematic training of Japanese, so that by 1885 it became possible for practically all railway construction, except for the design of bridges, to be carried out by the Japanese themselves.

Morel had only one and a half years in Japan before he died, sadly a year before the colourful opening ceremony for the first railway line on 14 October 1872, in the presence of Emperor Meiji. However part of his important contribution had been to send a letter on 28 May 1870 to Hirobumi Itō, a high-ranking official of the Finance Ministry, advising the establishment of a government office in charge of overall industrial administration. This advice was followed, and Itō was appointed as the first head of the new Ministry. Morel also suggested establishing an engineering school where promising young men would be trained in modern technology, adding that his own country, Great Britain, still had no such institution. So here is yet another example of Japanese success through following the advice of foreigners who were unable to implement their ideas in their own countries. Morel and his Japanese wife Kino were buried in the Yokohama Foreign Cemetery, which was rebuilt in 1934 and is now designated by Japan Railways as a historic Railway Monument.

In 1871 Hirobumi Itō joined the Iwakura mission to the United States and Europe. In London he called on a London trader he knew, H.M. Matheson, to ask him to recommend British teaching staff for the Japanese institute of technology recommended by Morel. Matheson sought the advice of his friend, L.D.P. Gordon, a professor at the University of Glasgow, who in turn consulted W.J.M. Rankine, the genius in mechanical engineering who had become rector of the University of Glasgow at the age of 24. Rankine recommended one of his students, Henry Dyer, then himself aged 24, to head a group of technical experts. Eight young Britishers arrived in Japan in 1873: Dyer, William Ayrton, an electrical engineer, David Henry Marshall, a mathematician, Edmund F. Mondy, a specialist in industrial design, William Craigie, an English scholar, and three assistants. Thus was founded, by Henry Dyer, the Imperial College of Engineering, which is now the premier school of engineering in Japan at the University of Tokyo, in many ways the powerhouse of Japanese technology. Its graduates, and those of Japan's other numerous universities, are now masterminding the transfer of Japanese expertise overseas, notably to Britain and the USA.

A prophet scorned

Henry Dyer wrote many articles and books aimed at reforming technical education in Britain. Amongst these are titles such as:

- Some lessons from Japan
- Revolutions of industry
- Engineering in Japan
- Japan in world politics
- Dai Nippon – the Britain of the East: a study in national evolution
- Education and national efficiency in Japan
- Japanese industries and foreign investments

One of his well-known phrases was 'The engineer is the real revolutionary.' As history was to show, that has indeed proved to be the case for Japanese engineering – and where, it might it be asked, is it yet to go in its domination of world technology?

But the real tragedy for Henry Dyer was that the more he insisted on the need for his compatriots to learn from the Japanese, the more he was disliked by the British. His fate was to be disowned and forgotten by his own people.

Other important British contributors to Japan's development

Both authors are electrical engineers, and therefore have particular interest in William Edward Ayrton, known as the father of Japan's electrical engineering. Ayrton was 25 when he arrived in Japan on 30 June 1873. He taught at the College until his voyage home on 29 June 1879. The story is told of how he supervised his students' experiment on a measurement of gravity until the last possible moment before hurrying to the railway station with his data. Unfortunately he missed his train, but because he could not bear to wait idly for two hours for the next one, he rushed back to the college to teach his students for those few extra moments. Ayrton became President of the Institution of Electrical Engineers (in which the British author is very active) in 1892. He was also elected a Fellow of the Royal Society in 1881, and was President of the Physical Society from 1890 to 1892. In other words, Japan has always been consistent in learning from the best in the world.

Another British engineer who played a key role in Japan's development, this time in terms of its sanitary infrastructure, was William K. Burton. In September 1877 a cholera epidemic broke out in Nagasaki, and quickly spread all over the country. As a result the introduction of modern waterworks was given a high priority in Japan's modernization. Burton became the official technical adviser to the Meiji government on matters related to sewage disposal and water supply on a national scale. He was the son of a famous Scottish historian, J.H. Burton, graduated from the Edinburgh Engineering School, and later studied at King's College, London. In 1880, at the age of 24, he set up a partnership firm with a relative, and in 1881 was appointed Senior Field Engineer of the London Sanitation Society. Burton went to Japan to teach sanitary engineering at the Engineering College of the Imperial University of Tokyo, predecessor of the present Faculty of Engineering at Tokyo University. His monthly salary of 350 yen was even higher than that of the highest-paid cabinet ministers. His book *The water supply of towns and the construction of waterworks* (London, 1894) was the sole textbook on waterworks in Japan at the time, and also very well received back in Britain. He stressed, for example, the importance of provisions against earthquakes and fires, which spread quickly through the crowded towns of wooden one-storey buildings. When he left the Imperial University in 1896 he was decorated with the Fourth Order of the Rising Sun.

On the campus of Tokyo University stands the statue of Josiah Conder, the father of modern Japanese architecture. His granite pedestal weighs down upon two crouching devils, personifying earthquakes, the greatest enemies of buildings in Japan. Conder came to Japan at the age of 24 in January 1877, soon after winning the Soane Medallion Architectural Prize; this was awarded annually by the Royal Institute of British Architects to promote excellence in architectural design. Among Conder's pupils was his successor as Professor of Architecture at the Imperial College of Engineering, Kingo Tatsuno, renowned for designing Tokyo Railway Station and the head office of the Bank of Japan.

In seismology, particularly important in a country with so many earthquakes, Japan received valuable help from John Milne. Offered a three-year appointment as Professor of Geology and Mines at the Imperial College of Engineering in Tokyo, he experienced an earthquake during his first night after arriving from Britain in March 1876. He resolved to study this alarming phenomenon in depth, and it soon became his lifework. Following a major earthquake in Yokohama and Tokyo on 22 February 1880, the Seismological Society of Japan was formed, with John Milne as its vice-president. He also invented the Grey-Milne seismometer. Another major contributor to Japanese seismology was James Alfred Ewing, who arrived in Japan in 1870 at the age of

25; he went on to be Tokyo Imperial University's first Professor of Mechanical Engineering.

Expertise was brought in world-wide

Even in basic science, there were experts in those early days of the Meiji period. Edward Sylvester Morse from Portland, Maine, in the USA, received a two-year contract to establish the Department of Biology at Tokyo University.

The acknowledged father of Japanese medicine was Erwin Balz, one of 15 German doctors who were brought in by the Meiji government to help to teach Japanese medical students. Balz arrived on 6 June 1876 at the age of 26 as a Professor of Physiology and Internal Medicine at the Imperial Medical Academy (which is now part of Tokyo University) at an annual salary of 16 200 Marks, payable monthly in gold, and remained for almost thirty years. Before leaving Japan he was decorated with Japan's highest honour, the First Order of Merit of the Grand Cordon of the Rising Sun, and on his return to Germany was raised to the Peerage as Erwin von Balz.

In many other fields, too, there were foreign advisers by the mid-1870s. Six Dutchmen advised the Board of Construction, 46 Frenchmen the Army (after the Franco-Prussian War, the Japanese remodelled their Army on that of the Prussian victors), and 87 British the Naval Ministry.

In 1872 Admiral Kawamura visited the Admiralty in London and persuaded them to send British instructors to the naval school at Yokosuka in Tokyo Bay. A 31-year-old Commander, Archibald Douglas, accepted a three-year contract from 1873 to 1875 as Director at Yokosuka. Again the Japanese had selected the best possible expert from whom to learn, for by the time of his retirement in 1907, he was Admiral Sir Archibald Lucius Douglas, KCB, KCMG, and Legion of Honour.

A cult-like admiration of the West

The first political parties appeared in 1874[9] and the Japanese Diet (parliament) was formed on 25 November 1890. It was based on the British model, with two chambers, the House of Representatives and the House of Peers, and was much influenced by British parliamentary procedures.

In the early days of the Meiji period the legal system was largely based on that of the French, who also provided guidance, with the English and German systems later having an influence. After 1945 the system changed yet again, under the guidance of the occupying Americans.

One of Japan's military heroes is Admiral Heihachirō Tōgō, who defeated the Russian Baltic Fleet in the Battle of the Japan Sea at Tsushima in May 1905. Tōgō was born the son of a samurai in the domain of Satsuma, Kyushu, in 1847, while Japan was still under the rule of the shogunate. In 1863 Satsuma was bombarded by a British warship in reprisal for refusing to open its ports to British traders. Aged 17, he joined the defenders, together with his father and brother. Realizing the importance of naval power, he joined the Japanese Navy in 1869, the year after the Meiji Restoration. Two years later he was sent to Britain for eight years to study Western naval strategy. By 1903 he had been appointed Commander-in-Chief of Japan's Combined Fleet. When Japan declared war on Russia in February 1904, Russia was a world power, and even the Japanese Prime Minister, Hirobumi Itō, declared, 'It is impossible to gain victory in this war.' However, Tōgō succeeded in defeating the world-famous Russian Admiral Makarov at Port Arthur in the Liaodong Peninsula, and went on to defeat another world-famous Admiral, Zincvii Petrovich Rozhestvenskii, who sailed the Russian Baltic fleet to join their Pacific Fleet, at the Battle of the Tsushima Straits. So here is yet another example of the ability of the Japanese to learn from the West and, by improving, to achieve the impossible. Ironically, the Meiji period, from 1867 to 1912, was one during which Japan developed an almost cult-like admiration of the West that included, for example, its forms of dress.

From the First to the Second World War

Before the First World War the Japanese leaders regarded Britain as the country on which they should model themselves and from which to learn. For both political and emotional reasons they sided with Britain during the First World War itself, and were therefore deeply upset by the political decisions affecting them in its aftermath. British delegates at the Paris Peace Conference adopted an anti-Japanese approach, and at the 1922 Washington Naval Conference Japan was forced to curtail plans to make itself a world-class naval power, with Britain and the USA imposing a 5–5–3 ratio for the US, British, and Japanese fleets. The reason for this was that the West had seen Japan's military adventures in Korea (invaded in 1910 and colonized until 1945) and China, and wished to curtail them. Japan, in turn, saw no reason not to join the Western powers in carving out its own empire, and thus were sown the seeds of Japan's tragic entry into the Second World War.

Emperor Hirohito had become Regent in 1921 on behalf of his father, Emperor Taishō, and formally took over as Emperor in 1926 on his father's death. There were right-wing militants in the army who felt it their duty to save the Emperor from Western influence. On 26 February 1936 some young officers staged a mutiny aimed at restoring samurai values to Japan, but were denounced by Emperor Hirohito, captured, and executed. Unfortunately the move towards a military government continued, with the Korean and Manchurian enclaves expanded by the invasion (the

Japanese Ministry of Education still uses the word *Shinshutsu* – 'advance into' – instead of 'invasion' in Senior High School textbooks) of Manchuria in 1931. This was followed by the invasion of China in 1937. After Germany's initial successes in 1940, Japan invaded French Indo-China, but was startled by the West's reaction. The USA and Holland cut off oil supplies, financial assets overseas were frozen, and trade embargoes were imposed. In return Japan decided to attack the Philippines, Singapore, Malaya, and Hong Kong in order to secure its oil supplies. Thus came Japan's pre-emptive strike on Pearl Harbor on 7 December 1941, and America's entry into the Second World War with 80 times Japan's industrial potential for war production and with 12 times Japan's GNP; the inevitable ultimate defeat came with the two atom bombs dropped on Hiroshima and Nagasaki on 6 and 9 August 1945, and the surrender on 14 August. During the war it is notable how Japanese industry innovated rapidly, showing skills which were to be used again for their 'commercial war' on the West after 1945.

The war left a legacy which has hindered Westerners from learning as effectively as they might from Japan, no doubt to Japan's great commercial advantage. On the other hand, Japan is increasingly harmed by the memories of those in the West of Japan's military expansionism and the atrocities committed so widely by her armed forces; equally, there is quiet admiration for the great courage and bravery of her troops, who often fought to the last man rather than surrender. Many Japanese, although not all of them, for their part, feel little guilt for the Second World War, seeing themselves as having been forced into it by the oil and trade sanctions imposed in 1940.

Psychological barriers

The purpose of this book is not to make value judgements on those terrible events, but rather to explain the consequent psychological barriers that hinder the West and Japan from learning from each other.

For example, Japan, unlike Germany, is extremely reluctant to acknowledge the facts of the Second World War, and this very much influences the view of Japan taken by the West. The word *shūsen* (the end of the war) is used instead of *haisen* (defeat). This is in stark contrast to Germany, which clearly recognized its defeat in 1945, and accepted guilt and responsibility for its aggression. In this difference between the two countries perhaps lies much of the psychological reason for America to indulge regularly in Japan-bashing; Germany has also had a very large trade surplus over America for many years, but without any hint of a Germany-bashing campaign as a result.[10]

After the Second World War – from Shōwa to Heisei

On 15 August 1945 Emperor Hirohito broadcast to his people. His famous indirect words were: 'The war situation has developed not entirely to Japan's advantage.' But by the mere fact that he was speaking for the first time ever on the radio the Japanese knew that the war was lost. Hirohito must in many ways have been much saddened by the war against Britain. In March 1921, while still Crown Prince at the age of 20, he had visited Britain, and as a result ever after ate bacon, eggs, and toast for breakfast following his stay at Buckingham Palace; the Emperor insisted that the bacon came from the rare Berkshire pigs farmed in England. In addition, having seen King George V in his dressing-gown, he never again wore a kimono. Given that he described his stay with the British Royal Family as the most beautiful time in his life, it was appropriate that the memories of the war were set aside and Prince Philip attended his funeral in 1989, despite the strong protests of British war veterans. It is also notable that Empress Michiko, wife of the present Emperor Akihito, was educated by Irish nuns in Japan and is fluent in Gaelic.

Such is the respect of the Imperial family for Britain that both of Emperor Hirohito's grandsons were educated at Oxford University, a very notable mark of respect for Britain given the great importance attached to education by the Japanese.

The Shōwa era

What is remarkable about the Shōwa period (the reign of Emperor Hirohito, from Christmas 1926 to January 1989) is the rate of growth of Japanese industry during those 62 years. Industry expanded nearly 25-fold, an annual growth rate of 5.75 per cent, despite an 85 per cent drop in production during the years of the Second World War. In contrast, during the previous 58 years from the Meiji Restoration in 1868, Japanese industry had expanded fivefold, an annual rate of growth of 2.75 per cent. The comparative industrial expansion of Japan in relation to the USA, Italy, Britain, France, and Germany between 1900 and 1965 is shown in Figure 2.1 Contrary to popular belief, it can be seen that Japan's relatively much greater rate of growth dates from long before the Second World War, and in fact has been operative throughout the present century.

General MacArthur – the American Shogun

The relative rate of growth, however, has been notably spectacular since 1945, and it is ironic, given the protests of the Americans in the 1990s of unfair Japanese trade practices, that it was General MacArthur who played a key role in reviving Japan's industry. He was, in effect, a 'Shogun' from 1945 until 1951 in his role as Supreme Commander for the Allied Powers (SCAP). Immediately

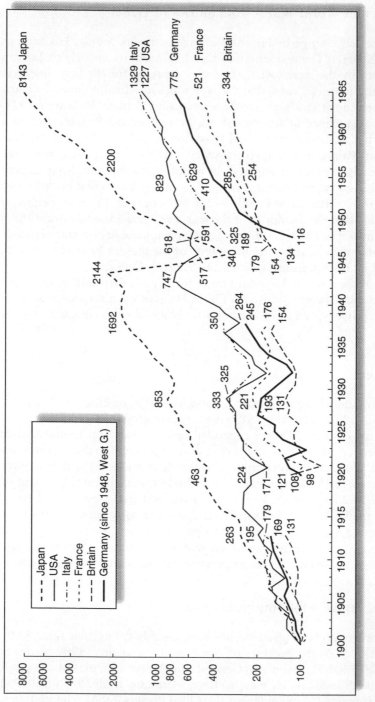

Fig. 2.1 Industrial expansion of six national economies, 1900–65. The figures are numerical indices of manufacturing production taking the base year 1900 as 100. *Source:* Hyōe Ōuchi *et al.* (eds) (1967). *Nihon Keizai Zusetsu* (*The Japanese economy illustrated*), 4th edn, p. 7 (graph prepared by Yutaka Kitagawa). Iwanami, Tokyo. Reprinted by permission from Takeshi Ishida (1971). *Japanese Society*, p. 2. University Press of America, Washington DC.

after the war there was intense economic hardship. Japan's industrial base had been bombed and burnt almost out of existence, and her people, with little in the way of natural resources, faced a grim future. Unlike the Soviets, who extracted severe financial reparations from Germany and Finland, the Americans adopted an extremely generous and positive approach to restoring Japan's, and of course Germany's, economies. A new democratic Constitution was implemented in 1946, the education system was reformed on the American model, mainly to remove the nationalistic emphasis, and women were given the vote. Overseas experts, most famously Deming and Juran (who were almost unknown in their native USA), were brought in by MacArthur, who was very much left to run Japan as he saw fit. The result was that decisions could be made quickly and effectively, and the economy was given a significant further boost by the Korean War (1950–3), for which Japan was able to form an important military and industrial base.

Interestingly, immediately following the American Occupation, MacArthur very much encouraged the spread of unions, which had been largely suppressed by the wartime regime. There were many bitter labour disputes and factory occupations. However, unlike the Western form of factory occupation, where production is suspended as a key part of the protest, the Japanese approach was for the trade unionists to evict the factory managers and show that they could actually *increase* production output; the logic was that the management would suffer enormous loss of face and be forced to concede the demands of the unions, while the employees suffered no loss of earnings. For example, strikers at the Mitsui-owned coal mine barred all management personnel from the pits and stepped daily output up from 250 tons to 620. Workers at Ashio copper mines operated during a 'strike', increased production, and doubled their own wages.[11] It was typical of the sophisticated and non-confrontational approach which still characterizes unions in Japan today. Industrial disputes are more likely to be effected by trade unionists' wearing black armbands during the lunchbreak (but not during working hours in case visiting potential customers should get a negative impression of the company) than by work stoppages. Japanese trade unions also have excellent research departments, in order to have a clear understanding of their members' views. However, in the 1940s, many trade unions fell under Communist influence, and there were a number of bitter disputes, resulting in a crackdown by MacArthur, with many union leaders gaoled and the formation of company-based ('enterprise') unions, such as were also developed in Germany at that time under Allied guidance.

Zaibatsu – the merits and demerits

One of MacArthur's decisions was to disband the 'Zaibatsu', the conglomerations of large manufacturing companies with close links to the banks. The Mitsui family, for example, had established their merchant house as long ago as the middle of the seventeenth century, during the Tokugawa era. These merchant houses were enormously influential in establishing the value systems of Japanese industry, which apply to this day – values such as the principle of lifetime employment with one company, and the sense of family throughout the organization. If a Japanese employee is asked today about his occupation, he will reply, for example, 'Hitachi employee', rather than 'electrical engineer' or 'technician'.

The 'Zaibatsu' only really developed during the Meiji period, with the support of the Japanese government, and by 1890 over half Japanese industry was owned by them. They had been very much responsible for the success of Japan's war-machine during the 1930s and 1940s; hence MacArthur's decree that they should disband. In typical Japanese style, the law was obeyed in the letter but not the spirit, and today Japan's large trading companies (Mitsui, Mitsubishi, Sumitomo, Fuyo, Sanwa, and Dai-ichi Kangyo Bank are the six largest) are inextricably interlinked with the banks, real-estate agencies, and insurance companies in major groupings known as *Keiretsu*. If a company is in financial difficulties experts are seconded to that company from other parts of the grouping, and support is given until the company is returned to financial health. Similarly, takeovers of companies are virtually unknown and there are close financial links between the major companies and sub-contractors, as well as the movement of senior managers to sub-contractor companies when they are approaching retirement; this is very effective in strengthening the technical and organizational links between the trading partners.

The value of political stability

Another key factor in Japan's success has been its political stability. The Liberal Democratic party was formed in 1955 as a coalition of the conservative parties, and remained in power until July 1993, despite a number of notorious scandals. A key figure in its formation was Nobusuke Kishi, a former member of General Hideki Tōjō's wartime cabinet. After overseeing Japan's economic policy in the puppet government of Manchuria, he returned to Japan at the beginning of the war as Vice-Minister of Commerce and Industry. After the war he was imprisoned as a Class A war criminal, but was released, in mysterious circumstances, the day after Tōjō and six others were hanged. He became Prime Minister from 1957 to 1960, and was responsible for pushing through the Revision of the United States – Japan Security Treaty despite massive public protest. His brother, Eisaku Satō, was Prime Minister from 1964 to 1972. He was successful in negotiations with President Nixon to end America's occupation of Okinawa, although there are still major US bases in these southern islands. For this achievement (the bloodless recovery of the lost territory), Sato was awarded the 1974 Nobel Peace Prize.

On 25 June 1994 the socialist Mr Tomi-ich Murayama came to power as Prime Minister in a coalition of the Liberal Democratic Party, the Japan Socialist Party, and Sakigake. World leaders wondered what major changes he would introduce; after all, when young he had sat in front of the Prime Minister's Official Residence protesting at the revision by Kishi of the US–Japan Security Treaty. Indeed, he agonized and could not sleep for many nights before he gave the Prime Minister's Address to the Diet on 18 July 1994. In the event he declared that:

1. he would maintain the US–Japan Security Treaty;
2. the Self-Defence Army is not unconstitutional;
3. he accepted the Hinomaru (the Rising Sun) as the national flag;
4. he accepted the Kimigayo (from the era of the Emperors) as the National Anthem.

All this implied both a continuity in national policy and a major change in the slogans of the Japan Socialist Party, which in 1995 renamed itself the Social Democratic Party.

In the 1980s Japan's rapidly growing trade surpluses led to '*Endaka*' in 1986 and 1987 – the strong danger of recession as a result of a considerable strengthening in the value of the yen. It is a remarkable tribute to the inherent strengths of Japanese companies that they not only survived '*Endaka*', but actually emerged even stronger as a result of the action taken, much to the amazement of foreign observers.

By May 1988, Japan's supreme advisory body on economic policy was recommending in a new five-year plan that priority should be given to improving the quality of life, shifting the nation's emphasis for the first time away from the major aim of commercial conquest.

The challenges facing Japan

A major political challenge facing Japan is that of publicly accepting responsibility for its part in World War II. Significantly, on 15 August 1995, 50 years after the war ended, Prime Minister Murayama addressed the Diet to try and end such controversy. He said: 'I acknowledge the damage and suffering inflicted upon other countries by Japan's colonial rule and aggression, and we will do our best towards the realization of world peace with a no-war pledge.'

Not everything is perfect for the Japanese economy. After the death of the charismatic Shōwa Emperor in 1989 the bubble economy burst. Increasingly fierce competition is faced from the NIEs – the Newly Industrialized Economies. The strength of the yen and the lower wages in the NIEs, together with the rapidly improving quality of their products, led to a rise in imports of goods into Japan from the Asian NIEs of 66 per cent in the first half of 1988 alone. It is both significant and worrying for the West, however, that the competition faced by Japan is from the Asian NIEs and not from the West.

The hard fact is that there is a continuing trend of defeat for Western companies and Western technology. An example of this may be seen in the case of NEC, which started life in Japan in 1899 as a joint-venture company with the American Western Electric of Illinois, a subsidiary of AT&T. In 1962 it signed an agreement with Honeywell to sell mainframe computers in Japan based on the US company's technology. By 1985 NEC had 78 000 employees world-wide in 51 manufacturing plants in Japan and 20 more in 11 other countries. It produced 15 000 different products, and Honeywell signed an agreement to sell NEC mainframe computers under the Honeywell name in the USA and Europe.

December 1991 marked the fiftieth anniversary of Pearl Harbor and the Japanese invasion of the British colony of Malaya. The notable fact is that most of the Americans returning to Pearl Harbor that month for ceremonies marking events fifty years earlier found they had no alternative but to stay in Japanese-owned hotels. And yet they had been the leaders of the countries which had overwhelmingly defeated Japan militarily for the first time in her history.

Both Japanese and Americans may well have been asking themselves who had really won the war triggered by commercial rivalry and ambition that half century before. Because for Japan, with no natural resources other than her people, the key to industrial survival and growing success has been simple; to learn every possible lesson from other countries and then to improve even further. 'Knowledge shall be sought for throughout the world, so that the welfare of the empire may be promoted', as Henry Dyer often quoted from the words of the Emperor Meiji.

Events now showed that the pupil had become the teacher, and was well on the way to becoming the master.

References

1 Stephen Turnbull, *The book of the samurai – the warrior class of Japan*, Bison Books, London, 1982, p. 117.
2 Inazō Nitobe, *Bushido – The soul of Japan*, Charles E. Tuttle, Tokyo, 1969, p. ix.
3 Inazō Nitobe, ibid., pp. 25–6.
4 Inazō Nitobe, ibid., pp. 173–4.
5 *Nippon – The land and its people*, Nippon Steel Corporation, Gakuseisha Publishing Co. Ltd., Tokyo, 1982, pp. 35–7.
6 Masanori Moritani, *Getting the best for the least – Japanese technology*, The Simul Press, Tokyo, 1982, p. vii.
7 Marvin J. Wolf, *The Japanese conspiracy*, New English Library, London, 1983, p. 201.
8 Michio Morishima, *The production of technologists and robotization in Japan*, Suntory Toyota International Centre for Economics and Related Disciplines, London School of Economics, pp. 2–3.
9 Joy Hendry, *Understanding Japanese Society*, Croom Helm, Beckenham, Kent, 1987, p. 175.
10 Hitoshi Hanai, *Nippon to Doitsu no sa* (in Japanese; English title: *The difference between Japan and Germany*), Gakushikai Kaihō No. 792, Tokyo, 1991, pp. 32–4.
11 *Time* magazine, February 18, 1946.

3

The first winning margin – education

'If you think education is expensive – try ignorance.'
– Derek Bok, President, Harvard University

Introduction

'Japan's success has nothing whatsoever to do with its system of education' said a senior educational expert from one of Britain's most eminent universities at a conference of academics in the UK in 1991.

This was in response to evidence, quoted by the British author in his own paper at the same conference, of a comparative study by Professor Sig Prais, at the National Institute for Economic and Social Research in London. This shows that the average 13½ year old English pupil's mathematical attainment is 2½ years behind that of an equivalent Japanese or German pupil.

There are perhaps three key questions to be asked:

- Is there any direct link between the educational qualifications of a nation's workforce and its industrial and commercial success?
- Is Japan's success a direct result of her characteristic approaches to education?
- Are there any lessons to be learnt by other countries from Japan's education system?

In opposition to the views of most British educationists, the authors wish to show evidence that the answer to all three questions is 'Yes'.

Japan has a long tradition of excellent education

One illustration of the Japanese commitment to education as a key part of her industrial strategy is shown in Figure 3.1, showing the expansion in the numbers of students enrolled in higher education from the Meiji Restoration onwards.

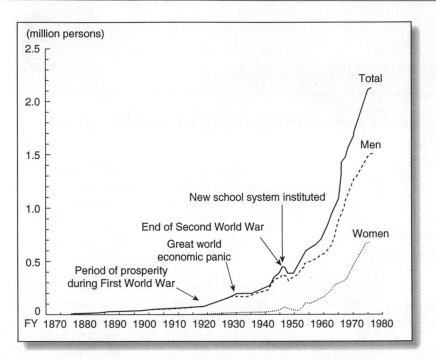

Fig. 3.1 Students enrolled in higher education in Japan, 1875–1980. *Source*: Kōji Hoashi (1978). 'Transfer to a higher-education society'. In *Dictionary of Japan's problems* (ed. Overall Research Development Organization). Gakuyō Shobō, Tokyo.

What is probably not often realized in other countries is that Japan has a long tradition of being one of the best educated nations in the world. This is in contrast to the popular image in the West of a Japan which has developed a high-pressure education system only over the last two or three decades, and in which the pupils suffer the world's highest suicide rate; both of these are to a certain degree myths. On the other hand, it is certainly true that many things which are possible in Japan cannot be directly transposed to the West. The lessons are more subtle, but are crucial to understanding how to compete with the Japanese – and how to beat them.

In his book *Modern Japan* Richard Sims explains the historical background:

There were 10,000 or so small local schools in Japan known as *terakoya*, mostly run by private teachers, although earlier Buddhist temples had played the leading part in instructing the commoners. By 1850 forty per cent of the total male population could read and write and more than ten per cent of the female, figures which compare favourably with many European countries at that time.[1]

He goes on to explain that a high standard of literacy was part of the Tokugawa (1603–1867) era's legacy:

The ability of over a quarter of the population to read provided a good foundation for the introduction of a national education system which by 1900 was giving over ninety per cent of Japanese children the basic knowledge and discipline essential to a modern workforce.[2]

In contrast to Britain, the Meiji rulers established an integrated education system encompassing both schools and universities. In 1872 a compulsory attendance system was promulgated for the first time with the words 'We look forward to a time when there will be no illiteracy in any village house, no illiterate in any home.'

Is it education's purpose to meet the needs of the State?

One fundamental principle on which Japan's education system is based is that it is very clearly established to educate pupils specifically to meet the needs of the State. This is made quite clear, for example, in the first clause of the Imperial University Edict of 1886, which states: 'The Imperial University shall have as its purpose instruction in the arts and sciences such as accords with the cardinal principles of the State and research into their deepest mysteries.'

This question as to what is the major purpose of education is a key one. In the UK, education is strongly influenced by the so-called 'progressives'. This school of thought demands that education is child-centred, on the basis of the theories of Piaget and Kohlberg. It is believed that education must focus on the interests and mentality of the child, rather than on directed aspects of knowledge to which the child has to conform. On the 11 June 1993, for example, a letter condemning the British Government's 'doctrinaire preoccupation' with grammar and spelling, and its insistence that fourteen year olds should study Shakespeare, was published in *The Times Higher Education Supplement*: it was signed by nearly 600 university teachers of English.

In September 1993 14 British professors of education published a document entitled *Education: a different version*.[3] In this they said:

We thoroughly condemn a strategy which sees children as commodities, parents as consumers, schools as competitive businesses, teachers as technicians, the curriculum as a set of bureaucratic requirements, accountability as narrowly conceived test scores put into crude league tables . . .

We have asserted values other than competition and the commercial view of education . . .

We sometimes discover, from comparisons, that some institutions are performing better than others. What we cannot do is identify with precision just which those institutions are.

These views to a large extent reflect the views of the vast majority of the British teaching profession. They are largely contrary to the value system which has applied in Japan since the Meiji Revolution, and which has been an important element in making Japan the highly successful nation that it is today in commercial terms. Let us therefore examine the relative successes of the Japanese and British education systems.

An extraordinary expansion in Japan's education system at all levels

By 1900 compulsory education in Japan started at the age of six and continued for four years, which was extended in 1907 to six years. As from that time there was a rapid expansion in the numbers and types of schools at all levels. It necessarily took time to expand the education system, so that:

In 1935, the percentage of elementary school students going on to the secondary schools of the time (middle school, girls' high school, and vocational school) was 18.5%, and the percentage going on to receive higher education (higher school, college, university) was 3%.

  In 1947 the education system was completely revised, and compulsory education was extended to 9 years.[4]

Imperial Universities and entrance examinations

The Imperial University Edict of 1886 led to the formation of the seven premier universities in Japan today:

The University of Tokyo	1886	Kyoto University	1897
Tohoku University	1907	Kyushu University	1910
Hokkaido University	1918	Osaka University	1931
Nagoya University	1939		

Two other Imperial Universities were also established in the then Japanese colonies in Seoul and Taipei. Each of these universities had its own independent history before being awarded the prime status of an Imperial University. The University of Tokyo, for example, had at first been called by the same name as it is now (Tokyo Daigaku), and changed to 'The Imperial University' at the promulgation of the Edict. It was then again renamed the Tokyo Imperial University when the second Imperial University was established in Kyoto. Tohoku University began as the Science College in Sendai and the Agricultural College in Sapporo, with the latter achieving independent status in 1918. The purpose of the Imperial University Edict was to establish universities as good as those in Europe (and better than those in America).

In order to produce first-class students, well schooled in English and one of either French or German before they started at university, five Higher Schools were established in 1886. The curricula at these schools were based on those of traditional European schools, such as the German *Gymnasium*. However, a major difference was that, in place of the classics of Greek and Latin, modern languages were taught as a tool for studying effectively from the West. Another feature was that every male who successfully completed middle school was able to proceed to a Higher School via an examination and thence, if good enough, to an Imperial University, giving him the possibility of becoming a minister and helping to run the nation.

The five Higher Schools were called the 'Number Schools'. The First was in Tokyo, the Second in Sendai, the Third in Kyoto, etc. Many boys wished to enter the First, and the school had to select the intake by examination. Crammers then soon appeared. Thus started the history of very tough entrance examinations, in contrast to the Western tradition of national school-leaving exams. Three more were soon added to the family of the 'Number Schools'. After 1920, however, many higher schools named after the district in which they were founded (for example Shizuoka, which Nakasone attended before he went up to the Tokyo Imperial University) were established. As a result the Imperial Universities began to introduce entrance examinations. By 1941 there were a total of 32 higher schools, including national, public, and private, with 22 000 students.

Private and new national universities

Along with the Imperial Universities, there were also, at the same time, a number of private universities established, most notably Keio University (founded in 1868 and given university status in 1890) and Waseda University (started in 1882, becoming a university in 1902), both in Tokyo. Both of these were founded by government ministers who went into opposition to follow their own ideals and obtained donations from private individuals. Others were founded with donations from companies such as Mitsubishi. Sophia was founded by the Jesuits. However, almost no entrance examinations were required by private universities, with the exception of Keio and Waseda, until 1940. On the other hand, various National Colleges were established for medicine, technology, agriculture, etc., and had their own entrance examinations. These were reformed to become the new national universities after the Second World War.

Japan now has the extraordinary total of 513 universities, of which 377 are private. But it was not always that way. There was a severe shortage of graduates at the end of the nineteenth century, and most were recruited by the government, with few going into industry. The progress over the first three decades of this century is described by Rodney Clark in *The Japanese company*:

A survey of 354 industrial managers active in 1900 reveals that only eight per cent had higher education. In the first two decades of the twentieth century, however, the older universities expanded, and those that did not already have them set up departments of law, economics, and commerce. New institutions were also established both by private groups and the state ... Beneath the universities in the educational hierarchy there was an increase in the numbers of students at technical and commercial higher vocational colleges. The flow of university graduates into management during these years was so rapid that a sample of 198 business leaders of 1920 shows that no fewer than forty-six per cent were university educated, and a further seventeen per cent had been to 'specialist schools' including the higher vocational colleges. A slightly later, larger sample of 500 directors in 153 companies in 1928 reveals that fifty-five per cent were university graduates, a proportion comparable with that in European industry today.[5]

Britain's industrial failures are closely linked to lack of education

This may indeed be the typical figure in most of Europe today, but it is not quite the case in Britain. A reference book published in 1991[6] showed that almost half the 10 000 executives from 1600 companies listed had no degree qualifications. A report in 1987, for which the British author was asked to provide some advice, showed that only 24 per cent of top British managers have degrees, compared to 85 per cent in each of Japan and the USA, 65 per cent in France, and 62 per cent in Germany.[7]

It is typical of the British disdain for education that, despite Britain's position in the van of the Industrial Revolution, it was not until 1908 that Oxford University set up its first chair in engineering, with just two undergraduates taking the first exams in 1910. Cambridge University only developed its outstanding reputation in engineering between the two World Wars and did not, for example, have a chair in electrical engineering until 1945. The British colleges of advanced technology were only established in 1960, some 120 years after Germany's equivalent. In the following decade the polytechnics and technical universities arrived in Britain, whereas Germany's equivalents had appeared over 70 years earlier. Is it really credible that the Japanese and German systems of education at all levels are not directly responsible for those nations' industrial successes over the last century? Or that the British industrial failures are unconnected to her ineffective and inadequate education system? As Geoffrey Holland, then Director of Britain's Manpower Services Commission said in August 1984 when launching *Competence and competition – training and education in the Federal Republic of Germany, the United States and Japan*, a widely publicized and much discussed comparative report, 'We're not only not in the same league, we're not in the same game.'

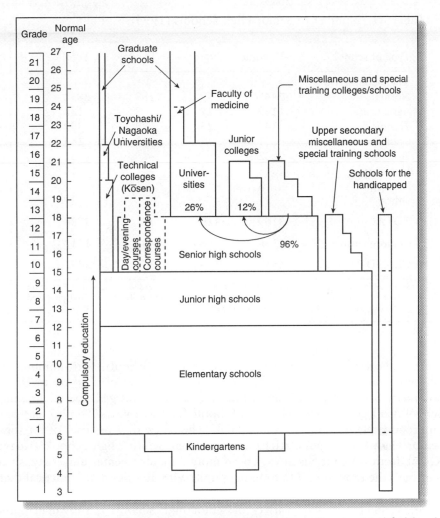

Fig. 3.2 Organization of the Japanese educational system. *Source*: Modified by the authors from: Ministry of Education (1993). *Statistical Abstract of Education, Science, and Culture*, p. 6. The Ministry, Tokyo.

The Japanese education system

The Japanese education system before 1945 followed a model originating in Europe, with 14 years of schooling preceding a three-year degree course. This was completely overhauled by the Americans after the Second World War and is now, not surprisingly therefore, based on the American 6–3–3–4 pattern. As is shown in Fig. 3.2, there are six years at Elementary School, with compulsory education starting at the age of six. Then follow three

Table 3.1. Number of Senior High Schools (1994)

Type of school	Daytime	Night	Dual	Total
Single-course				
Normal	2448	97	287	2832
Agriculture	169	12	7	188
Technical	247	23	129	399
Commerce	231	5	47	283
Fisheries	32	–	–	32
Homecare	13	3	–	16
Nursing	8	–	1	9
Others	21	–	–	21
TOTAL	3169	140	471	3780
Comprehensive	1368	46	303	1717
GRAND TOTAL	4537	186	774	5497

Source: Rearrangement of data from *Gakkō kihon chōsa hōkokusho*, English title: *Report on basic data on schools*, edited by Monbushō (Japanese Ministry of Education) and published by Printing Bureau of the Ministry of Finance, 1995, Tokyo.

years at Lower Secondary School (Junior High School), with compulsory education finishing at the age of 15. However, 95 per cent go on to Upper Secondary School (Senior High School), Technical Colleges, Special Training Schools/Colleges, or Miscellaneous Schools for three years. Some 7 per cent (approximately 400) of the Senior High Schools (with 9 per cent of the total Senior High School population) are Technical Senior High Schools (Kōgyō Kōkō), from which it has always been more difficult to enter university, since they have the reputation of attracting pupils with abilities more practical than academic.

The number and wide variety of senior high schools is shown in Table 3.1, with the numbers of senior high school students shown in Table 3.2. A relatively small number of junior high school graduates enter the 64 technical colleges ('Kōgyō Senmon Gakkō', generally known as 'Kōsen'), of which there is one in each prefecture.

According to statistics from Monbushō[8] (the Japanese Ministry of Education), in 1992 there were 54 739 students in 62 technical colleges, 389 807 students in 3 202 miscellaneous schools, and 861 903 in 3 409 special training colleges/schools. The latter two types are mainly private, but the majority of the miscellaneous schools are crammers for some 140 000 'Rōnins' (those who have failed the university entrance exams, or not passed those for a university of their choice, and are going to have another attempt) and about 72 000 in learner driver schools. While the technical colleges mainly specialize in engineering disciplines, as well as in associated subjects such as industrial chemistry and architecture, the special training colleges/schools provide a wider range of courses in vocational and practical training. Perhaps the most impressive statistic of all is that almost 40 per cent of senior high school pupils enter universities or junior colleges.

First-degree courses at universities are four years long (six years for medicine and dentistry), while masters' degrees take two years. Doctoral degrees, which are almost always only taken following a master's degree, require another three years, and can only be awarded after a certain number of research theses have been published in authorized learned journals. There are also many doctoral degrees awarded for research undertaken over a longer period by engineering and scientific staff working in industry. For this there is no prior academic qualification required; these are an excellent means of increasing the links between universities and industry. It is also important to note that the prime role of universities in Japan is seen as teaching rather than research, to a much greater degree than in the UK, where university research has a higher importance and profile.

Junior colleges provide two- or three-year courses, mainly entered by women, which follow on from senior high school. In the past they tended to concentrate on the skills required to become a good housewife, such as cookery and flower arranging. These days they are much more aimed at providing a basis for careers in practical occupations such as software engineering, sales, teaching, health, and administration.

Table 3.2. Numbers of Senior High School students

	1987	1989	1991	1993	1994
Normal					
Male	1 933 697	2 052 087	1 981 081	1 812 616	1 757 081
Female	1 992 654	2 117 348	2 055 374	1 896 968	1 846 228
Technical					
Male	459 028	465 257	445 193	408 101	394 561
Female	19 520	24 059	27 611	29 980	31 119
Commerce					
Male	165 876	171 836	167 659	154 232	148 643
Female	412 951	416 905	393 710	346 655	325 696
Agriculture					
Male	104 710	105 370	100 572	94 005	91 562
Female	49 028	50 959	48 784	44 273	44 000

Source: Same as Table 3.1.

The benefits of a broad education system

Unlike the narrow post-16 educational system in England and Wales, the Japanese receive a very broad education throughout their schooling, and this is exactly what is required by Japanese industry. The President of a large Japanese company has said that a good engineer must have three qualities:

1. He must have a broader ability than his own specialism, and should develop his wider abilities.
2. He should have a broad view.
3. He must have a high level and wide knowledge, and be good at teaching others.

This commitment to ensuring both flexibility and skills in tutoring others is extremely important. Their presence as key value systems throughout Japanese industry and commerce is at the core of their ability to provide the quality, innovative, well-designed, and good-value products which have increasingly dominated world markets. Their absence in British industry has had the reverse effect.

But if the Japanese educational system is so broad, how can it be justified as suitable for Japan's specific industrial requirements? The answer is that it is precisely because the output from the schools, in particular, is so thoroughly well educated.

A notoriously high-pressure school system

Japan is well-known for its pressure cooker school system, and what is known as 'shiken-jigoku' (the examination hell). To what extent is this image correct? And why and how does it operate, and is it good for Japan? The answer to the first question is that the international image of a high-pressure school system is basically correct. so what drives it? The incentive to tolerate this enormously pressurized school system is that status in Japanese society is very largely determined by which university one has attended. No doubt it is the Confucian ethic of respect for learning which lies at the heart of this obsession.

Of the 513 universities in Japan, 95 are National (funded by the Ministry of Education), 39 are Public (funded by the Prefectures), and two are Governmental (funded by Ministries other than the Ministry of Education). On the whole, these are considered the best, although several of the 377 private universities, most notably Waseda, Keio, and Sophia, also have a very high reputation. In addition there are 32 National, 51 Public, and hundreds of Private Junior Colleges.

In large companies, in particular, and in the civil service, it is clear that those promoted to senior levels have almost invariably up to now come from the best universities (although there is some evidence that this may be changing) and are groomed for the top very largely on that basis.

There is therefore extraordinary pressure at all levels of society to enter these best-regarded universities. A further major incentive is that the fees at the national and public universities, as well as the staff-to-student ratios, are much better than at the private ones. In order to get into one of these few best universities, it is important to have been at one of the best senior high schools. In practice, there is an acknowledged hierarchy in the reputation of all schools at all levels, just as there is in the universities. This is reinforced by the system of entrance exams for schools, each of which sets its own, just as do all universities. Therefore, in order to get into the best senior high schools, students need to obtain a place at the best junior high schools, and so on down to the best kindergartens. The pressure is such that in recent years there has been the emergence of 'Jukus' (private cramming tuition colleges) for pre-school children between the ages of one and five in order to enable them to enter the best elementary schools!

Astonishingly, 40 per cent of medical students at Tokyo University, which is known as the most difficult to enter, come from the top four private high schools. This does not, interestingly, mean that Tokyo University students are the most successful in the National Certificate Examination for qualifying as a doctor; that particular accolade went to Tsukuba University in 1992 and the University of Occupational and Environmental Health in 1993.

Pupils are driven to their best efforts by their mothers

Just in case there is any hesitation on the part of any pupil, then behind every one of them stands the *Kyōikumama*, the school-minded mother. In fact it can reasonably be argued that the *kyōikumama* is another major factor in Japan's success. She will often attend the crammer together with her son or daughter in the early years, and will not see her job as done until her offspring has safely entered one of the best universities. Even then she may not rest until her son has joined a good company. Small and medium-sized companies complain of the strong influence of mothers in encouraging their sons to obtain jobs in large companies featured in television commercials.

It is worth exploring this important relationship between mother and child. Fathers in Japan are rarely seen at home until late at night, and are often working or socializing with colleagues even at weekends. Wives seem to have a philosophical view about this, recognizing the importance of their husbands' success at work. Indeed, most of them would actually be highly concerned if their husbands were to be seen regularly at home; the neighbours would assume that the man was not successful at his work if he could be regularly spared, and that would involve considerable loss of face. Japanese housewives therefore have a saying that the perfect husband is 'healthy and rarely seen'!

Throughout early childhood Japanese mothers remain physically close to their offspring, even to the extent that the child sleeps with the mother in or next to her futon, as well as bathing together with her. Unlike what happens in the West, childhood rarely involves any punishment. It is assumed that children are born inherently good, and they are encouraged to become highly dependent on their mothers. The implied threat to the children is that the mother's indulgence will be withdrawn if they misbehave or refuse to conform. It is therefore right from birth that Japanese are socialized to understand that conformity is critical to survival in their society; but this is done in a secure and indulgent environment which makes childhood an enjoyable experience so that in later life there is an inbuilt self-confidence among the Japanese in their role in a structured society. That structure teaches that it is the role of women to care for their husbands in every possible way. As the men pursue a career which puts them under great pressure, and often stress, they tend to see their wives as substitute mothers, as they hanker back to those early days of childhood.

The Japanese never stop learning

It would be a mistake to underestimate the widespread inclination to learn amongst most Japanese. The circulation of Japanese newspapers has long been the highest in the world, reflecting the almost insatiable Japanese thirst for knowledge. In July 1987, for example, the circulation of the *Nihon Keizai Shimbun* was 2 622 000, against the 2 070 392 of the *Wall Street Journal* and the 344 584 of Britain's *Financial Times*. In 1931 Inazō Nitobe wrote:

The best showing of which compulsory education can boast is seen in the wide diffusion of periodicals and the vast circulation of newspapers, two of which print 1,500,000 copies daily. A still more apparent evidence of the universal literacy of the Japanese is shown in the fact that nearly all the daily newspapers devote the first page entirely to book and magazine advertisements.[9]

Japan now has a huge book-buying population. In contrast, in Britain 67 per cent of adults rarely if ever visit a library, according to a 1991 report by the National Institute of Adult Continuing Education.

Japanese teaching is a one-way affair

The Japanese education system may be dedicated to providing the raw material for her government and industry, but that is not to say that it is narrow or applied. In fact the opposite is true. The education is very broad, with little attempt to explain the applications of the teaching.

Indeed teaching in both schools and universities is mainly one-way lecturing, with no questions from the pupils or students. This is a Confucian approach (interpreted in Japan as the teacher being superior to the pupils and not to be questioned) which would definitely not be appropriate in the West, although even in Japan one-way teaching is often thought undesirable and teachers do increasingly frequently encourage questions. It is also probably only in the East that an education system could be tolerated in which there is such a pure divide between the largely academic, non-practical, and non-applied content of school and university curricula, and the practical application of that knowledge in industry and commerce. The objective in Japan is to provide a firm theoretical base through education which then forms the basis for thorough training throughout the individual's career. In addition, it is expected that people will make every effort to extend their knowledge after the end of their formal education, be it by reading, correspondence courses, or any other means, including in-company tuition. Most importantly, the formal profession of and informal role of teaching others (*sensei*) is considered a highly honourable and prestigious duty.

In schools, teaching is a rather sterile affair – largely a matter of duplicating the contents of the pupils' textbooks, which lie open on the desks before them. There is no discussion between pupils and teacher or description of the practical applications of the subject-matter. The practical equipment available for science teaching, for example, is generally much more basic than in an equivalent British school, largely because the experimental work is no more than three or four hours each term. Nor are there the practical demonstrations that are such an important part of British science teaching. School-leavers in Japan have very little practical experience of science, but a great deal of theoretical knowledge.

The average Japanese student, up to and including university level, does not actually expect to see any direct use for his or her learning, presumably merely seeing it as a tool to achieve a place at a top-ranking university. When a professor at the Tokyo Institute of Technology was challenged by the British author about the view that Japanese education is largely about rote learning, he accepted the criticism as containing some truth; he pointed out, however, that students must first understand the basics. The first three years of a degree do this, and then in the final year the students work together in a laboratory and learn to apply the theory. These final-year research groups, called *Kōza*, are usually made up of a professor, an associate professor, two assistants, and a number of undergraduate and graduate students. By the time science or engineering students graduate, they probably actually have more experimental and practical experience than their American counterparts.

It is also common for professors to have no funds for a secretary, and therefore to have to deal with all their own correspondence, as well as designing and building much of their own equipment. This no doubt both teaches their students how to develop their practical skills and re-emphasizes the basic Japanese ethic of humility.

There is great pressure to conform

A revealing insight into the high pressure and close observation to which
Japanese school children are subjected was given in an article by Rosy
Clark in the September 1985 edition of *Winds*, the in-flight magazine of
Japan Air Lines. The article is entitled *'The new Japanese teenager'*, and
explains that:

Most parents and school administrators support the rule of conformity because . . .
they feel it's easier to educate children under tight controls. To help parents and school
officials recognise a budding 'delinquent', the Tokyo Metropolitan Police Office widely
distributes a document that offers pointers on deviant appearance. The worst of it
appears to be cigarette burns on the hands or a Checkers haircut (Checkers is a
popular Japanese rock group that affects a neo-punk image). But other aberrations
described in the police handout include coloured stockings, pink nail polish and a
pinky ring for girls, while boys who carry a pocket knife or remove the school badge
from their school uniforms are suspect. And it's believed that girls who carry a disco
key ring and a quilted tote bag probably change out of their school uniforms once
away from the campus, a definite affront to the school.

This pressure to conform, to achieve academically and to do so in an
environment of one-way teaching, runs totally counter to the value system in
the West. Educationists therefore frequently quote Japanese pupils as suffering
the world's highest suicide rate; in fact it is lower than in either Britain or
the USA.

   Even in Japan, however, there is acceptance that these pressures are at times
taken too far. There was shock in July 1990 when a girl of 15 was killed when
the school gate was slammed on her because she was one second late for class in
the city of Kobe; in that case the teacher was rapidly dismissed amidst outraged
publicity. A year later a 14-year-old girl and a 16-year-old boy died at a private
reform school near Hiroshima; they had been locked in a cargo container after
being caught smoking, and died of dehydration and heat-stroke. Such extreme
examples are rare, but they do stir national debate in Japan over the severity
of school discipline.

   The very positive side of Japanese schooling was noted by the British
Secretary of State for Education when he visited Japan in 1991. His
Principal Private Secretary, Christina Bienkowska, who accompanied him
on his twelve-day visit, commented:

They don't seem to have a sub-class of kids who have dropped out of the system, nor
the problems of illiteracy that we have. It is not at the top of the range that there is a
difference because I feel that their best and ours are probably matched. What is most
startling is how their average and below average pupils advance through the system.
Their average is far higher than ours.[10]

Overseas visitors comment on the pace of the school day and the effort and
enthusiasm which pupils of all ages devote to school long after the school

day and term finish. The Japanese school day (normally from 8.30 a.m. to 3.30 p.m.) is slightly longer than in the UK, and is followed as often as not by two hours of compulsory 'voluntary' activities. Furthermore, 36 per cent of all students nationwide (58 per cent of students in the Tokyo metropolitan area) either attend *jukus* (evening and weekend crammers) or have private teachers.[11]

The extraordinary pressure at all levels of society to enter the best universities, moreover, leads a high proportion (about one third) of senior high school graduates to become what are known as *Rōnin* ('leaderless samurai') and attend a crammer for a further year in the hope of achieving a place at a top-flight university, rather than accept a place at a second-rate one, since the likelihood is so great that the outcome will strongly influence their future career prospects.

Westerners may be dismissive or highly critical of such a demanding educational system, but the evidence is overwhelming that it is highly effective in providing Japan with the best-educated population in the world. This inevitably gives Japanese industry the raw material on which it can build the practical competence and skills for which it is so renowned.

Are British educationists really in any position to criticize?

Perhaps the strongest and most vocal critics of the Japanese system are the British educationists. Unfortunately they are hardly in a strong position to criticize a system so much more effective than their own. Professor Sig Prais from the National Institute for Economic and Social Research participated in a scientifically-organized international comparison of the mathematical attainments of secondary school pupils carried out in 1981 among some two dozen countries. This shows, as quoted at the beginning of this chapter, that the mathematical attainment of a Japanese 13 1/2-year-old is approximately equivalent to that of a 16-year-old English pupil. Since Japanese compulsory education starts at the age of six and that of an English pupil at the age of five, the evidence is that the Japanese learn their mathematics about 50 per cent faster per year of schooling. More worrying still for the British experts in education:

Nonetheless, a closer comparison restricted to those questions that were identical in both the 1964 and 1981 mathematical tests shows a slight advance by Japanese pupils – from 62 to 63 per cent of correct answers; but a fall in the attainments of English pupils – from 50 to 44 per cent of correct answers. England was the *only one of the ten countries* for which these comparisons were possible which showed a fall in average scores in *all* three main components – arithmetic, algebra and geometry.[12]

Explaining the likely reasons for this difference between the two countries, he says:

Higher Japanese schooling attainments have apparently not absorbed a greater share of national resources than in England (5.0 per cent of GDP in Japan, 5.8 in UK, and 5.2 in Germany). The main factors contributing to controlled costs are probably: larger class-sizes are typically taught by a teacher in Japan (40 as compared with under 30 in England); a restricted curriculum *within* each school, with few optional subjects (but allowing for diversity of curricula *between* schools at later ages); a longer school-year, that is fewer school holidays (243 school-days a year in Japan, compared with 193 in England); and pupils' assistance in ancillary tasks at schools – cleaning classrooms, operating the school library, helping with mid-day meals, and the like.[13]

The willingness of pupils to help with tasks such as cleaning is an interesting insight into the upbringing of Japanese children (this is perfectly normal in German schools as well). It must reflect in their later careers, for example, in their preparedness to spend several months working on a production line – something which is anathema to a British graduate. In *The Japan diaries of Richard Gordon Smith*, he notes in his entry for 21 December 1905 in Kobe:

While coming up the hill and passing the upper girls school I saw the young ladies cleaning the window glass and frames. What an excellent idea, and what a lot of good it would do both our boys and girls if they were made to work out and clean systematically the whole of their classrooms. It requires discipline of an almost military mind to get it done properly.[14]

A further reason for the Japanese advantage appears to lie in the standardization of textbooks. As Professor Prais says:

Remarkably enough, the whole class in a typical Japanese Lower Secondary School is taught together, without streaming, and follows systematically one of the officially-authorised textbooks. Pupils are expected to attempt the many problems printed in their textbooks; a certain quota of pages in the text is covered each week. 'Japanese education is textbook centred' (as Professor Anderson put it); in English Comprehensive Schools, on the other hand, the teacher often prides himself on *not* using textbooks, and relies on many individually – and laboriously – produced duplicated sets of problems and other teaching material. Japanese textbooks are attractively set out with graded exercises, including additional exercises for slower pupils and more difficult exercises for faster pupils. The proportion of the school timetable devoted to mathematics is not very different in the two countries, but more mathematical homework is set in Japan.[15]

It has to be said that the level of homework required of pupils at senior high schools is highly demanding. There is a well-known saying in Japan in relation to the amount of homework necessary for passing the exams for entry to universities of 'Four hours sleep – pass; five hours sleep – fail.'

There were a number of reports published in 1990 and 1991 showing the depth of the problem in Britain. For example, the Assessment of Performance Unit, a government-funded monitoring body, showed in 1990 that 60 per cent of 15-year-olds could not put hat sizes of $7\frac{1}{8}$, $7\frac{3}{4}$, $7\frac{5}{6}$, and $7\frac{1}{4}$ in order. A survey by Public Attitude Surveys that same year indicated that 47 per cent of over-15s were baffled by percentages. Another report in 1990 by the Adult Literacy and Basic Skills Unit showed that one young person in four between the ages of 16 and 20 has difficulties with reading, one in three has problems with spelling, and nearly half rarely or never read books. A survey by the National Foundation for Educational Research for the Department of Education and Science in 1991 found that 28 per cent of children aged 7 could not read with any accuracy, a quarter could not spell simple words such as 'car', 'man', and 'hot', and a third were unable to count up to 100 or add and subtract numbers up to ten, while fewer than one in seven could do simple multiplications such as 5×5. Similar problems were discovered in tests on 14-year-olds.

It is surely inconceivable that such educational incompetence does not affect Britain's ability to produce quality products in increasingly tough world markets. Britain is being used as an example in comparison to Japan since the effectiveness of the two countries' educational systems is so obviously at opposite ends of the spectrum that it is perhaps thereby easier to draw out lessons. It is, however, important to emphasize that this is rather more a British problem than a Western one. Germany's mathematical performance according to international research by the International Association for the Evaluation of Educational Achievement is similar to that of Japan, and it is notable that Germany, too, has a very successful industrial track record. The German education system is rather different from that in Japan, but it has the same rigour, quite unlike what is found in Britain. For example, a pupil in Germany will only progress from one grade of class to the next by passing the exams at the end of the year. It is unknown in Britain for a pupil to have to repeat a year in a class for failing such end-of-year exams, for one reason because such exams do not generally exist as yet, and for another because giving a child reason to see itself as a failure is unacceptable to most of the British educational establishment.

One lesson, surely, is that the disciplines of achieving required minimum standards, with penalty for failure, together with the challenge of competition, is the basis for success both by individuals in their future careers and for the economies of nations. Again it has to be noted that British educationists are, in the main, obsessed by the idea of competition leading to losers as well as winners, and are therefore vociferously opposed to it.

International comparisons of educational attainment

In view of the way in which the Japanese education system has been based on the American one since 1946, it is particularly interesting to compare the effectiveness of those two systems 45 years later. In 1991 the National Education Goals Panel found that less than 20 per cent of American schoolchildren were competent in solving basic mathematical problems. The findings put the United States behind Japan, South Korea, and Britain, the countries with which comparisons were made. American students also trailed these countries in science studies. The Secretary of Education, Mr Lamar Alexander, said, 'The gap between what students know and what they need to know is so large that it's almost shocking.' Like Britain, the USA suffers from an indisciplined school system and a soft culture in which pupils are all too often not stretched to achieve their real potential.

Japanese educated outside Japan face major problems

The very great difficulty experienced by Japanese pupils who have received part of their education outside Japan is a major issue. There have been two key problems. The first is the one of readjusting from a relatively low-pressure foreign education system with a different syllabus to the system back in Japan in an environment of such intense competition. The second is the cultural one, where those educated overseas have been seen in many cases as having been tainted by foreign values and as having lost some of their Japanese identity. These problems have been seen as being so great that an overseas posting for a Japanese businessman has very often been a great sacrifice. Either he had to sacrifice his childrens' future career prospects by bringing his family with him, or he had to leave his family behind in Japan.

In the case of the first difficulty, there are now many Japanese schools being established in those countries with significant numbers of Japanese expatriates. One example is the Japanese Gyōsei International School in Milton Keynes in England, which opened in 1987. Pupils are woken at 6.00 a.m., and perform physical exercises before starting a 17-hour day of classes, private study, meals, and 'supplementary lessons'.

In the case of the cultural problem, it is beginning to be perceived by some Japanese companies that education overseas is a definite advantage in a world where they have to improve their understanding of those overseas markets and cultures.

Japan has a very large number of technologists

There is a complete contrast between the relative numbers of engineers and scientists graduating each year. *Competence and competition* showed that in Japan in 1982 19.4 per cent of undergraduates were engineers, but only 3.2 per cent were scientists.[16] In contrast, the *Butcher IT Skills Shortages Committee – First report* in 1984 showed that the annual output in the UK of home science graduates was about 24 000, compared to those graduating in engineering of 14 000;[17] these represent respectively about 23 per cent and 13 per cent of total graduate output. It may reasonably be argued that Japan produces far too few scientists, while the UK produces far too few engineers.

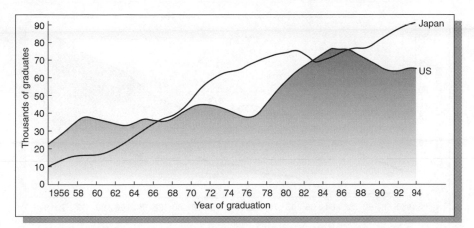

Fig. 3.3 Comparison of first-degree technology graduates in Japan and the USA 1956–82. *Source*: L.P. Grayson (1983). 'Japan's intellectual challenge: the strategy'. *Engineering Education*, December 1983, p. 4, updated by the authors from data in the USA and Japan.

Lawrence P. Grayson of the American National Institute of Education has shown how Japan overtook the USA in terms of the total number of engineers graduating annually in 1967. This is shown in Figure 3.3. Given that the population of the USA is twice that of Japan, this Chart actually shows that at that point Japan was graduating *twice* as many engineers *pro rata* each year as the USA. Indeed, by 1980 there were 35 engineers employed in Japan per 10 000 population, compared to only 25 per 10 000 in the USA. In contrast, Lawrence Grayson also shows how Japan lags behind the USA in the numbers of master and doctoral degrees awarded annually in engineering, as shown in Figures 3.4 and 3.5.

This very significant international advantage in the numbers of technology graduates is extremely important. This is particularly so given the equal advantage in their numbers of technicians, which will be discussed in later chapters. How else, after all, can an industrially based economy thrive and grow? As Figure 3.6 shows, there is a direct correlation between the cumulative numbers of bachelor, master and doctorate degree graduates in technology from Japanese universities and the progressive increase in Japan's GNP.

Despite this, all Japanese companies are emphatic that Japan has a severe national shortage of electrical engineers, and that twice as many would be recruited from the universities each year if they were available. That is even in spite of the fact that Japanese universities are producing three times as many such graduates each year *pro rata* as British Universities. This national shortage in Japan is supported by responses to a survey by Denki Rōren (the Japanese Federation of Electrical Machine Workers' Unions) in October 1979, in other

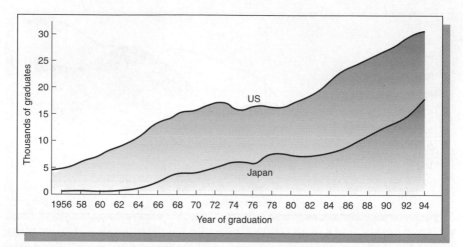

Fig. 3.4 Comparison of masters' degree technology graduates in Japan and the USA 1956–82. *Source*: L. P. Grayson (1984). 'Japan's intellectual challenge: the system'. *Engineering Education*, January 1984, p. 17, updated by the authors from data in the USA and Japan.

words before the even greater successes of the Japanese electrical engineering industry in the 1980s. This showed that the major problem regarding working conditions as seen by engineers was the shortage of staff. Some 55.9 per cent of Sanyo, 51.2 per cent of Toshiba, and 46.4 per cent of Fujitsu engineers referred to this problem.[18] The key lesson is that, by producing large numbers of well-educated engineers, who are then well trained and well managed, Japan has been able to dominate world markets to such an extent that shortages of skilled staff become the main restraint on even faster expansion.

The benefits of a well-educated and adaptable workforce

To Western eyes it appears that the Japanese grow up and mature much later than in the West. The combined result of this 'immaturity', together with their high level of education, is an extremely well-educated and adaptable workforce. This gives Japan an enormous advantage over the West. Small companies find it almost impossible to recruit engineering graduates; they nevertheless find it perfectly feasible to recruit non-technical graduates, with degrees in subjects like economics, and train them to do technical maintenance and marketing jobs.

Another small example of this adaptability was observed by the British author at a Toshiba computer factory, where he observed that even the storemen were giving all components and sub-assemblies a visual inspection as they issued them in trays for further assembly from a highly automated storage system. These are but two examples; but Japan scores because so many people at so many levels are so extremely adaptable.

A study by Richard Lynn, a British psychologist, in 1982 showed that 77 per cent of young Japanese have IQs higher than the average European or American: 10 per cent of all Japanese have IQs higher than 130, compared to only 2 per cent of Europeans or Americans.[19] Other comparative studies by the American psychologist Harold Stevenson in the USA and Japan indicate that these results are due to the educational system, rather than to nutritional or hereditary factors.

Nakasone's educational reforms

Despite the undeniable successes of the Japanese educational system, in 1984 the then Prime Minister, Yasuhiro Nakasone, set up a three-year Provisional Council on Educational Reform. In his speech at its first meeting on 5 September 1984 he said:

Today we are facing dramatic changes in our circumstances, both domestic and overseas, as well as great changes in the times. I am convinced that the time has

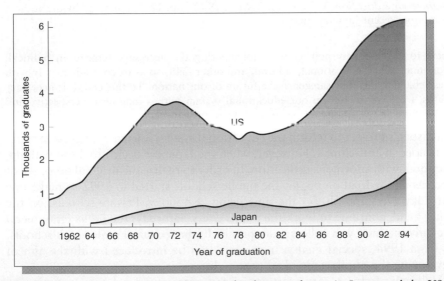

Fig. 3.5 Comparison of doctoral degree technology graduates in Japan and the USA 1962–82. *Source*: L. P. Grayson (1984). 'Japan's intellectual challenge: the system'. *Engineering Education*, January 1984, p. 18, updated by the authors from data in the USA and Japan.

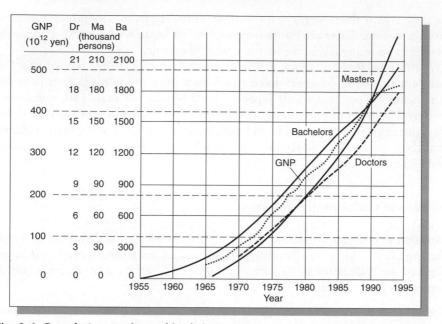

Fig. 3.6 Cumulative numbers of bachelors', masters', and doctoral degree graduates in technology from Japanese universities shown in relation to the increase in Japan's GNP. *Source*: Motokazu Nakamura (1990). 'My opinion concerning a reason why the Japanese have made such economic progress'. *Journal of the Japan Society for Engineering Education*, Vol. 38 No. 2 (Mar. 1990), pp. 12–16, updated by the authors from more recent Japanese data.

come to develop new policies for implementing the necessary reforms in political, economic, social, educational, cultural, and other fields so as to cope adequately with these changes and thus safeguard the future of our nation. To this end, it is necessary for us, I believe, to reform our educational system with a long-term perspective and make this a responsibility of the entire Government.

Nakasone's project to reform the educational system started with great fanfare, but ended in anti-climax. However, when the Japanese decide to do something, they do it with enormous dedication. In order to realize the original objective of decreasing the load on pupils, the public schools started in 1992 to make one Saturday every month, for the time being, a holiday. Private schools, on the other hand, continue to work the pupils every Saturday; the *jukus* (crammers) are only too happy to collect more pupils. In the technical senior high schools, as from 1994, special final-year projects will be introduced with the aim of developing the pupils' individual personalities.

University reforms are starting in the area of liberal arts courses. As examples, let us take the cases of the two most eminent universities, Tokyo and Kyoto. The liberal arts courses in the former Imperial Universities had their origins in the old Higher Schools. Before the 1947 reforms, the curriculum at the Imperial Universities was a specialized three-year one. The Higher Schools which the students attended before going to university taught languages, mathematics, and liberal arts subjects, as well as giving their pupils a good opportunity to develop their personality over three years. When the new university system was introduced under American guidance, the first half was for liberal arts, with the second half for specialized subjects. When this system started the liberal arts courses attracted students because they could maintain a breadth in their studies. However, today's liberal studies courses have changed into ones where students can pass the course just by taking easy subjects. This reflects immaturity in the students. Kyoto University has therefore decided to abolish this course. As from 1993 both liberal arts subjects and specialized ones are taught in parallel to freshmen.

The students successful in Tokyo's highly demanding entrance examination study liberal arts at the Komaba Campus, which used to be the First Higher School, for at least two years before transferring to the Hongo Campus for their specialized studies. This liberal arts course is reforming its curriculum; the reason given is surprising. One of the professors says: 'We must give suitable guidance to those students who cannot follow the classes and who do not show much enthusiasm. Some students cannot read English even to [Japanese] junior high school level. The worse problem, however, is lethargy . . .'

We must also be careful about another significant aspect of the Educational Reform review. As Akira Takanashi, [20] a Council member for the Educational Reform says:

The Provisional Council for Educational Reform was triggered by the bullying problem in elementary and junior high schools and over-heated entrance exams. The author understands the reason (or necessity) for the PCER, which was established beyond the frame of Monbushō (the Ministry of Education); this has been because the terms of reference of the Council are to discuss education reform in the context that life-time education is much more than school education alone.'

Further he says:

1992 saw the peak in the number of 18-year-old boys and girls, and hereafter the population of youngsters will certainly decrease. In contrast, the number of older people will increase. We are entering the era of a society of the aged. Japan's past rapid economic progress has been supported by young graduates – highly efficient low-wage manpower. This basis will begin to be lost from now on. Middle- and old-aged people are generally less adaptive to technological change. Unless Japan can succesfully create an environment which will maintain the conditions to make these people adaptive, her economic rate of growth will decline at the end of this century. It is necessary to maintain a refreshed state in every Japanese in such areas as skills, expertise, and social knowledge. For this very reason, education and re-training of the adult is an important subject in educational reform.

The Council reported on the need for a 'Third' education reform to Mr Nakasone. (The 'First' reform being the one implemented after the Meiji

Restoration, while the 'Second' was that implemented in 1947 under American guidance.) By this was meant an epoch-making transfer to lifetime education, with four characteristic Japanese features:

1. Learning from the best experiences in other countries.
2. Traditional culture, including: the tea ceremony, flower-arranging, calligraphy, *kendo/judo*, gardening, and *waka/haiku* poetry.
3. Traditional in-house training/education associated with lifetime employment.
4. The custom of providing the opportunity of education/training at a Japanese or overseas university.

This concept affected the 1992 revision of the 'New Vocational Training Law' to the 'Human Resources Development Promotion Law', which will be dealt with in Chapter 6. There is therefore hardly any danger of Japan losing its world-leading competence in industry by neglecting the importance of education.

Japan is now looking outwards, not inwards

From a position where the average Japanese student at the age of 18 is as competent at mathematics as the top 1 per cent in other competitor countries,[21] Japan clearly has the capacity to consider some liberalization of its system of education. It has to be said, however, that there are as yet few signs that it will actually do so.

After all, some 120 years after bringing in those European and American educational and technical experts, Japan has reached the stage where in 1990 Sumitomo Trust and Banking Company gave £1 million to Eton for the teaching of Japanese. This followed on the £1 million gift to the Oxford Union from the Mitsubishi Trust and Banking Corporation in 1988. Nissan has given £1 million for an Institute at Oxford in its name and Suntory and Toyota have donated £1.5 million each to the London School of Economics, from which the British author benefited as a Research Associate as part of the background research for this book. Japan's internationalization in education is such that it has started to invest in British universities, with Teikyo University leasing part of Durham University in 1989 for 99 years to provide 130 Japanese students a year with facilities for English language and culture study.

So when will the West start to learn from Japan?

Japan has always been a nation totally prepared to learn from others. Since both authors are electrical engineers, we will finish this chapter by noting that a classic book[22] written in 1861 by Michael Faraday, one of the fathers of electrical engineering, *The chemical history of a candle* (in which he quotes the construction of the Japanese candle – shown in Fig. 3.7 as a good structure for burning, since it has a hollow wick), is still recommended reading in the summer holidays for Japanese schoolchildren. When American and European schoolchildren are taught to show equal thirst for learning, then perhaps Japan's industrial conquest of the world will start to slow.

Fig. 3.7 The construction of a Japanese candle.

References

1 Richard Sims, *Modern Japan*, The Bodley Head, London, 1973, pp. 19–20.
2 Richard Sims, ibid., p. 50.
3 *Education: A different version*, Institute of Public Policy Research, 30–32 Southampton Street, London WC2E 7RA, September 1993.
4 *Nippon – The land and its people*, Nippon Steel Corporation, Gakuseisha Publishing Co. Ltd, 1982.
5 Rodney Clark, *The Japanese Company*, Yale University Press, New Haven, 1979, p. 36.

6 *Who's who in industry*, Fulcrum Publishing, 1991.
7 Manpower Services Commission, National Economic Development Council and the British Institute of Management, *The making of managers – A report on management education, training and development in the USA, West Germany, France, Japan and the UK*, HMSO, London, April 1987.
8 *Statistical Abstract of Education, Science and Culture*, Ministry of Education, Science and Culture, Japan, 1993 edition, Tokyo, p. 70.
9 Inazō Nitobe, *Japan – some phases of her problems and development*, Ernest Benn, London, 1931, p. 235.
10 *Japan*, No. 517, 9 July 1991.
11 *Japan Hand Book, JETRO's Desktop Economic Encyclopedia*, Japan External Trade Organization, Kodansha, Tokyo, 1985, p. 93.
12 S. J. Prais, *Educating for productivity: comparisons of Japanese and English schooling and vocational preparation*, National Institute Economic Review, London, February 1987, p. 200.
13 Ibid., p. 203.
14 *The Japan diaries of Richard Gordon Smith – edited by Victoria Manthorpe*, Viking Rainbird – Penguin Books, London, 1986, p. 189.
15 S. J. Prais, op. cit., p. 204.
16 Manpower Services Commission, *Competence and competition – training and education in the Federal Republic of Germany, the United States and Japan*, HMSO, London, August 1984, Table 4.5, p. 60.
17 *The human factor – the supply side problem*, Department of Trade and Industry, IT Skills Shortages Committee, First Report, HMSO, London July 1984, Table 3.
18 Denki Rōren (the Japanese Federation of Electrical Machine Workers' Unions), *Survey No. 160*, October 1979. Tokyo
19 Richard Lynn, 'IQ in Japan and the United States shows a growing disparity', *Nature*, 20 May, 1982, pp. 222–3, (quoted in L. P. Grayson, 'Japan's Intellectual challenge: the future', *Engineering Education*, February 1984, p. 32).
20 Akira Takanashi, *Shōgai gakushū to gakkō kyōiku kaikaku* (in Japanese; English title: *Lifetime studying and school education reform*), Eidel Institute, Tokyo, 1992.
21 Richard Lynn, *Educational achievement in Japan – lessons for the West*, Macmillan Press, Basingstoke, 1988, p. 9.
22 Michael Faraday, *A course of six lectures on the chemical history of a candle* (Delivered before a Juvenile Auditory at the Royal Institution of Great Britain during the Christmas Holidays of 1860–1), Griffin, Bohn, & Co., London, 1861, pp. 142–3.

Recruitment in Japan

'It has become clear that what makes companies competitive is, above all, the quality of the workforce.'

– Sir John Cassels, CB

Introduction

Whether at company or national level, Japan takes a much more analytical and strategic approach to recruitment than its competitors.

There is a perspective brought to bear in analysing the means required to achieve long-term objectives, up to 250 years in the future, which is a key factor in actually attaining those objectives. One essential element in that strategy is the broad and long-term view taken of the types and sources of recruits required, supported by a flexible and well-thought-out approach in its implementation.

Recruitment strategy exists at both national and company levels

One well-publicized example of manpower needs debated and analysed nationally is the case of software engineers. The Ministry of International Trade and Industry identified the between the supply and demand from 1985 until the year 2000 as shown in Figure 4.1. The Information Manpower Committee of the Industrial Structure Deliberation Council reporting to MITI estimated in 1984 that by the year 2000 the Japanese software market would have expanded almost tenfold to 34 600 billion yen, requiring 2 145 000 software engineers. On the other hand, the supply by then was projected to reach 1 180 000 at most, unless education, industry, and employment were restructured. As a result the £100 million SIGMA PROJECT was launched in 1985 to increase software productivity; this was aimed at reducing the projected 965 000 manpower gap at the end of the century to 450 000. In the event SIGMA was less successful than had been hoped, and was replaced by a much more

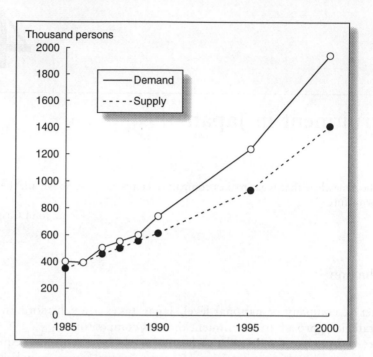

Fig. 4.1 Demand for, and supply of, software engineers in Japan. *Source*: MITI (Japanese Ministry of International Trade and Industry) (1993). *Shin jōhō kakumei wo sasaeru jinzaizō* (in Japanese; English title: *Manpower needs to support the new information revolution*), Computer Age Company, Tokyo, pp. 99 and 108.

modest project in 1990. Japan therefore has still to solve its future software skills problem; but the way the problem has been identified and approached illustrates a long-term philosophy rarely found in other countries.

Masanori Moritani is the author of *Japanese technology – getting the best for the least*, one of the best-known books on the Japanese approach to technology. He told the British author that technology has now become very wide and deep. Japanese companies therefore do not look for specialist skills in recruits, but rather basic ability, and especially character; they see themselves as building on the broad education of recruits by developing their abilities in-company throughout their careers. This strategic view is supported by the Research and Development Institute of Vocational Training:

... although there is a difference between big enterprises and small enterprises in their policy for personnel employment, the difference has begun to be considered not a fundamental one but rather a matter of degree. Generally speaking, the factors which enterprises in Japan put most emphasis on at the time of personnel hiring are not what prospective employees can do at present, but their potential to learn and adaptability to changing situations.[1]

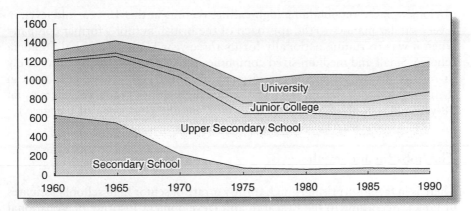

Fig. 4.2 Highest qualification levels of school-leavers entering the labour market 1960–90 (thousands of persons per highest level of qualification). *Source*: Japanese Ministry of Education (1993). *Basic statistical survey of schools*, quoted in The Japan Institute of Labor (1993). *1991–92 Japanese Working Life Profile – Labor Statistics*, p. 19.

... there are more cases of employment of prospective skilled personnel which 'takes preference of those whose general scholastic ability and adaptability is higher over those who can immediately handle their given duties' (47 per cent), than the cases that 'take preference of those who have received education/training related to their job so that they can immediately handle their given duties' (21 per cent).[2]

Recruiting school-leavers

With 95 per cent of pupils entering senior high school, only a very small proportion of company recruits enter employment directly from junior high school at the age of 15. The declining proportion of such 15-year old recruits entering the labour market is shown in Figure 4.2.

As one example, Table 4.1 shows the qualifications in 1992 of the employees in a medium-sized precision motor company with an eighty-year history of continuous profits.

Most companies recruit locally from senior high schools for factory assembly, office clerical, and similar vacancies. In contrast to Britain, where such positions are usually filled by 16-year-old school-leavers with generally mediocre academic qualifications, the Japanese equivalents are therefore not only much better educated, but are recruited and trained for a wide range of possible jobs. The overall competence and flexibility of the Japanese workforce is thus very much greater than that of its British competition.

For more skilled technician jobs, larger companies establish contacts nationally with the best senior high schools, and such recruits may therefore work in a plant which is hundreds of miles from the school. Enormous emphasis is obviously placed on obtaining high-calibre recruits at this 18-year-old level, in a very similar manner to the approach of the British author's former company when it was recruiting nationally for its three-year Higher National Diploma scheme. Small and medium-sized companies are of necessity much more likely to restrict themselves to the recruitment of senior high school graduates in their local area. (In Japan, the term 'senior high school graduate' refers to an 18-year-old school-leaver, rather than implying the possession of a degree.)

The 'jobs for life' myth

There is in fact a surprisingly high turnover rate of senior high school graduates in Japan. According to the Research and Development Institute of Vocational Training:

In Japan, in spite of the so-called life-long employment system, 50 per cent of new senior high school graduates leave their first job in three years. It appears that there are many young people around 25 who are searching for more suitable jobs, wanting to develop their occupational capability, to rechallenge themselves and readjust to new occupations.

It is very significant that the initial training courses of public vocational training [details of these will be described in Chapter 7] are used as education/training facilities to assist these young people who leave a job to rechallenge themselves.

One of the important tasks expected of public vocational training institutions is that they assist small and medium-sized enterprises to secure skilled workers, as it is difficult for those enterprises to provide the training necessary for fostering the skilled workers they need by themselves.[3]

This turnover of senior high school graduates must predominantly occur in small and medium-sized companies, since it would be highly unusual for anyone to give up the status and job security of a large company, as well as the relatively better pay. Figure 4.3 and Table 4.2 show the distribution of employment by size of establishment in private industry.

Table 4.1. Qualifications of employees in a very successful medium-sized precision motor company (1992)

	Junior High School	Senior High School	Junior College	Bachelors' degree	Masters' degree	TOTAL
Male	44	190	13	148	6	401
Female	95	193	61	0	0	349
TOTAL	139	383	74	148	6	750

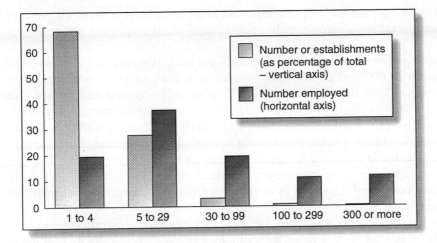

Fig. 4.3 Distribution of employment by size of establishment (private firms) in Japanese industry, 1986. *Source*: Management and Co-ordination Agency (1991–2). 'Establishment census of Japan, 1986'. In The Japan Institute of Labour (1993) *1991–92 Japanese Working Life Profile – Labour Statistics*, p. 21.

This of course raises the question of the general level of labour turnover in Japan. The Ministry of Labour say that approximately 14 per cent of skilled employees leave their employers each year, of whom about 2.5 per cent are retirements. Allowing for marriages (at which time a high proportion of Japanese women automatically give up work), the private sector turnover must be a little less than 10 per cent. However, it appears that large companies only suffer a turnover rate of 2 or 3 per cent, so these statistics indicate a

Table 4.2. Number of establishments and insured employees covered by employment insurance by industries and size of establishments.

Size of establishment	Number of establishments	Number of insured employees covered by employment insurance
All sizes	1 866 278	33 071 811
1–4 employees	1 032 786	1 919 993
5–29	655 819	7 315 380
30–99	126 907	6 544 685
100–499	44 030	8 580 008
500 or more	6 736	8 711 745

Source: Year Book of Labour Statistics 1993, Policy Planning and Research Development, Minister's Secretary, Ministry of Labour.

relatively high turnover of employees in most companies of over 10 per cent (since, as Table 4.2 shows, only 11.6 per cent of all employees are in the 0.1 per cent of all private companies which have 300 or more employees).

With an unemployment rate of under 3 per cent, as shown in Figure 4.4, and between 20 000 and 25 000 bankruptcies each year, an obvious conclusion is that the bulk of the workforce in Japan is so well educated and trained that there is little difficulty in finding immediate alternative employment elsewhere. As will be shown in Chapter 7, only a relatively small amount of government money is available to support training in companies. Therefore these statistics are a significant tribute to the quality and effectiveness of On-the-Job Training in small and medium-sized companies, which will be explained in more detail in Chapters 6 and 7, as well as to the vocational retraining facilities provided by the State.

At a strategic level, therefore, Japan has an inestimable advantage commercially in having such a flexible, well-educated, and well-trained workforce, from whom employers can readily recruit at all ages if they either voluntarily leave their previous company or are forced involuntarily on to the employment market. From the individual's point of view, this also gives a much wider choice of employment than, for example, is found in the UK. A comparison of the frequency of job changes in Japan, the USA, and the UK is shown in Figure 4.5.

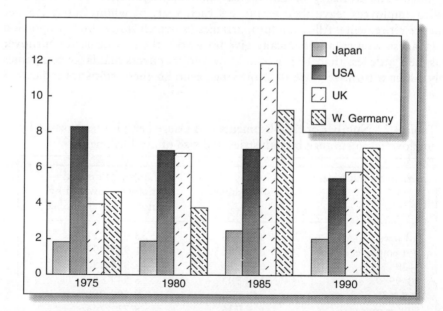

Fig. 4.4 Comparative rates of unemployment in four countries (per cent), 1975–90. *Source*: International Labor Organization (ILO) (1991–2). *Bulletin of Labour Statistics*. ILO, Geneva.

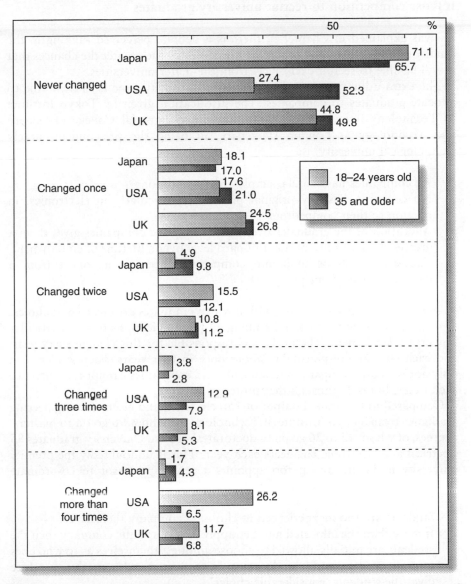

Fig. 4.5 Frequency of job changes in the 10 years to 1979 in Japan, the USA, and the UK (percentages of working population under and over 35). *Source*: *Census of, Work Attitudes* (in Japanese only). Prime Minister's office, Tokyo, 1979. Quoted in JETRO (Japan External Trade Organization) (1982). *Japanese corporate personnel management*, JETRO Business Information Series No. 10, p. 7. JETRO, Tokyo.

Intense competition to recruit university graduates

As was explained in Chapter 3, there is a definite perceived ranking in the quality of universities, and the larger the company the greater the chances that it will be able to recruit exclusively from the better universities.

The extraordinary fact is that the better universities see it as their role to allocate graduates to companies. The justification given by Tokyo Institute of Technology (which is roughly equivalent to Imperial College of Science and Technology at London University, in being the pre-eminent largely technological university) is:

1. All companies have similar employment conditions.
2. No company has any original products, particularly in electronics, in relation to their competitors.
3. Allocation of the graduates over a wide range of companies gives them a greater chance of promotion to Board level over a lifetime of employment, since there will be minimum competition between a cohort from a particular year of entry.

In order to effect this allocation, within which graduates are given some choice, a professor is given the task of handling all job applications from a particular university department. The professors responsible for this change every year, and each will take responsibility about once in four years. Each student can only apply to one company, and students and companies cannot talk direct to each other, but only through that professor.

Compared to the annual output of 150 electrical and electronic engineering graduates from Tokyo Institute of Technology (of whom 90 go on to masters' degrees, of whom 15 to 20 go on to doctorates), Tokyo University graduates 85 electrical and electronic engineers each year. This is undoubtedly the premier university in Japan, and it too appoints a senior professor to co-ordinate recruitment. The justification given is:

1. Students are too inexperienced to choose a company themselves.
2. If more than the allocated number apply to any specific company then the students are initially allowed to choose amongst themselves as to who goes to that company and who does not. In the university's eyes this therefore gives the students 'considerable choice'.

In this department no more than eight 'letters of recommendation' are available to any company, and no company would consider it in its best interests to recruit a graduate without one. There is therefore a strict allocation of a maximum of eight to each of a spread of large companies, with only one or two going to smaller companies. Some advice about companies is offered to students if they ask for it.

To most Westerners, all this must seem a quite extraordinary role for professors. Even for the Japanese themselves it must be asked whether professors do not busy themselves so much with these and similar matters that they are unable to concentrate sufficiently on research and writing.

One example of how this system works is that in 1985 10 electrical engineering graduates from Tokyo University wished to join Toshiba's Training Centre at Kawasaki, but only four were allocated to that company by the University. Toshiba's General Manager, Personnel, regretted that the graduates' freedom is restricted in this manner, and commented that professors at the national universities are trying to persuade some graduates to join small companies. There are similar problems in the private universities, he explained, with 10 job offers to each graduate. Of some 700 graduates recruited in 1984 by Toshiba 55 per cent were in electronics, and the majority were allocated by their professors. Those nominated by professors take a Toshiba entrance exam, and 85 per cent pass. Toshiba also offer one month of work experience during the final year's vacation; but there is no direct connection between offering such vacation work and recruitment.

Professor Takuo Sugano at Tokyo University believes that because there is such a severe shortage of electrical engineering graduates they tend to be recruited into development jobs, while science graduates are recruited for research. However, he says, some science graduates do not like the idea of going into industry, and therefore stay on to do research at university.

Less than 10 per cent of electrical and electronics graduates across Japan go on to masters' degrees, and less than 1 per cent to doctorates. Yet at Toshiba's research and development laboratories, only 37 per cent of all graduates employed have only bachelor degrees, while 43 per cent have masters' degrees and 20 per cent doctorates. Of 2500 recruits into Toshiba nationally in 1984, 1500 were senior high school graduates (recruited directly by the factories), 650 had bachelor degrees, and 350 had masters' degrees or doctorates. These figures are similar to those provided by other large companies. The only possible conclusion, therefore, is that graduates with higher degrees are almost exclusively recruited by large companies, and almost all are employed in research and development laboratories. Of all the graduates in Toshiba's Research and Development Centre, the degree disciplines are:

> 40 per cent Electrical and Electronic
> 15 per cent Mechanical
> 15 per cent Physics
> 15 per cent Chemistry
> 15 per cent Metallurgy, Mathematics, etc.

Despite this spread of degrees, Toshiba say that they have difficulties in finding sufficient numbers of high-calibre graduates. In many ways this is hardly surprising: for example, such are their successes and ambitions, that between them Hitachi, Matsushita, NEC, Toshiba, and Toyota are spending more on research and development than the whole of British industry put together. As a result there are some 700 000 vacancies for graduates each year, but only about 320 000 graduates to fill them.

The competition to recruit these graduates is such that reports started in 1989 of companies breaking the gentlemen's agreement not to start recruiting until the official date of 20 August. Many companies started giving students unofficial offers of employment (*naitei*) as early as 30 June. Applicants in many instances then found themselves subjected to *kōsoku* (physical restraint), by being so repeatedly invited to functions that they had no time to visit other potential employers, or even by being transported for up to a week to Japanese holiday resorts – or, in some cases, to California, Hawaii, or Hong Kong! Nikkeiren, the Japan Federation of Employers' Associations, established a telephone hotline at its employment and education policy departments, and received some 400 complaints of 'kidnapping' in 1989, including cases where students turned up for one-hour interviews, but found themselves trapped all day, and unable to make appointments arranged with other employers.

How do companies beat the graduate shortage?

So, in view of this very competitive national picture for the recruitment of university graduates in Japan, how do companies set about achieving their recruitment targets? It will have become clear that the larger companies have to direct their efforts, in the main, at the professors responsible for allocating graduates, for which there appear to be three main methods. First, generous funds are donated to the best universities. Second, there is intensive lobbying of the recruitment professors by Personnel Directors. And third, young graduates are sent back to their alma maters to talk to their old professors and the new generation of students some one to three years after they graduate.

It is even more difficult for small and medium companies. Nidec, for example, has several thousand employees, and claims a 75 per cent share of the market for particular high-precision DC motors for the computer industry. It was founded by Mr S. Nagamori in 1973, and is based in Kyoto. He has frequent meetings with professors at Kyoto University (one of the seven Imperial Universities). He is only able to recruit very few graduates from the best universities, and he estimates that his graduate recruits are equally split from second- and third-rank universities. More will be said in Chapter 5 about how Mr Nagamori achieves such success from such relatively unpromising material. In the meantime it should also be noted that he spends about one-third of his time on recruitment, using any available opportunities. He explains how, for example, he recruits engineers he sits next to by chance on aircraft and trains, and how weddings are excellent sources of recruitment; he is often asked to make a wedding speech, and devotes eight of the ten minutes to advertising his company. In the three hours of the reception he will meet all the bridegroom's friends, and then at a later date personally invite the best to a coffee shop and tell them how badly they are doing in their careers in their own companies! He has no hesitation, either, in headhunting engineers when he visits customers' research and development laboratories or from his parent bank.

Another small company is Yokogawa Digital Computers Limited (YDCL). This was founded by Mr T. Yamada, the President and Chief Executive Officer, in 1972, and by 1985 employed 350 people, of whom 100 were in 20 satellite companies. All but three employees were university graduates. Half the recruits each year join from medium-sized companies, the rest direct from universities. There are about 25 of these direct university recruits each year, of whom slightly more than half have electronics degrees and the rest are mathematicians; but there is equal difficulty recruiting either. Rather more engineers are recruited from the private than the national universities. Mr Yamada explains that he has a policy of giving his machines free to about thirty of the national and public universities for the professors to develop software as part of their research with their students; and the deal is that they then give that software back free to YDCL. In this way the firm hopes to be able to attract good-quality graduates from the national universities. They also offer vacation training to about forty students each year over the spring and summer holidays, but do not pay them (or, as they explained, expect the students to pay YDCL for it either!). It is hoped that many of these students will then decide to join YDCL on graduating.

A co-operative approach to recruitment

Yet another approach to graduate recruitment is adopted by Air Conditioning Services Limited. Mr Inoue is the Managing Director of this service company with 50 employees, which has been established for 30 years. Twelve of his staff are university graduates, 10 are from technical college, and the rest are equally split between senior high school and technical high school backgrounds. Half his employees have been with the company for all their working lives, and the rest joined from other companies.

Ten new starters joined the company in April 1985, four from technical college, three from senior high school, and three from universities. Of the graduates, one had an engineering degree and two were economists; this reflects the difficulty small companies have in attracting engineering graduates. However, Mr Inoue is also Director General of an Association of small and medium companies with 287 members. Usually university graduates prefer, he explains, to work for large companies for reasons of job security; but they are reassured by the idea of joining a company which is a member of such a large association. In fact, until about 1980, poaching was the policy for small companies, since they believed it was impossible to recruit direct from the universities. However, the general feeling was that those poached did not then identify with the company in the same way as a lifelong employee. As Mr Inoue explains, if you attract a man by offering a higher salary, then the chances are that he will eventually leave you for an even higher salary elsewhere.

This association makes presentations to 2 000 students each year, and in 1984 recruited 402 graduates from 126 universities; of these, 312 were arts and 90 were engineering graduates. Over the period 1980 to 1985 Mr Inoue recruited 8 university graduates out of 28 total recruits, and all were still with him. In fact, of the 3 who had left out of those 28, all were Senior High School graduates. This is certainly an interesting approach to university recruitment, well illustrating the inventiveness of the Japanese in the face of difficulties. Each of 27 Prefectures (out of 47 in Japan) has a similar organization, with a total of 19 000 member companies. Mr Inoue also showed the British author a 15-minute recruitment video made for ACS by a friend of his.

Opportunities are not quite the same for women!

Japan is one of the most male-chauvinistic countries in the world, and few women can yet expect to reach senior positions in their careers. An opinion poll in 1986 by a leading Japanese daily newspaper, the *Asahi Shimbun*, showed that 68 per cent of Japanese men are not prepared to take orders from a woman boss under any circumstances. Less than 1 per cent of Japanese working women occupy managerial posts, in comparison with 10 per cent in EEC countries and 35 per cent in the United States.

Only about 1½ per cent of those graduating in electrical and electronic engineering each year are women. However, a significant proportion of graduate recruits into electrical engineering companies are female, because many enter with science and non-technical degrees, and are trained in software. It is also true that many 'office girls' (the Japanese do not have the concept of a secretary, as in the West, and need special training when posted overseas to have it explained to them how to work with one!), receptionists, and guides are graduates, and are often recruited largely on the basis of their good looks.

In May 1985 the Equal Employment Opportunity Law was enacted. The book *Women and Japanese Management* by Dr Alice Lam explains:

This new legislation was also partly a product of international pressures on Japan to bring her legislative framework on women into line with international standards. From the western perspective, the Japanese EEO Law may appear rather peculiar. It has granted women very few new rights and imposed only limited legal obligations on employers. The legislation makes a distinction between 'prohibition' and 'exhortation' in its provisions for ensuring equal treatment between men and women. Prohibition against discrimination applies to basic vocational training, fringe benefits, retirement and dismissal – areas in which substantial changes had already taken place before the law was introduced. With regard to the most important stages in employment including recruitment, job assignment and promotion – the law 'exhorts' employers to treat women equally as men. The hortatory provisions appear to be highly ambiguous and their enforcement is dependent upon the administrative guidance (gyōsei-shido) of the Ministry of Labour.[4]

Matsushita recruit about 4000 employees each year; of these, 3000 are senior high school and junior college graduates, and the remaining 800 to 1000 are university graduates, of whom 200 have masters' degrees. About 100 of these university graduates are female, mainly scientists, with 70 per cent to 80 per cent being employed as computer systems engineers, and 20 per cent in research. However, while the male graduates are recruited centrally by Matsushita, the female graduates are recruited directly by each plant. Both sexes then undergo induction training for three weeks centrally before starting work in specific plants. There are then three types of graduate training scheme, one for males with bachelors' degrees (seven months long), another for males with masters' degrees (three and a half months long), and the third for female graduates, consisting of one month's basic education in computers. It is claimed that this apparent sex discrimination is because 'few female graduates are technologists, and it would in any case be unsuitable to give them experience in manufacturing or retailing'. At least it would appear that British employers have a slightly more positive view on careers for girls in engineering than yet seems to be the case in Japan!

There is, however, increasing evidence that the 1985 Equal Employment Opportunity Law is beginning to have a positive effect on the career opportunities open to women. One example is in the number of female student enrolments at the Japanese author's Polytechnic University of Japan. The rapid increase in the early 1990s is shown in Fig. 4.6. Even in 1986 one girl enrolling said 'I had long worried about being born as a girl, and therefore having limited career opportunities. A teacher at my senior high school recommended me to the Polytechnic University of Japan, telling me that teaching or instructing in public schools is not segregated.' It is likely that there are two reasons for this sharp increase in female enrolments:

- After the promulgation of the 1985 EEO Law it came to be accepted that technical subjects were no longer appropriate only for boys.
- There was a special campaign to increase the number of females enrolling on these courses, aimed at increasing the number of female instructors in vocational training.

Future trends in Japan and elsewhere

The Ministry of International Trade and Industry have been urging the Japanese government to double public spending on research and development over the 1990s, from 0.46 per cent of GNP to 1.0 per cent. This compares to slightly more than 1 per cent of GNP in the USA, West Germany, and France, and just under 1 per cent in Britain. However these countries devote around half their government R&D budgets to military research, whereas Japan spends substantially less. The future trend, therefore, would seem to be one where Japan is moving towards having the world's largest civilian R&D budget, just at the same time as the Western nations are slashing their military research as a result of the collapse of the former Soviet Union.

There is, however, a labour-shortage crisis increasingly facing Japan's employers. The current labour shortage is such that in 1988 the Japanese Newspaper Association offered 120 work-study scholarships in Japan to delivery boys from Taiwan, with free tuition at a language school. In 1991 the 'Hanamachi' ('Flower District') of the Asakusa area of Tokyo offered to recruit and train foreign women as Geishas. In rather more vital areas of Japan's economy the future also looks grim, as the average birth-rate hit an all-time low of 1.53 children in 1990. Japan's population profile is rapidly changing, so that the retired population will increase from 12.1 per cent to 25.4 per cent between 1990 and 2025, while the working-age population will decline from 69.8 per cent to 60.1 per cent over the same period, as shown in Figure 4.7. A government report in 1991 predicted that the then population of 123.6 million would peak at 129 million in 2010 and then continuously decline, falling to 100 million by 2069 and halving by the end of the twenty-first century.

The competition for recruits within Japan will therefore rapidly intensify. One option open is to recruit foreign labour on a much greater scale than in such limited cases as newspaper boys and geishas. Mitsubishi Electric,

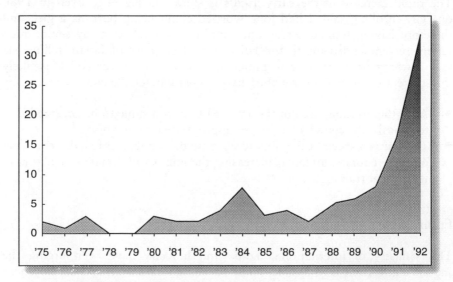

Fig. 4.6 Enrolment of female students at the Polytechnic University of Japan, Sagamihara, Kanagawa (internal data).

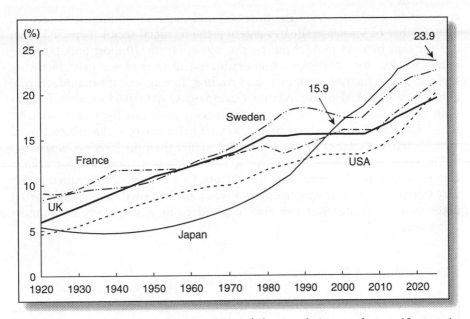

Fig. 4.7 Actual and projected proportions of the population aged over 65 years in five countries, 1920–2020. *Source*: Ministry of Labour, Japan (no date). *Labour administration – seeking a more comfortable life for workers*. The Ministry, Tokyo.

for example, started recruiting foreign graduate engineers in 1990 as part of its globalization programme. In 1992 the company planned to recruit nine graduates from the USA and eight from Europe to work in Japan for two or three years before returning to their own countries. Many other Japanese companies have introduced such schemes over the last few years, and there are quite a number of graduates employed more permanently in Japan. However, the numbers involved now, or likely to be involved in the future, are negligible compared to the increasing labour shortages. Japan has always jealously guarded her racial identity, and the massed importation of foreign labour seems inconceivable. Instead, the much more likely policy will be the basing of an increasing proportion of Japan's research and development, as well as factories, overseas. From a strategic point of view this must make sense in several ways. First, as military R&D declines in the West there will be many well-qualified engineers and scientists seeking alternative employment. Second, R&D facilities located in overseas markets are better placed to identify effective solutions to commercial opportunities. Third, it will increasingly become politically necessary, as Japan's commercial successes lead to protectionist reactions in North America and Europe.

Within Japan itself the recruitment market will become ever more competitive. Japanese industry in the late 1980s faced increasing competition for engineering graduates from the financial and mass communications sectors. The number of science graduates entering the financial sector increased from 2.9 per cent in 1984 to 15.9 per cent in 1988. Of the 30 most popular companies in 1988 for male engineering graduates, 12 were in non-manufacturing sectors such as finance, insurance, and trading. In response the manufacturing companies launched public relations campaigns, with steel companies running television commercials featuring actresses, including Sigourney Weaver. Smaller and medium-sized companies, as well as foreign ones, have been forced to offer starting salaries up to 10 per cent higher than the larger companies.

The labour shortage in the 1980s reached such a point that even the *yakuza* gangsters advertised in magazines for recruits. One 19-year-old recruited in this way told police after he was arrested, 'I was a bit surprised to find I was being taken on as a gangster. But it seemed fun, and the money was better than most companies pay.'

The challenge of flexibility

In many ways the Japanese are highly flexible and inventive. For example, large Japanese companies have several different types of employees; there are regular employees, part-time employees, subsidiary company employees, and subcontractor employees. Subsidiary companies are relevant in the context of recruitment for these two reasons, amongst others. First, they are used to recruit graduates from the lower-ranking universities, who are then employed on lower salaries than regular employees. Second, they can be used to attract those with skills that are in short supply, such as software skills, enabling them to be paid more than the regular staff. In both cases the subsidiary company employees literally work alongside regular company employees.

On the other hand, Japanese employers have a long way to go before they move away from the simplified classification of most university graduates according to the ranking of the university they attended. In May 1991 Sony led the way, and announced that applicants would no longer be asked to name the university they attended on their application form. 'What we want are staff with the ability to come up with ideas and capable of setting their own agendas', said a Sony spokesman.

These are the challenges now facing Japan. Can they, for example, find more effective ways of releasing the real talents of women, other than in their traditional subservient and home-based roles? Are there not much greater challenges for which women might be recruited? And there are many lessons still to be learnt by Japan in how to resolve its forthcoming critical labour shortage by recruiting many more foreigners to work both in Japan itself and in their own countries.

Japan's job centres, previously known as Public Employment Security Offices ('Kōkyō Shokugyō Anteisho', generally known as 'Shokuan'), were renamed as 'Hello Work' in 1990 as part of a 'Refreshing Labour Exchange Service Campaign' aimed at providing a better service to the 1.4 million unemployed and encouraging them to use the facilities to return to employment and reduce the national skills shortage. Such imaginative solutions and positive thinking are typical of Japan's inherent strengths, and should provide much food for thought for her competitors.

The Japanese way

The recruitment of a new employee is potentially a massive long-term investment for any organization; done effectively the opportunities open to the employer are almost unlimited, while done badly or haphazardly the long-term damage to both company and recruit can be immense.

It is clear that there is far-sighted strategic vision shown by both Japanese companies and the Japanese government. Employees are predominantly recruited, therefore, for their learning ability, rather than their immediate knowledge. On the other hand, the clear ranking of schools, colleges, and universities makes it very difficult for smaller companies to recruit the quality of employee they need to thrive and grow. Indeed, a major challenge to companies of all sizes in Japan is to recruit employees in a country where the continuing success of the economy is endangered by a reducing proportion of the population of working age; furthermore, Japan is surely the only country in the world where the major world recession of the early 1990s had no effect in significantly increasing the extremely low level of unemployment.

Japan's increasing demand for skilled employees at a time of falling need for highly qualified staff in the world's defence industries raises one final important question: will this be a great opportunity for Japanese companies to recruit even more of the best talent in other countries?

It will be ironic, will it not, if it is increasingly the peoples of Japan's competitor nations who are recruited to destroy the technological bases of their own countries – particularly if it is the collapse of their own defence industries in a time of peace which enables it to happen?

References

1 Research and Development Institute of Vocational Training, Employment Promotion Projects Corporation, *Country report on the planning, programming and evaluation of vocational training – Japan*, Sagamihara, December 1984, p. 25.
2 Ibid., p. 26.
3 Ibid., p. 24.
4 Alice C.L. Lam, *Women and Japanese management – discrimination and reform*, Routledge, London, 1992, pp. 19–20.

5

The second winning margin – management and the commitment of employees

'Growth begins when we start to accept our own weakness.'
– Jean Vanier

Introduction

The concept of management in Japanese companies is fundamentally different from that in the West. Above all else the Japanese manager is selected, trained, rewarded, and promoted on the basis of his ability to develop the skills and careers of his staff, to be a good communicator, and to encourage good teamwork.

The will to win – a clear vision

The foremost and universal objective, within which one must view the approach to management of Japanese companies, is the aim to be *Ichiban* – Number One. Every company knows where it stands in the sales league, whether locally, nationally, or internationally, and this information is usually volunteered at an early stage to visitors.

Hitachi, for example, have a booklet entitled 'Introduction to Hitachi and Modern Japan'; on page 4, immediately after the profile on the company, it shows that they ranked in 1982 as second largest in sales in Japan, seventh in the world league of electrical and electronic equipment manufacturers, and 35th in world ranking of all world companies by total sales according to *Fortune* magazine. The same booklet also shows that Japan's total GNP is now only second to that of the USA, with the implication that becoming *Ichiban* in that as well is a target to which all are committed. The real point is that not only senior management in Japanese companies are aware of these statistics – but so are all employees, and they are totally committed to improving them until they really are *Ichiban*. Furthermore, they will use all the strengths and tactics of Bushido in order to achieve that aim.

As Boris Becker said in 1991, after being beaten in the Wimbledon final for the third time in four years, 'In the final, tactics alone are not that important. It's who has the strongest mind.' Just as top tennis players have discovered that mental attitude is a crucial part of any player's arsenal, so Japanese companies, managers, and employees have a greater will to win than most of their competitors – and therefore, not surprisingly, go on to do so. As in sport, so in industry; if one team really wants to win, and the others are not so committed, then the outcome is almost certainly already determined.

An obsessive attention to detail

The Japanese give enormous attention to detail, and a very high priority to satisfying the customer. They also expect suppliers to give the same commitment. In April 1986 Alan Sugar, Chairman of Amstrad Consumer Electronics, said that

it was dealing with the Japanese that crystallized his thinking, and gave him the managerial tools to start beating them at their own electronic and audio-visual game. "It was their follow-through that impressed me, the way that they finish things off and carry everything through to the bitter end. When they don't like the colour of something they don't say, 'We'd like it a bit more white-ish' like a British or even American company; they send you a colour-card with shades marked from 1 to 15 and specify exactly which white they want. And then they send a team to make sure they get it."[1]

One Westerner describes the purchase in Japan of a second-hand car; six months after the purchase the salesman arranged a one-hour visit to check on the customer's satisfaction, to note any points of dissatisfaction or suggestions for improvements in the product and to discover when another vehicle would be purchased. All these details would have been fed back to the manufacturer and systematically analysed and acted upon. Indeed, rather than employing market researchers, Japanese companies rely instead on direct feedback from their dealers and by sending their managers out to talk to the customers. The extraordinary success of the Japanese car industry, linked to extremely fast product development, testifies to the effectiveness of this hands-on approach – another obvious lesson for Western competitors!

Attention to detail is such that the Japanese subsidiary of Alcan Aluminium succeeded in reducing the changeover time for a large set of rolls on their big mill from eight hours to eight minutes. John Hawkins, who was a Divisional Managing Director of British Alcan at the time, describes his amazement at seeing the new changeover process on his last visit to Japan. 'As the last strip of aluminium went through, the team-leader blew a whistle. Everyone in the production area immediately moved to preassigned positions and the first of eight lights went on above the rollers. It was just like a ballet, with each man knowing exactly what had to be done. At the end of the first minute, the second light went on, and so on until, at the end of eight minutes, the rolls had been successfully changed.' As a result, the production process became much more flexible, and work-in-progress was substantially reduced. This approach is at the heart of the famous Japanese Just-In-Time system, which originated in Toyota with the *kanban* system, and which relies on tool changes reduced from hours to minutes – in another case from two days to two minutes!

The West's concept of 'management' is damagingly wrong

One major disadvantage suffered by much of Western industry is that they have accepted the American concept of 'macho' management – with management consisting of leaders who spend much of their time either personally solving problems or seeing themselves as strategists. Master of Business Administration (MBA) courses tend to emphasize both of these aspects as skills required of senior managers, providing a heavy diet of lectures and case-study material in such matters as business strategy, finance, marketing and 'Japanese manufacturing techniques'. The 70 000 MBA graduates produced by the USA each year seem to have been signally unsuccessful in stemming the tide of Japanese commercial victories. In contrast, Japan has just one major, not particularly well regarded, MBA course at Keio University, producing relatively few graduates each year; this MBA started in the mid-1970s. Two other private universities, Aoyama Gakuin University (in Tokyo) and the International University of Japan (in Niigata) have also recently started MBA courses, and there is also one run by the University of Tsukuba, a national university.

What therefore is the Japanese concept of management?

The prime competence required of Japanese managers is not that of technical ability, the skill to undertake challenging tasks themselves successfully, or of being strategic thinkers. All these are, of course, of some importance, but they are not the basis on which managers are selected, trained, rewarded, or promoted – and that is a vitally important difference from the value system in most Western companies.

Their battle-winning concept of management is that of the ability to develop the highest possible level and breadth of skills in their staff. To most Westerners, one of the extraordinary aspects of Japanese management and training is the very high proportion of a supervisor's, manager's, or director's time which is devoted to developing and training their subordinates. One estimate of the proportion of their time given to this activity is between 20 per cent and 30 per cent. A number of British engineers who have worked in Japan even suggest that this is a conservative estimate. Even at director level, senior representatives of British companies in Japan testify that Japanese senior managers and directors have specific dates (typically 5 days each month) set aside in their diaries for their involvement in the in-house training of their employees. Interestingly, these British representatives usually find it relatively easy to obtain access to Japanese companies at these senior levels; much more significant, however, is the fact that there is absolutely no way that these same Japanese senior managers and directors are prepared to agree to business meetings on these dates pre-allocated for training.

It seems apparent, therefore, that the development of staff is seen as the single most important responsibility of a Japanese manager. It is emphasized on many occasions in Japan that a high level of development in their subordinates reflects well on managers. This is the prime basis on which managers are selected, the skill which is predominantly developed in the training they are given when appointed, and, most importantly, the major consideration in rewarding and promoting them. In how many Western companies can this be described as being the value system?

Some Western companies do have the right management values

One very successful American company in which this value system does apply is Digital. Ken Olsen, its original President and Founder, refers to its senior managers as 'coaches': their role is not to focus on the operation itself, but, instead, to make sure that *their staff* are capable of achieving the company's objectives. Digital say that this prime role of senior managers has been made very, very clear. This style of management is reflected in the way that employees are encouraged to take risks. They point out that in taking a risk there are two possible outcomes: the first is a success, and the second is a powerful learning experience – and both are good. In Digital there is a heavy emphasis on taking reponsibility for one's own personal development, just as in most Japanese companies. Digital say that it is easier to obtain forgiveness than permission; staff own their own growth and destiny, and their manager is there to help them.

In contrast, the managing director of one very large British engineering company is notorious for demanding that managers who make mistakes are fired; not surprisingly, as a result, that company has a reputation for cautious management. On the other hand, John Hawkins of Alcan believes that the number of managers he had to dismiss during a long career could be counted on the fingers of one hand, and testifies to the concept of good management as being the ability to coach the best contribution possible out of employees.

Only companies which encourage risk-taking by their employees can develop and grow. Management by fear patently does not work. The evidence is that

Japanese companies increasingly encourage their employees to challenge the existing systems and procedures; the result is that both the individuals and the companies are developing and growing at the fastest possible rate.

Management = Training = Assisting others

This concept of management in Japan is undoubtedly strongly reinforced by the strong cultural inclination of the Japanese to assist each other. It appears to be generally unthinkable for a Japanese supervisor or manager not to devote an enormous amount of his own time to training a new member of his team, for example, face to face and by demonstration. This is very apparent to those spending time in Japan, and is one of the tremendous strengths of Japanese industry. In contrast, the failure to adopt this value system in most Western companies is their single greatest weakness, and the major reason for their collapse in the face of the Japanese industrial onslaught. One director of training of a major British company, as an example, admits that he has never once been appraised himself during a long career. Job descriptions of managers in Western companies are almost invariably task-oriented; in Japanese companies they are always focused on the responsibility of managers to develop the skills of their staff and to foster good communication and teamwork – in other words, process- rather than task-oriented.

It is also interesting to analyse the management value systems in France and Germany, both countries with cohesive education and training systems, unlike Britain. The French system is highly élitist, and the development of staff is not a priority in the minds of status-conscious French managers. Germany has a system for the initial training of employees which is every bit as effective as that in Japan, but there is far less emphasis on lifetime learning. German management is bureaucratic, with decisions often made at senior levels and transmitted down the organization for implementation by subordinates. This contrasts with the much more organic style of Japanese management, and explains why, for example, in 1992 Mercedes-Benz announced it was planning to cut 20 000 jobs over the following three years out of a total of 238 000. Mercedes, part of Daimler Benz, Germany's largest industrial group, found increasing difficulty in competing with competition from Japanese cars such as the Toyota Lexus, the Honda Legend, and the Nissan Infiniti.

Customers can only be satisfied through quality products

Of Japanese companies, 90 per cent see customer service as the most important priority facing them in the 1990s.[2] On the other hand, another survey showed that only 6 per cent of Japanese companies thought that profitability is the sole goal of a company; in the same study the USA was top of the league in putting profits first, with Britain around the middle of a number of countries.[3] There is increasing evidence, however, that the importance of profitability is increasing amongst Japanese companies.

One well-known approach to improving the quality of products is through Quality Circles and the Zero Defect Movement. Quality Circles originated as an idea from Professor W. E. Deming, an American, after the Second World War, and Japan is of course renowned for their implementation. This is co-ordinated by Japanese Union of Scientists and Engineers (JUSE), established in 1946, which has a membership of over 1600 companies. JUSE has awarded an annual Deming Prize for the past forty years to the Japanese manufacturer achieving the best quality performance; the status of the award is such that the annual ceremony is now televised nationally.

Most Quality Circles take place in employees' own time. They are voluntary activities, but there is a general understanding that everyone is expected to participate. At the Toshiba laptop computer factory at Ome, on the north-western outskirts of Tokyo, all production employees are members of a Quality Circle, and devote two hours each week to such meetings without pay. In fact Quality Circles and Zero Defect Movements in most companies have now developed into Small-Group Activities covering most employees. In Hitachi, for example, they are described thus:

Each small-group consists of some ten company employees, and its activities are directed to finding solutions to problems closely related to the jobs of the members. The merits of such activities are:

1 They promote a feeling of mutual respect among the employees, and increase the will to work.

2 They invigorate the company and promote greater creativity.

In Kyocera (the Kyoto Ceramics Company, which is very large and highly successful) it is called the New Amoeba Campaign, and the basic doctrine is:

To improve problems close to oneself by group activities in which all employees must participate with a view to mastering the genuine spirit of Kyocera's philosophy. It is also to strengthen mutual relations by seizing true pleasure as an employee of Kyocera through accomplishment of each one's target. At the same time it is to activate the Amoeba Campaign by elevating each one's participating mind into management and operation.

In Kyocera's Gamo factory near Kyoto there are 200 circles, to which all 1600 employees belong, with members all usually from the same department, with a minimum of two and a maximum of 16 in each group. Charts of each group's activities line the canteen, showing that some meet regularly and others hardly at all, but always in their own time. There is a co-ordinating committee consisting of the Plant, Personnel, Accounting, Maintenance, Purchasing, and Quality

Assurance managers. To back this up there are detailed training programmes.

This supportive training as part of the the total approach to quality control in Japan must be heavily emphasized. For example an official document states:

... since the latter half of the 1970s, there has been a great change in the environment and conditions surrounding public vocational training.

... there was a big change in the competency expected of skilled workers for the technological progress centring around microelectronics, and the level of requirements for quality control has become extremely high.[4]

Japanese workers are of high quality

One major reason why Japan can implement Quality Circles and quality control in general so successfully is precisely because of the high average level of education. Employees are therefore readily able to grasp the basic statistics involved, and appreciate the wider aspects of quality control. At Seiko Instruments and Electronics, as an example, quality control education systems are seen as very important. Special quality control texts have been written, part of them by the General Manager. One of these is a 100-hour QC course which includes statistical methods, and is designed as a self-study evening course, backed up by a few lectures. Students work on real QC problems, together with group discussions. It is worth realizing that the Japanese spent the decade up to the 1960s training upper and middle-level managers in all aspects of quality. Thereafter the training in quality for foremen and other employees followed, so that now hundreds of thousands of managers and supervisors, as well as millions of other employees, are thoroughly acquainted with quality control – an exercise only possible because of the very high level of educational backgrounds among Japanese employees.

The lower educational levels in other countries may well be one reason why Japanese subsidiaries overseas rarely use Quality Circles – an example of the very pragmatic approach used by the Japanese in their management practices outside Japan. A 1981 large-scale study by Harvard University found no Japanese subsidiaries in the USA using Quality Circles, while few in the UK do now.

Japan has long led the world in obtaining the greatest efficiency and quality in manufacturing. Toyota pioneered the *kanban* ('Just-In-Time') approach to production. Apart from the well-known principle of delivering parts immediately before assembly (an idea generated by observing the system used in American supermarkets, incidentally), Toyota have put enormous emphasis on shortening set-up times of machines. This makes it economical to run short batches, which itself tends to show up production problems more quickly.

It is generally accepted that production involves three factors: People, Machines, and Material. In the West the big sin is usually seen as allowing either or both of the first two to stand idle; but that is not the case in Japan, where the only sin – and it is seen as a major one – is to allow Material (Work-in-Progress) to stand idle.

Production operatives in Toyota and other Japanese companies are given two types of button to press on the production line – one to indicate they need assistance, and the other to stop the line itself if a quality problem appears. The tendency is for foremen to reduce the number of operators on the line until too many press the assistance button; this not only encourages the operators to work at maximum effort, but also soon shows up any problems. In fact the idea of Total Quality Control is *not* to schedule at full capacity (as tends to happen in the West), but to build in slack time for maintenance and for discussions on ways to effect improvements. Maintenance staff actually often spend most of their time training operators to maintain their own machines. There is also evidence that a Japanese production plant has a much higher ratio of production supervisors to operatives than is usually found in the West, and that these are working team-leaders who train and develop the skills of their team members, rather than being the type of authoritarian foreman found in Europe and North America.

It is common practice for companies such as Toyota to visit suppliers' plants and suggest improvements. On the track itself it is also normal not only to see displays of the day's production achievement against target, but that of anticipated production achievements by rival companies as well! But despite this high pressure to reach production targets, shopfloor employees with a new idea are given leave from the track to develop it, which not only encourages bright ideas for improvement, but also builds on the high educational levels of the average Japanese employee. Above all, the foreman will be thoroughly well trained, and expected to manage in a real sense. Sanyo in the UK, for example, take the view that British companies tend to employ foremen promoted from the shop-floor, who are then surrounded by 'experts' in time-study, production engineering, etc.; they have decided instead to employ well-qualified people, many of them graduates, as foremen, and all activities such as work-study and production engineering – tasks for which they are properly trained – are done directly by them.

This rigorous selection of those appointed to supervisory and management positions, together with the requirement that appointment is only made on successfully passing the exams at the end of the pre-appointment training course, is another important difference between Japan and most of the West. The nearest Western equivalent is the *Meister* system in Germany, where foremen are usually only appointed after obtaining the nationally recognized *Meister* qualification, which is aimed at giving them pedagogical skills as well as more detailed technical knowledge in their specialist trades. After Japan, it is of course Germany which has a world-wide reputation for quality; it is surely no coincidence that both countries adopt a rigorous approach to training supervisors that is based predominantly on their ability to develop the skills of their staff.

A nation open to new ideas

The eagerness with which Japanese companies receive new ideas, and the readiness with which their managers implement them, is a strategically decisive advantage. The development of Quality Circles, however, although now thought to be an inherent part of Japanese management, was implemented only with great dedication and effort. In 1962, for example, there were just three such circles. The commitment to the idea, however, was such that:

By 1973 there were over one million of them in Japan, and in 1972 the first one was set up in the USA by the Lockheed Company.

A fairly recent survey comparing Japanese and British companies has shown that, whereas in Japan an employee makes on average 18 suggestions per year for improving the system within which he works, in Britain there is only one suggestion per 78 employees per year! Clearly this factor reflects vast differences in work attitudes and participation. These differences are also conclusively reflected in the yen – sterling exchange rate.[5]

The dramatic spread of suggestion schemes is such that the Japanese Suggestion Scheme Association put Matsushita top with 6.5 million suggestions in one year, followed by Hitachi with 4.6 million, Mazda with 3.0 million, and Toyota with 2.1 million. The highest number of suggestions per head on average was at Okidenki, with 570! Toyota publish a table showing the number of suggestions submitted and the proportion adopted. In 1979 there were 575 861 suggestions submitted, with 91 per cent adopted, representing 13.3 adopted suggestions per employee; by 1982 this had increased dramatically to 1 905 642 suggestions, with 95 per cent adopted, averaging 38.8 per employee. In 1988, a record 80 per cent of all employees in Japanese private companies put forward suggestions, with an average 31 suggestions per employee; the average cash award to these employees was US$71, while the greatest financial return from any one suggestion was US$7.8 million.[6]

This commitment to utilizing new ideas from any source is complemented in a very important way in their use of patents. In 1984 Toshiba's laptop computer factory at Ome started to install an optical disk database for patents. This was supplied by a private Japanese agency, and was designed to be expanded to 50 disks, each capable of storing details of 60 000 patents from any country in the world. This was linked via a 100-megabit Local Area Network to Visual Display Units across the site. VDU users could access this enormous database, enlarging any section of a particular page for closer inspection on a high-resolution screen. This system is an improved version of one which had been in operation in the USA for a number of years, and is a very powerful tool. One typical use is for negotiating patent-exchange agreements, such as between Toshiba and Siemens. Furthermore, in most large Japanese companies all engineers are given training on patents once a year. In addition, all these engineers are strongly encouraged to register at least one patent a year each, and in the more commercially aggressive companies a minimum of four a year is expected.

Between 1987 and 1989 the British author was responsible for a joint Anglo-Japanese comparative research project, together with Professor Keith Thurley at the London School of Economics. This will be described in more detail in the next chapter, but there were very interesting results from the background questionnaires the 91 engineers participating in Japan and the 57 in the UK were asked to complete as part of this research. As Table 9.4 (p. 186) shows, the number of patents registered by the Japanese sample is very significant.

It is notable that of the 57 participating British engineers, only four had registered any patents, in each case only one. Even allowing for the much easier and less rigorous system of patent registration in Japan, this is a highly significant difference between the two countries. Not only are British engineers not registering many patents, but they are not consulting patent literature either. On 28 August 1991, Mr Ted Blake, Director of Marketing at the British Patent Office, told a symposium that about £20 billion was wasted in duplicating research across Europe for this reason.

In contrast, in Japan this aggressive approach to innovation using patents and suggestion schemes is sharpened even further by the manner in which cohorts of graduates from the same university working in different companies and in the civil service keep in regular touch with each other.

A nation expert at sharing information

For any organization to survive and grow there has to be sharing of experiences and expertise. In this sense there is nothing unique to Japan in its ability to do this. What Japan has as a key advantage is the historical and cultural background which enables her people and her companies to do this much more easily and consistently than in other nations. That is not to say, however, that Western companies, for example, cannot apply these basic principles in effective and practical ways.

Japanese companies see the sharing of information as a vitally important competitive advantage. Many Japanese manufacturers receive a daily flow of information from *each* of the overseas countries (in some cases over 70!) in which they are selling for *each* of their products (perhaps 100 or more); this information is then circulated systematically to *everyone* to whom it might be useful, not only within the company, but also to subcontractors and suppliers. Are there really cultural barriers preventing any Western company from doing the same, particularly with the advent of software such as Lotus Notes? Another example of highly effective information sharing which frequently strikes visitors to Japanese factories is the use of visual control techniques. These include visual displays in production areas showing the status of machines, real-time output achieved versus that scheduled and picture-based process instructions at workstations.

A nation committed to effective communications

Effective communications are considered very important in Japan. One of the booklets made available free to visiting businessmen by the Japan External Trade Organization (JETRO) explains:

Indeed, if a Japanese manager is in doubt as to whether he ought to bother informing his colleagues of a piece of information, he is far safer to inform them. One top executive of a major Japanese corporation reflected for a long time on his sudden fall from favour and concluded that his single mistake was to heed the advice of a subordinate who considered some data inconsequential and suggested that it not be circulated. His colleagues admitted that the data concerned was not particularly vital, but their confidence in his willingness to share information was damaged and they could not function in confidence with a manager guilty of withholding information.

The degree of informal communication which occurs in Japanese firms can be called distinctive with greater certainty. Even when the piece of information is not significant enough to merit a memo, Japanese managers are prone to call up a colleague who might be interested in it. They know who might be interested in the information because job rotation has exposed them to the perspectives of various sections and departments and they have developed personal relationships with staff members throughout the company. Sharing information is not just a favour done for a friend or merely in keeping with good business practice; a manager's effectiveness depends on his keeping well informed, which in turn requires the mutual assistance of his peers.

On the whole, one can conclude that Japanese companies possess more intensive and extensive in-house information networks than Western firms. These formal and informal information channels carry information both up and down in the corporate hierarchy, and from side to side between the various bureaus of a Japanese company, largely at the discretion of lower and middle-level managers.[7]

There is also much more emphasis on formal communications than is generally found in the West; it is simply that there is a universal recognition that the better the information available to everyone, the more likely it is that the best decisions will result. One British engineer working in a Japanese company in Tokyo described the quarterly magazines from the company, the division, the site, and the particular specialist area in which he was working. All employees had to stand for five minutes each Monday morning while the company President addressed them over the loudspeakers on the state of the company's business. The departmental safety officer, too, talked to them for five minutes as a group. This approach appears fairly typical in Japan. The British author recalls finding his taxi unable to reach the front entrance of a Toshiba factory because all the employees, in their company uniforms, were lined up in military formation in the forecourt at 2.00 p.m. being given a briefing. At NTT there is a house magazine which is distributed monthly to all 230 000 employees. This is supported by no less than another 560 regular house magazines across NTT. Even more amazing is the way in which in 1982 NTT started producing a seven- to ten-minute video briefing each week. This is broadcast on-line to each regional office every Thursday, with a further 3200 tapes sent by mail to every site. This is shown to every employee every week, but in unpaid time. The videos contain information on new products and services, or feature a top executive explaining management policy. There is no discussion after the videos are shown, but regular questionnaire surveys are used to gauge reaction to the video briefings and house magazines.

Simple, but highly effective, ways of sharing knowledge

Even more important than all this is the way in which there is every effort made to ensure that there is the greatest degree of on-going learning in the organization. One example comes from a British engineer who was working in NEC on a Winston Churchill Travelling Fellowship at the same time as the British author was in Japan funded in the same way:

... each researcher has to present what he has done over the past 6 weeks to the whole division. This takes a whole day at the moment but will soon be split into two half-day meetings in order to save time.

Each piece of work has to be written up as a short internal report and most people average about 5–10 reports a year. In addition, and this is something that astounded me, they each *have* to write 4 patents each a year. Unlike the UK, patents in Japan are unvetted so anybody can patent anything, whether original or not. The patent is only tested during a dispute in Court over patent rights. Each researcher does a 3-day course in how to write in the legal jargon of patents. Clearance to publish a paper requires an appropriate patent to be written first.[8]

Another British engineer seconded from GEC to Toshiba in Japan for six months commented:

Reporting here is excellent. Every week we have a two hour meeting which is good information flow (no waffling or argument). Everyone summarises their work down to one page for transfer upwards of information. This produces clear thinking as to what has really been done. When I had my opening discussion with each engineer, just a few summary sheets of previous work gave a superb outline.[9]

Here it is an important part of the system that information disseminates downwards and sideways as well as upwards. Reporting via wall charts is almost universal in Japanese factories. In the working area at Himeji there are several charts, all giving clear summaries . . . From these wall charts it is possible to very quickly get a picture of recent progress, or lack of it. It is very important that these charts are not hidden away in senior managers' offices (not that many managers have offices here anyway).[10]

Group harmony and consensus decision-making require more staff

There are clearly differences of management style between Japanese companies, but one thing tends to remain the same – the emphasis on consensus decision-making. Group harmony is supremely important. One Japanese

Managing Director describes this style as 'bottom-up'. Everybody must feel part of the team and must believe that decisions are made jointly. He emphasizes this as being most important, and describes it as *sanka ishiki* – a feeling of participation – and illustrated it with the concept of Total Quality Control. He describes how Japanese managers will work hard to obtain consensus on a decision. Indeed, consensus decision-making, as much as anything, involves politicking to ensure that, not only is everyone involved in a decision, but they are all identified with that decision whether it succeeds or fails, thus saving any one individual from the potential humiliation of being totally identified with a mistake.

The efforts required in reaching a consensus are necessarily time-consuming, and this time is generally consumed during normal working hours. Therefore after 5 p.m. most staff will stay on until 9 p.m. or 10 p.m. to do the work which in the West would have been carried out during the day. This is particularly notable since most of these employees will then face a one- or two-hour train journey home.

The pace of work in a typical Japanese company certainly appears in offices (not in production areas) to be slower than in the West. Not only is enormous effort given to reaching a consensus on decisions, but a very high priority is also given to training others, about which more will be said in Chapter 6. One British engineer working in Japan describes how in his section there were four section leaders and eight engineers. The engineers, because of their non-specialist technical backgrounds (the result of their broad degrees) would often have to wait for their section leader to come and help them, and in the meantime would do no work. In one extreme case the section leader was in the USA, and the engineer sat and did nothing for five days until he returned. This illustrates a key inherent weakness in the Japanese management system – the discouragement of individual initiative, and a consequent reluctance to delegate. Indeed, in these respects, the Japanese weakness is the British strength. The same British engineer describes the approach to modifications of printed circuit boards in his Japanese development laboratory. In Britain he would have drilled components out and modified the circuit in a rough and ready way to see if the circuit worked. In Japan, in contrast, the printed circuit board was taken to a special craftsmanship section, where two and a half hours would be taken to do what would have required just 15 minutes in his own company in Britain, albeit with a better-looking prototype board at the end of it. This again illustrates how an inherent strength, the emphasis on quality of work, is also a potential weakness. He also describes Japanese meetings as being very slow and laborious. There are long periods of silence while suggestions are considered, there are many people present to ensure that all viewpoints are aired, no notes are taken so that no individual can be blamed for a decision, and, above all, meetings are time-consuming because of the inherent imprecision of the Japanese language.

The observation of this British engineer, therefore, is that this Japanese company requires at least twice as many development engineers for any particular purpose as his own required in the UK. Nevertheless he believes that, given time, the Japanese will produce a better product, because they will push the design to the limits of perfection, with an emphasis on doing things right the first time. In fact, other British engineers working in Japan have estimated that the Japanese require more like four or five times as many development engineers as Western companies to complete a particular design, but then, as was demonstrated in Chapter 3, they educate and train many more engineers *pro rata* than their Western competitor countries, and can therefore afford that luxury.

That luxury can of course only be afforded if the unit price to the customer is at least comparable to that of Western competitors, so how is that achieved? The answer is probably twofold. The Japanese are superb at marketing, and therefore achieve the necessary volume to write off their development overheads at a low price; and they are also superb at manufacturing, which also reduces the unit price despite a high level of quality. Thus overall the Japanese are increasingly able to produce a better-engineered product at a comparable price to, or even a lower price than, their competitors. Inherent in this success is the ability to get things right first time more often than, say, British companies, who usually concentrate on completing the design of a product as quickly as possible, and then pay a large penalty in correcting problems which arise at great expense at a later stage in the manufacturing process.

A very flexible approach to the use of employees

While from a Western point of view the Japanese may appear to require greater human resources than might appear justified, the fact remains that in many ways they use those human resources with greater flexibility and to better effect. Nikkeiren – the Japanese Federation of Employers' Associations quotes one large electrical company as having a computerized database of the specialist knowledge of each of their engineers, who are then brought in to solve any problem anywhere in the company requiring such specialist knowledge.

An American engineer working in Japan describes what he calls 'ghost-workers':

During a trying period in one of my projects, we were falling behind schedule because the computer program to analyze magnetic fields for our prototype device was not entirely user-friendly. Our section manager summoned what I thought were three young apprentices to help with the project. They painstakingly scrutinized the data and put in enough overtime to complete the work on schedule.

When I later asked my boss about these 'apprentices', I was surprised to learn that one was an engineer of my rank, another was the author of the computer program, and the third was the author's collaborator. They were not apprentices at all, but expert consultants. They were what I call ghost-workers – employees who often turn up when there is an engineering problem and, once the problem is solved, vanish.[11]

Japanese companies, furthermore, have a very flexible (even perhaps a Macchiavellian) approach to categorizing employees. All large companies have four different types of employees working on their sites:

- regular;
- part-time;
- subsidiary company; and
- subcontractor.

At first the British author found the explanations he was given as to the reason for there being such a high proportion (often 50 per cent) of subsidiary company and subcontractor employees on major sites a little baffling. Eventually one senior executive explained the reasons to him – on condition that he was not identified as the source of the information! There are four main reasons for subsidiary companies being formed:

1. A large company's head office will specify the number of university graduates to be recruited by each operating company each year. However, the actual number required is often much higher, although it is usually impossible anyway to recruit more than the official number of high-calibre graduates from the best universities. Subsidiary companies therefore recruit lower-calibre graduates on lower salaries and with lesser promotion prospects, although they will quite probably sit at the same desks as the main company's regular graduates.
2. In some situations special skills which command premium salaries, such as software, are required. Subsidiary companies then allow higher wages to be paid than for the regular engineers. Software engineers, for example, might effectively have to retire between the ages of 30 and 35, requiring special methods of payment and special retirement systems.
3. Most companies have an official retirement age of, say, 56. Directors can continue in employment with the company beyond that age, but all other employees must retire. Therefore particularly skilled and valuable employees are re-employed by a subsidiary company formed for that purpose, and everyone is satisfied, since the main company has officially kept to the strict retirement rules.
4. In a recession, the subsidiary companies are the first to shed employees, and therefore the concept of lifetime employment is maintained.

Subsidiaries are also often set up as an autonomous part of a company and operate in a specialist field, where they do not necessarily need to trade with the parent company, although they would normally do so. Staff will then usually remain with the subsidiary, and see themselves as employed by the subsidiary rather than by the company as a whole.

Increasing flexibility by using subcontractors

There is also a very flexible labour market amongst subcontractors. There was a remarkable increase in the numbers of contract engineers in software in the 1980s, for example, for two major reasons; there was a national shortage of software engineers, and using contract employees avoided the need to train them in the company. These contract engineers were often those failing to get themselves recruited by a large company, and many were non-technical. Software houses provided basic intensive training for three months, followed by on-the-job training in a large company working next to the company's regular engineers. The salary of a contract engineer is lower than that of a regular company engineer; and, in addition, the main company does not have to pay such costs as retirement or welfare. These contract engineers are employed both by independent companies and by subsidiaries of main companies. The largest independent software contractor company has 2800 employees working for various periods with 450 companies. This company recruits 800 university graduates each year, and therefore obviously suffers a very high turnover rate. Those leaving go to other types of non-software jobs, to other agencies with better employment conditions, or to establish their own companies. It is however, apparently very unusual for them to be recruited by a large company.

Broad experience is an essential condition for flexibility

The subject of career development will be covered in more depth in Chapter 8, but it is important to realize here in the context of management that providing broad experience for employees is a key aspect of the Japanese approach to developing staff who are flexible. A British engineer seconded to Toshiba's Mechanical Engineering Laboratory in Yokohama noted:

The MEL is funded by Toshiba head office and supports the manufacturing effort within the corporation. Of about 400 engineers, almost one-sixth are visiting for 1 or 2 years from a Toshiba factory in order to learn some new technology or for general experience as part of their career development. A similar number of MEL engineers are on secondment to Toshiba factories. This transfer between lab and factory is an important part of the success they have in making the company work as a team and preventing the credibility gap often seen between engineers who have spent their whole careers only in research or in manufacturing. A typical engineer moves job every 3 years or so and is expected to become broadly based technically.[12]

Yet another way in which career flexibility is built in is in the separation of position and rank. Since a cohort of graduates will generally be promoted together, they will usually all have the same rank at any given time, but their job titles and actual responsibilities may differ considerably – a system with great subtlety!

Total commitment is expected of employees – and is given

There is strict discipline in Japanese companies. There is no smoking or consumption of alcohol on company premises, and absenteeism is heavily frowned on. Sickness absence normally has to be taken out of one's holiday entitlement.

Companies encourage employees to remain on the premises at lunchtime by providing heavily subsidized meals, and often provide only one choice of menu each day in order to avoid wasting the employees' time in choosing between menus. To speed up lunches many canteens have yellow lines on the floor to guide employees. Finally, some also take regular samples of employees' blood pressure, and use the result to adjust the level of salt in the meals.

Total commitment is expected of employees, and is usually given. On his first flight to Japan the British author sat next to the Statutory Auditor of the Nomura Research Institute. He was returning from a fortnight's holiday in Europe with his wife to mark his forthcoming retirement. However, that was his first holiday for 10 years – ten years ago he had had a three-day holiday; while 15 years before that he had had a five-day holiday.

Nevertheless, there are signs that things are changing slowly, The Deputy Director of the Economic Co-operation Department at Keidanren, the equivalent of the Confederation of British Industry, said in 1985 after returning from three years as Keidanren's Representative in London that he had found it was becoming much more normal for everyone in the Tokyo office to take their holidays, even to the extent of displaying a holiday wallchart. Even in 1979 Denki Rōren, the Japanese Federation of Electrical Machine Workers' Union, with 570 000 members in large Japanese electrical companies, of whom 120 000 are graduates, found that 'sport and hobby' ranked higher than 'work and study' in a survey of the desires of their members for those under the age of 30; however, 'the pleasure of a happy home' trailed a bad third to either at all ages.

An extreme example of a company's requirement for employee commitment is Mr S. Nagamori's Nidec Corporation, a medium-sized company which typically faces difficulty in recruiting high-calibre employees. His view is that large companies evaluate employees on the basis of their university background, whereas in Nidec the key measures are enthusiasm, energy, and dedication. Every employee must carry a copy of a little green booklet at all times; this contains, amongst other things, the company song, the annual company slogans, and Mr Nagamori's own 100 maxims. He educates new employees using 50 lessons which essentially function through emphasis on the emotions such as sorrow and joy, and by means of scolding. Each lesson takes two hours, but he was reluctant to explain his method to the British author in any detail, since he said it would only be misunderstood. He has devised this approach himself and bases it on his childhood. He admitted that he has been criticized for it, but does not care, as long as he retains those staff sympathizing with the company's aims. The lessons take place not only in a lecture room, but also during the employee's meals and at his own home. One-third of the training is in the lecture room, with 40 per cent conducted by Mr Nagamori himself and the rest by specialists. About 90 per cent of new graduates can stand this approach, but one-third of those recruited from large companies cannot, and leave. Employees usually either leave within three months or are completely 'Nidecized' after one year.

In 1984 Mr Nagamori wrote a best-selling book on educating employees based on these experiences, which has so far sold several hundred thousand copies. In this book we find how outstanding he is at grasping each employee's abilities and emotions and giving them appropriate messages and encouragement. One key objective is increasing the abilities of the graduate from an ordinary university. He often says to the new graduates, 'Believing that you are not superior to others is a splendid thing. You will respect others and endeavour to obtain better wisdom from people in client companies.' Thus, 'The Customer is King' is a fundamental truth in Nidec. Another Nagamori motto is: 'Do not make excuses to postpone a problem till tomorrow, but instead do it today.' The Japanese author feels that the corporate practice of these two doctrines is the key to Nidec's rapid growth and successes. Computer manufacturers, which are generally large, needed small motors to ventilate their personal computers and drive memory disks without failures. Nidec's engineers listened to what customer engineers said and responded much quicker than those of subcontractor motor suppliers of PC manufacturers. Through trial-and-error approaches to solving problems quickly, they often found suitable solutions.

Mr Nagamori does not expect his employees to socialize outside work and believes that there is no need to have a hobby if one's work is making sufficient use of one's abilities. Mr Nagamori quotes a very large company as having several hundred doctorates in the field of electric motors and an astronomical number of researchers in their laboratories, yet they have never designed better motors than Nidec. Thus major computer manufacturers rely on Nidec for the supply of many of their key components.

It is notable that their corporate internal meetings and training seminars are held at weekends so that Nidec are always ready to respond to customers by phone and to welcome visitors during weekdays.

Clearly such dedication to the company would be completely unacceptable in the West, even if Nidec is an extreme example, and it is only the oriental approach to the marital relationship that allows the average Japanese man to have such total commitment to his company. Even in less pressurized companies than Nidec the working hours are so long that the male engineers have no time left for courting; in such cases they will usually either turn to their managers or their mothers to find them a bride. If they turn to their managers, then they have no alternative other than to marry the girl he chooses, otherwise face will be lost. Hitachi's booklet 'Introduction to Hitachi and modern Japan' shows on page 76 that in 1978 40 per cent of all marriages in Japan were arranged. If the question is asked as to how Japanese wives tolerate such long working hours by their husbands, then it is worth bearing in mind the saying of Japanese wives that 'A good husband is healthy and rarely seen'; by this they mean that a husband successful in his career will rarely be seen at home, and that is a good state of affairs, particularly in terms of status in the neighbourhood!

There is nevertheless a deadly serious side to this overwork. A government survey in February 1992 reported that a majority of adults complained of physical fatigue and emotional stress. The 12 June 1984 edition of the *Asahi* newspaper reported:

The highest incidence of suicide since 1900, when the government began keeping records, was 24970 in 1983. One of the causes is said to be the increasing rate of suicide among middle-aged managers. It is reported that the Japanese male of the 40 and 50 age group accounts for more than 35 per cent of the total cases.

The Economist reported on 24 October 1987 in an article headed 'Death at the top':

Suicide remains an honourable way out for the Japanese who believe they have failed. In the battleground of business, 275 company directors killed themselves last year. This was the highest number since 'management class' suicides were first distinguished in 1979. In the management class as a whole (which includes members of parliament, senior civil servants and non-board-level managers as well as directors), more than nine suicides a week happened during 1986.

Most of the suicides appear to be the result of far from terminal misfortunes: share scandals, business disappointments, export problems as a result of the high yen. Lower down the bowing order, some 50 workers on Japan National Railways took their lives in protest over its forthcoming break-up. One union leader killed himself after failing to prevent the closure of his coal mine.

Stress is also taking its toll even without a helping hand. So far this year, the chief executives of a dozen of Japan's very top companies have dropped dead – three times as many as in the whole of 1986. Japan's biggest trading house, biggest cosmetics company, biggest aluminium producer, its number two airline and its number three steelmaker and paint maker have all lost their top men. Most were in their 50s or 60s and had heart attacks. A comparative study of executives at American Telephone and Telegraph and Nippon Telegraph and Telephone blames the early deaths on the westernisation of Japanese life.

The commitment of employees contrasts with low job-satisfaction

It will have become clear that the degree of commitment given by the Japanese to their employers is extremely high, and is an important factor in their success. However, questions need to be asked such as whether this commitment is given willingly, whether it will continue in the future, and whether it is transferable overseas. The reply of the authors is 'no', 'maybe', and 'no'.

Even in 1979 a survey by Denki Rōren showed a significant minority interested in leaving their employers, as is shown in Table 5.1. International comparisons of job-satisfaction by the Japanese Prime Minister's Office, shown in Figures 5.1 and 5.2, indicate that the level of job-satisfaction of Japanese employees is lower than in the USA and UK, for example, and that this is due to long hours and the relative salaries. Both no doubt reflect the necessity of working a considerable amount of overtime, often unpaid, and the social pressure to minimize holidays. Yet another indication that all is not well under the surface is that a survey amongst section chiefs of 100 top-ranking companies in the *Nikkei Sangyō Shimbun* newspaper showed that as many as 40 per cent of them had given thought to seeking employment elsewhere. One reason, however, why managers are highly reluctant to leave the security of large companies is that they would then become *personae non gratae* amongst their former colleagues and contacts. One well-known Japanese company even expunges all references to employees who have left.

As to whether this will change in the future, this is a major question which

Table 5.1. Denki Rōren survey of the commitment of Japanese engineers to remaining with their companies (percentages of employees)

View on changing job	Production sites (%)	Research development (%)
Lifetime employment	54.7	40.0
May move to another job if better conditions are offered	24.0	35.9
Intend moving in the near future	3.8	3.5
Wish to continue work until getting married and having a child	0.4	0.2
Do not know	15.5	19.4
No answer	1.6	1.0

Japanese employers must address. There must, however, be considerable doubt whether this high-pressure system of Japanese industry will change, just as there is whether it is likely that the high-pressure system in Japanese schools will change. It is surely in Japan's best interests in raising the quality of life of its citizens, as well as in terms of the resentment stirred overseas by those seeing this as unfair competition, to modify both.

The international implications of Japanese management

One company which has carried out a survey of the views of its non-Japanese international managers is NEC. In order of priority, in their view the most positive aspects of Japanese management were:

1. lifetime employment;
2. consensus in management;
3. the 'family' atmosphere;
4. communication style;
5. the education and training system;
6. the long-term basis of management (market share more important than profits); and
7. patience and far-sightedness.

The negative aspects, as they saw them in order of priority, were listed as:

1. slowness in decision-making (a bottom-up approach, although NEC emphasize they now adopt quite a bit of top-down decision-making);
2. lack of understanding of local culture and business rules;
3. placing less confidence in local staff;
4. unwillingness to share information with local staff;
5. poor communication ability (a language problem);
6. the job-rotation system; and
7. the inflexible seniority system of rewards.

Japanese companies have in many respects been very pragmatic and successful in adapting their management and personnel systems in their overseas subsidiaries. Companies like Nidec, not surprisingly, have found that the approach which works in Japan is not directly transferable overseas. What is however transferable is dedication to detail, and in particular the systematic development of skills in all employees, which leads directly to the high quality in products on which their reputation is based. There are nevertheless still four key problems which Japanese companies have to solve if they are to adapt even more successfully overseas.

The first is what the authors will call **Hourism** – the fixation which

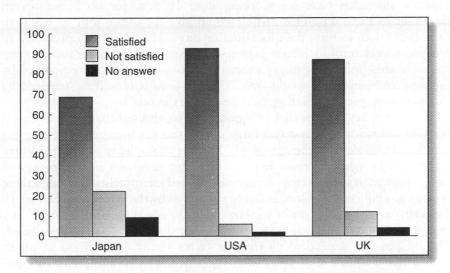

Fig. 5.1 Workers' job-satisfaction in Japan, the USA, and the UK (percent). *Source*: Prime Minister's Office (1979). *Census of work attitudes*. Prime Minister's Office, Tokyo. [In Japanese only.]

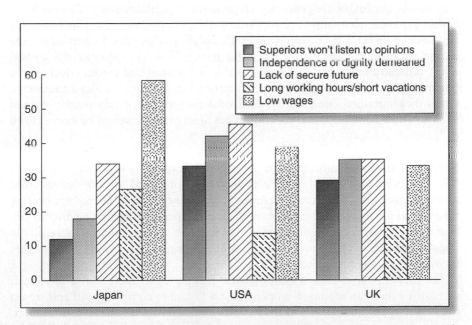

Fig. 5.2 Reasons for workers' dissatisfaction with their jobs (per cent) in Japan, the USA, and the UK. *Source*: Prime Minister's Office (1979). *Census of work attitudes*. Prime Minister's Office, Tokyo.

Japanese managers have for working until 10 p.m. for no better reason than that to leave the office earlier would give the impression of less than total dedication. In turn, their local-nationality management feel pressured to remain at work until the senior Japanese manager has left, and this is a great source of frustration, not to say exhaustion, for local managers employed by Japanese companies the world over. Greater sensitivity will be required by Japanese managers in adapting their behaviours in this area.

The second key issue is that of **Ageism**. In Japan itself there is less than 3 per cent unemployment, but to a large degree this has been achieved by great sacrifices by those over the age of 45. Pay, for example, is to a large degree determined by age, with those over 45 suffering significant salary drops, and being required to suffer a large degree of enforced job mobility (although these are on the whole not problems suffered very often by the better-qualified staff). Typically, a Japanese engineer's salary might be made up as follows: 50 per cent according to his age and 35 per cent according to his job responsibility, with 15 per cent dependent on the size of his family. In addition he might receive two bonuses each year, each equivalent to two-and-a-half months' salary, plus or minus 15 per cent, depending on the company's performance. Motivation of middle-level employees is becoming more difficult, as promotion opportunities are more limited as the rapid expansion of Japan's economy slows down; this is particularly problematical because tradition demands that a cohort of graduates are generally all promoted simultaneously. The evidence is that Japanese companies are far from fully solving how they translate these personnel policies at home into pragmatic solutions overseas. In particular, the major assumption that anyone over the age of 45 is less valuable has caused many difficulties. There was a considerable amount of bad media coverage, as one example, when a large Japanese electronics company in Wales announced, when they obtained complete control of a factory previously jointly owned with a British company, that all employees aged over 45 would be encouraged to leave.

The third issue is that of blatant **Sexism** on the part of Japanese men. According to an opinion poll in 1986 by a leading newspaper, the *Asahi Shimbun*, 68 per cent of Japanese men are not prepared to take orders from a woman manager. Less than 1 per cent of Japanese working women occupy managerial posts, compared to an average of 10 per cent in Europe and 35 per cent in the USA. As career opportunities for women becomes an increasingly important issue in the West it will be more important for Japanese managers to overcome their prejudices.

The fourth issue is that of **Colonialism**. It is no more likely that a European or North American manager working for a Japanese company will end up on the Board in Tokyo than it was that an African or Asian should be promoted to the corridors of power in Whitehall under the British Empire. This philosophy is rather better understood by the British, who after all invented colonialism, than by the Americans, who forced the British to relinquish their Empire. At present the only Japanese company indicating that promotion to the Board in Japan might be possible for a foreigner is Sony. In November 1990 Akio Morita said that he hoped that within twenty years it might be possible to have a Westerner succeed him as Chairman. However, Sony has always been a maverick company in Japanese terms, and at present it continues to be a major frustration and demotivator for foreigners employed by Japanese companies that their promotion opportunities are ultimately restricted.

Humility – a key strength

Another basic Japanese ethic is humility. Young university graduates are quite prepared to spend several months doing basically monotonous production work on the shopfloor, or in a retailer selling the company's products directly to customers, in order to learn the basics of the company's business. That readiness to roll up their shirtsleeves (or even, in some companies, to turn off the airconditioning system in the heat of the summer after the secretaries have left in the evening and continue working stripped down to their underwear!) indicates a mentality open to any sacrifices in order to learn. It means both that Japan has not only much more broadly experienced managers and employees in general, but also a willingness to lead from the front, much in the style of the British armed services officer.

A telling story concerns the visit of the British author to Yokogawa Digital Computers Limited, one of the companies referred to in Chapter 4. When he arrived he was shown into the office of the President, Mr T. Yamada, by Miss Nishioka, the Manager of their software Information Centre. His office was very luxurious, with a large meeting table in the main office and executive chairs, on which they sat, in the anteroom. At the end of his discussions with them, Miss Nishioka offered to show him around their facilities, and, as he left Mr Yamada's office, a group of executives went in for a meeting. About three-quarters of an hour later, at around 7 p.m., Miss Nishioka showed him their main software development laboratory. Like most such laboratories in Japan it was open plan, with the engineers working relatively close to each other. There, in the middle of the laboratory, was Mr Yamada; Miss Nishioka explained that he was at his normal work desk, having discussions with his engineers.

This style of management has many inherent strengths. Managers are closely involved in the action and the decisions, and they have an extremely good understanding of the strengths and weaknesses of each of their staff. Most importantly, when one of their subordinates is promoted to a managerial position he or she really does know what management is about. He or she has seen and heard his or her managers doing their jobs over many years. This is incomparably more effective at developing managerial skills in those promoted to management than the Western idea of managers being hidden in their own offices and of new promotees being given an off-the-job training course in management skills.

This is fundamentally why Western management is built on false premises, such as the notion of MBA courses as the solution to the development of management skills. How many of those courses tell the students to remove their office partitions and other barriers between them and their staff? After all, the Japanese management development approach of learning by observing those doing it well is precisely the one which has so successfully served the officers of the British armed forces, generally considered the most professional in the world!

Can Western companies beat the Japanese?

Nothing stops any company beating its Japanese competitors other than the lack of competence of its managers to develop and direct the skills of all employees to the ultimate degree possible. Not only do so many Western companies not do this, but they usually have very little, if any, concept that such is the role of managers. But how else can quality be built into the product or service? And without the highest, and a constantly increasing, level of quality the customers will simply transfer their custom elsewhere, and that 'elsewhere' is all too often to the Japanese, who do indeed see very clearly what the role and priorities of management are about.

Flexibility of skills, including the use of skills databases, well-informed employees, systems to maximize the contribution of everyone, such as highly effective suggestion schemes, and a complete openness to new ideas are at the heart of Japan's commercial victories.

One final question – and perhaps the most important one: are Japan's competitors willing to learn the key lessons about the skills of management, to build on their existing strengths, to take advantage of Japan's weaknesses (such as the low ability to delegate decision-making), and thus to stem the otherwise inexorable tide of Japanese victories?

References

1 *Sunday Times*, 13 April 1986.
2 *Sunday Times*, 16 February 1992, quoting research for *Quality – total customer service*, a book by Linda King Taylor to be published in April 1992.
3 *Sunday Times*, 8 April 1990, quoting research by Dr Fons Trompenaars, Managing Director of the Centre for International Business Studies in the Netherlands, and David Wheatley, Head of Advisory Services at Employment Conditions Abroad.
4 Research and Development Institute of Vocational Training, Employment Promotion Projects Corporation, *Country report on the planning, programming and education of vocational training – Japan*, Sagamihara, December 1984, p. 55.

5 Neil Pedlar, 'The man who gave Japan the "quality" edge – the story of Edward Deming and "Quality Circles"', *Japan Digest*, January 1991, p. 12.
6 Yasuhiko Inoue, *Key to improving productivity*, Japan Productivity Centre, Tokyo, p. 10.
7 JETRO (Japanese External Trade Organization), *Japanese corporate decision making*, JETRO Business Information Series 9, JETRO, 1982. Tokyo.
8 Colin A. Warwick, 'Methods and management of microelectronics research in Japan', Report on Winston Churchill Travelling Fellowship, Royal Signals and Radar Establishment, Memorandum 3909, December 1985, p. 7.
9 M. Urwin, 'Six weeks with the Toshiba Manufacturing Engineering Laboratory, preliminary report', February 1987.
10 M. Urwin, 'Work in Toshiba Manufacturing Engineering Laboratory, six-monthly report', July 1987.
11 Daun Bhasavanic, 'An American in Tokyo: jumping to the Japanese beat', *IEEE Spectrum*, September 1985, pp. 72–81.
12 Mike Urwin, 'A year in Japan – Part 2: Research to production in Toshiba', *IEE Review*, December 1988, p. 451.

6

The third winning margin – training

'Total quality begins and ends with training.'
– Professor Kaoru Ishikawa

Introduction

Training in Japan is both subtle and effective; subtle because it is an inherent aspect of Japanese management, and effective because everyone is involved in and totally committed to it.

The last chapter explained some of the ways in which training and the company's objectives are integrated. It is certainly not by having Training Managers or Training Departments that consider themselves the sole custodians of training expertise in their organizations. Rather, it is by commitment at all levels across the organization to On-the-Job Training (OJT), which is the predominant approach to training everywhere in Japan. It is now time to examine in some detail the philosophy, implementation, and value of OJT. Without that it is impossible either to understand one of the fundamental secrets of Japan's industrial success, or to structure the strategies for skills development that every organization wishing to become world-class, or indeed, often, to survive at all, needs to put in place.

However, it is also important to recognize that, as from 1985, there has been an increasing degree of emphasis placed on Off-the-Job Training (OffJT) in Japan. Indeed, their formalized OffJT is now better organized and on a larger scale than is generally seen in the West. This chapter will therefore also show why this is happening, and explain the balance required between OJT and OffJT. Just as Japan's greatest strength has been the emphasis on the former, so has the West's greatest weakness been its over-reliance on the latter. And just as we saw in the last chapter that quality in Japanese products is the result of decades of investment both in basic education and in education on quality itself, so we must realize that Japan's use of OffJT is only effective to the degree that it is because of decades of investment in OJT.

A cohesive and integrated approach

In the West much of the investment in formalized (and expensive) OffJT is wasted because it is not underpinned by a real learning environment; it is perfectly common for delegates on training courses, for example, to have only a limited understanding of why they have been sent on a course and how it will be followed up. It is even fair to say that most Western managers show little or no interest in helping or encouraging their staff to implement any learning or changes on their return from most training courses. The environment for successful learning, both day-by-day through the job itself and by building on lessons from formal training, is simply not there as an inherent and important part of the value system of these companies.

And yet that need not, and should not, be the case. In Japan, above all else, education and training are seen as a supremely important part of a manager's reponsibility, even at the most senior levels of a company. **One of the most important messages of this book is very simply this:** THE ROLE OF MANAGEMENT MUST BE SO REDEFINED THAT IT IS UNIVERSALLY ACCEPTED THAT THE **PRIME** ROLE OF MANAGERS IS THE DEVELOPMENT OF THEIR STAFF.

In the television portrait of Queen Elizabeth II in 1992 Her Majesty remarked of her own professionalism, 'You can do a lot if you are properly trained.' The tragedy of British industry is that most of her subjects have never understood that simple, but vitally important, truth.

Companies really do own the concept of training!

Before going any further, therefore, let us look at a typical example of a Japanese company which does indeed operate such a value system, *with* **REAL** *commitment from its President downwards*.

Hitachi is one of the largest and most successful Japanese companies, and on page 2 of their philosophy on education and training they say:

The highest responsibility for education throughout the company resides with the President. This philosophy is indicative of high prioritization of education at Hitachi.

And perhaps most significant is the statement on page 7:

We also believe that the use of top management is a unique aspect of our education programme. Even the President may make over twenty trips a year to our educational facilities to talk with students at all levels of management courses and the introductory assembly education for college graduates.

Do readers know of *any* Western company where such a value system applies? For herein lies a key secret to Japan's success and the West's failures.

A thorough and committed approach to induction

First impressions count in most situations. Nowhere more so than with respect to training in Japanese companies. Here, therefore, are a number of examples of how new employees are inducted into a new company. It is not just a matter of giving them the skills they will require to contribute effectively as quickly as possible. It is even more about developing right from the start an employee whose whole way of thinking is compatible with the traditions and value system of the organization.

In **Fujitsu** new employees are given a three-month correspondence course on the company *even before they start*. This is common practice in Japan, and reflects the high level of importance attached to inducting the new employee into the company's culture. Fujitsu's subsequent one-year Induction Programme is notable for the prominent part played by human skills training, including training in the many formal terminologies of the Japanese language which are so important in role relationships, and which are inordinately complicated, requiring many years to master. Even more important in that induction, unlike what happens in the West, is *the prominence of hands-on factory experience*.

All new employees in **Mitsubishi Motors**, without exception, spend at least six months on the shopfloor; in the case of new graduates it is up to two years.

Toshiba is another company with a typically detailed Manpower Development philosophy. Their approach to Induction Training, which also takes place over a one-year period, not only again emphasizes practical experience in the factory, but also includes a period *actually selling the company's products*.

A typical Induction Programme for new university graduates joining **Hitachi**, in this case their Musashi Works, is:

1. Orientation by Head Office (2 weeks).
   Lecture by top management. History and outline of Hitachi. Discussion of Company regulations. Visit to Hitachi's major factories.
2. Introduction to Musashi (1 week).
3. Fundamental Training (5 months).
   On-the-Job Training in manufacturing section (blue-collar job).
4. Assignment to a Section (18 months).
   Computer training (1 month).
   Basic Semiconductor Course (100 hours, 8 hours/week).

On-the-Job Training in a specialized field.

Preparation of a treatise, with the subject chosen by the managers in each trainee's section.

5. Oral and Written Thesis Presentation.

In **Matsushita** all university graduate entrants have a common induction together for three weeks. This length of initial induction is common amongst large companies, and the company President and other Directors always play a prominent role in explaining the company's philosophy to the new recruits. They are made to understand that they are now Matsushita, Fujitsu, Toshiba, Hitachi, NEC, etc., men or women. What these Presidents and Directors are doing is to explain the value system of their company to their newly joined colleagues, and sharing their visions for the future. Interestingly, in March 1992 Tim Waterstone, one of Britain's most successful booksellers, said at a lunch given by the Industrial Society to mark the publication of a book, *Leaders*, in which he featured, 'I am a firm believer in dreams. Success comes from great dreams. It is this aspiration that is most important. What is sad about British society today is that some of the dreams have faded away.' What better way of sharing those corporate values and visions than directly from the most senior company officers and as the first and most important experience of new recruits?

Japanese employees at all levels simply have a much better understanding of their organizations' products, processes, people, and potential. There is nothing mystical or magical about this; the Japanese generally win because they deserve to do so. Western companies generally lose entirely due to their own incompetence and stupidity.

Learning through 'conferences'

In large companies, following the induction period for university graduates of one or two years, there follows what the Japanese call **Conferences**. These are 20- to 30-minute presentations by graduates as the culmination of the first major project they have been given as their first real work. The whole of an annual cohort of graduates at a particular plant will gather together for one or two weeks to listen to each other's presentations. Far more importantly, also present will be the graduates' managers, managers from other sites who have a technical interest in the presentations, and company senior managers and directors. Often Managing Directors themselves will make a point of personally always attending these 'Conferences'.

This concept has a number of important advantages:

1. The graduates are motivated to learn everything possible in the year or two prior to their 'Conference'.

2. Their managers have a very direct incentive to do everything possible to ensure that the graduate is properly supervised and developed during that period. There is otherwise too much potential for losing face in front of their directors if their graduates do not make a good presentation.
3. The senior managers and directors are able to spot talent at an early stage in the young graduates' careers.
4. Finally, and very importantly, there is a certain amount of valuable transfer of technical knowledge, the lifeblood of Japanese companies (or of all companies world-wide, were they to recognize its importance).

Hitachi initiated this approach in the mid-1950s, and the idea was taken up by the other large companies. In fact it has proved to be so valuable that Toshiba have three or four such events during the first ten years of an engineer's career, and Fujitsu organize them twice a year for systems engineers.

It is important to note that this approach does to a degree depend on the graduate remaining in the same job and on the same project during that one or two-year period. This is not a problem in the typical Japanese long-term career environment, which is centrally directed in a lifetime employment context, but would need reinterpretation in other countries. The examples of Toshiba and Fujitsu show some of the ways in which this can be done.

It is also important to note that in Japan all Departmental and General Managers are present for the duration of these 'Conferences' (with Section Managers and Senior Engineers attending specific presentations) – another demonstration that the development of subordinates by managers plays a real and vital role in Japanese companies; but why do Western companies have such difficulty understanding the high priority that must be given to this?

The key role of OJT

In the UK, until the Japanese influence in the 1980s, these initials used to refer to Off-the-Job Training. This difference neatly epitomizes the differences in training approaches and priorities between the two countries.

The characteristics of Japanese Human Resources Development (HRD) are described in one Research and Development Institute of Vocational Training publication as follows:

The HRD systems facilitating the post-war rapid growth of the Japanese economy were based on OJT (On-the-Job Training). The high ratio of people with a secondary education has been one of the prerequisites supporting OJT as an effective learning method. In addition to the fact that workers have enough readiness to accept OJT there were motivational factors supporting independent self-development practised by workers. A view of work as a means of human development and role allocation based upon individual competency was made a premise of the approach.[1]

So what is this OJT and why is it considered so effective in Japan?

The Research and Development Institute of Vocational Training (now renamed the Polytechnic University of Japan) which determines training standards across Japan, explains:

One training method which enterprises give a lot of importance to is OJT. For instance, according to a 1982 survey of the Vocational Training Bureau of the Ministry of Labour, the training methods that enterprises listed as the most important were, first, OJT (36%) and, second, internal group education (28%).

The OJT referred to here is not a synonym for 'sitting by Nelly' which means 'learning from watching the work of their superiors and senior colleagues.' **The OJT mentioned here is a set of diverse experiences: one in which the employee is given an easy job at the beginning and then gradually assigned to higher-level jobs along with his experience, in the process of his internal promotion; planned rotation so that an employee can handle several different duties; internal guidance on a man-to-man basis with a specific instructor being assigned to each new employee.**[2]

Some examples of company OJT policy statements

The importance and effectiveness of OJT is so ill understood in the West that it is worth describing its importance as seen by some major Japanese companies.

For example, **Mitsubishi Heavy Industries'** 'Basic Policy of Education and Training' states:

Development of the employee's capability to perform his job so largely depends on daily coaching by managers or supervisors that the basic approach shall be education or training provided by the managers or supervisors of their subordinates' daily work (the so-called 'On-the-Job Training').

Dr Shigeru Asakawa, then **Toshiba**'s Corporate Technical Representative for Europe, in a paper presented in London on 27 March 1985 on the subject of 'Research and Development at Toshiba Corporation' said:

'On-the-Job' training, though it is not always formal, is thought to be more important than off-the-job training. It is attained through everyday work, and a great deal of knowledge, experience, skill, know-how and other important factors are gained by on-the-job training. To bring young people to an expert level is one of the essential duties of senior staff like managers or leading researchers.

Hitachi's policy statement on Education and Training says:

The foundation of our education programme, however, is On-the-Job Training. Managers and supervisors are responsible for the education of their subordinates through OJT. We believe that 'to hire a person and not train him is a failure of management; but that to train him and not be strict in guidance is negligence on the part of his superior.' **In order to have capable managers to provide OJT, there is an emphasis on the training and education of superiors to ensure that they will be able teachers.** Only the most skilful workers and the most able staff with an international outlook will be promoted, so that superior knowledge and experience will be passed on to the other employees.

OJT therefore means many things, but amongst them are daily work assignments (including those culminating for new graduate recruits in 'Conferences'), job rotation, and a career-development programme.

Japanese managers give time to developing their staff

One of the extraordinary aspects of Japanese management and training as seen by Westerners is the very high proportion of a supervisor's, manager's, or director's time which is devoted to developing and training his or her subordinates. Even at a conservative estimate the proportion of time devoted to this activity is between 20 per cent and 30 per cent – and some observers have suggested it is often higher than this.

Put quite simply, *the most important responsibility of a manager is the development of his staff.* This should apply in any company around the world (and indeed does in the American company Digital, for example), but in practice only predominantly does in Japan. But there is absolutely no reason why any organization should not accept the importance of this fundamental principle, which the British author has facilitated very successfully in many companies in his capacity as a consultant. The only effective way, however, in which it can be done is if the Chief Executive understands this very clearly and insists that it is a core value of the organization. **Managers have to be appointed predominantly because they are expected to be good at giving time to developing their staff; they must be trained to do it well, and their rewards and promotion must be intimately connected to their success or failure in so doing.** Again we must ask the question as to how many Western companies understand or accept this.

The British author recalls meeting the senior representatives in Japan of a number of large British companies. The first point they made was that Japanese senior managers and directors have specific dates (for example five days each month) set aside in their diaries to be involved in the in-house training of their employees, and there is absolutely no way that they are prepared to entertain the idea of business meetings on such dates.

It is soon apparent to all visitors to Japan that developing staff is universally seen as the single most important responsibility of a Japanese manager. They will have it emphasized to them on many occasions that successfully developed subordinates reflect well on their managers in Japan. This importance to giving time to developing staff is absolutely crucial to the successful implementation of OJT. This cannot be emphasized too strongly. It appears, for example, to be generally unthinkable for a Japanese supervisor or manager not to devote an enormous amount of his own time to training a new member of his team both face-to-face and by demonstration. This is one of the tremendous strengths of Japanese industry.

Another aspect of OJT is the emphasis on formalized updating and training in company time and at the workplace. One Hitachi engineer describes, for example, how he and his colleagues have study meetings, reading the technical literature on other companies' technology once a week for three or four months at the start of a project. Another explains how the ten people in his group meet once a week for two hours in company time; they take it in turns each week to make a presentation on matters they have learnt from studying technical books and magazines in their own time. In Toshiba an engineer would typically describe how he participates in similar two-hour weekly meetings with his team to exchange information on the activities, and learning and ideas gathered from the preceding week, this exchange being backed up by one-page written summaries which each team member circulates to his colleagues.

Achieving a balance between OJT and OffJT

What is the real reason for this enormous emphasis on OJT in Japan? Because it is far more than the fact that in its own right it is a highly cost-effective way of enabling employees to acquire the skills and techniques needed to do their jobs. Rather there is an emphasis placed through the instruction on developing the right attitude and way of thinking in the employee. This is such an intrinsic value in Japanese companies that most are far more concerned with recruiting people who have 'the right attitude' to learning than in selecting those with the best existing skills for a job.

For this reason it is essential to develop an employee's competence predominantly through the job itself, with constant reinforcement day-by-day. This is also intimately connected with the seniority system of promotion, where great respect is paid in Japan both to superior experience and to the role of imparting knowledge and expertise.

Even in those Japanese companies with a significant investment in Off-the-Job training facilities, there is always a major theme on their courses such as 'the way of thinking, attitude, and conviction of a company man'. Increasingly Japanese companies are establishing their own training centres; but the approach is such that in reality they are an extension of OJT.

OJT is undoubtedly very effective for solving day-to-day problems. However, it is often not an effective approach for obtaining forward-looking insights, understanding the latest technologies, or predicting the future. There is a limitation on how OJT can be used to deal with technical innovation in the rapidly changing environments that have been typical since the latter half of the 1980s.

OffJT has the greater potential in vocational education in enriching and broadening knowledge independently of a company's existing viewpoint and mindsets. One of the important decisions for managers is deciding whether to use OJT or OffJT in particular situations. Large companies have their own training facilities, and employ both. Generally, small and medium-sized companies do not have such facilities; there is therefore an important role here for public vocational training centres.

Historically, there have been a number of stages that the legal provision for vocational training has gone through in Japan.

- 1958   Promulgation of a Vocational Training Law.
- 1969   Total revision to the 'New Vocational Training Law' to establish a system whereby individuals may undergo adequate training until their retirement ages.
- 1978   Partial revision to emphasize lifetime training.
- 1981   Another partial revision to reinforce assistance to employers in the provision of employee training.
- 1985   Renaming to the 'Human Resources Development Promotion Law'. The main stream of vocational training shifted from a focus on training for craft skills towards a diversified approach to the development of occupational capability throughout individuals' lifetimes. Public training facilities were further developed to provide retraining for employees, particularly in small and medium-sized companies.
- 1992   Partial revision to allow for more flexible implementation of training, reflecting the recommendations of the Provisional Council for Educational Reform.

Evidence for this increasing emphasis on OffJT comes from a survey into training carried out by the Ministry of Labour in 1986, to which 83.4 per cent of employers responded that the role of OffJT would become more important in the future. At the same time the Ministry said that Japan must aim at a new 'Japanese-style development of lifelong vocational capability' by devising a systematic approach to introducing education and training outside a company.

An international research project

Let us now look at some evidence of the different existing approaches to training and career development in Britain and Japan.

First, in a study by the British author in 1985 with the late Professor Keith Thurley, Professor of Personnel Management at the London School of

Economics (LSE), it became obvious that the three key problems in British companies in providing effective Continuing Professional Development are:

- Inadequate ongoing *technical and management training*.
- Insufficient *career development*.
- Giving engineers enough *challenge* in their jobs. They are both misutilized and underutilized.

In 1987 a two-year research project was then initiated by the author, together with Keith Thurley, funded by the Suntory Toyota International Centre for Economics and Related Disciplines (STICERD), which is part of the LSE. It involved some 50 engineers in electronics companies in both the UK and Japan, from the following companies:

UK

GEC Hirst Research Laboratory
GPT
Honeywell Bull
Marconi Communication Systems
Marconi Research Laboratory
Thorn-EMI Electronics

JAPAN

Hitachi Research Laboratory
Meidensha
Mitsubishi Electric
NEC
Sanyo Research and Development
Toray Engineering
Toshiba Research and Development

The purpose was to study in depth the training experienced by a limited number of engineers over a six-month period. The stages of the research project were:

- Participants completed a background questionnaire.
- They were asked to complete details of their On-the-Job and Off-the-Job Training experiences, using the Institution of Electrical Engineers' Professional Development Record (a personal development planning document which the British author suggested and helped design, pilot, and launch), and forwarded the results to the research team for a total of six months (an example is shown in Figure 6.1).
- Feedback sessions were arranged to keep the participants interested and to test the results.
- All participants were interviewed in depth at the end of their six months about their training experiences.
- Conferences in the UK and Japan were organized in 1989, with delegates from both the participants and their managers.

The framework used in the analysis is shown in Table 6.1.
   The importance of these results is that it illustrates a vitally important

```
Name XXXX XXXX      PROFESSIONAL DEVELOPMENT RECORD    ON-THE-JOB
```

Period	Contents of OJT	Your evaluation	Follow-up
9/3 1 hour 16/3 〃 23/3 〃 30/3 〃	◆自己啓発 Self-study ◆グループ輪講 Group reading of a foreign book	◆将来の研究テーマ発掘 Helpful in looking for research themes in the future	◆定期的な輪講の開催 Practising on regular basis ◆週1回 Once a week
17/3 0.5 day	◆学会全国大会聴講 Attending general convention of academic society	◆他の研究者が注目して いるポイントの理解 Understanding other groups' interests ◆将来の研究テーマ発掘 Helpful in looking for future research themes	◆学会・研究会資料の 調査 Reading journals/ research reports
23/3 0.5 day	◆社内研究発表会 Research presentation inside the company	◆他のグループが研究し 重要と考えていることが 明確になった I could understand what other groups find important in their studies.	◆他のグループとの交流 によって多くのディス カッションをする Carrying out many discussions with other groups
6/4 1 hour 13/4 〃 20/4 〃 27/4 〃	◆自己啓発 Self-study ◆グループ輪講 Group reading of a foreign book	◆将来の研究テーマ発掘 Helpful in looking for research themes in the future	◆定期的な輪講の開催 Practising on regular basis ◆週一回 Once a week

Fig. 6.1 An example of a completed sheet of the Institution of Electrical Engineers' Professional Development Record.

advantage possessed by Japanese companies; their approach to the skills development of their staff gives them a breadth and depth of talent in their employees which provides enormous flexibility. This is a key strategic advantage in the world marketplace, and is summarized in Table 6.2, which compares the relative emphasis on specific and general technical skills development on-the-job in the UK and Japan (with the figures shown being extracted from the previous table).

Table 6.1. Comparison of knowledge and skills acquired On-the-Job and Off-the-Job (percentage figures)

		ON-the-Job		OFF-the-Job	
		Japan	UK	Japan	UK
Specific	(present)	13.4	53.7	5.2	8.7
technical	(future)	11.0	23.9	3.4	17.4
skills					
General	(present)	14.6	4.5	5.2	–
technical	(future)	34.2	1.5	48.3	26.1
skills					
Non-technical/		24.4	13.4	8.6	4.3
organizational					
skills					
Managerial					
skills		1.2	3.0	24.1	39.2
Others		1.2	–	5.2	4.3
TOTAL		100.0	100.0	100.0	100.0

There is an interesting comparison of the approaches to On-the-Job and Off-the-Job Training in the two countries to be seen in Tables 6.3 and 6.4. Japanese companies take a long-term strategic view of the skills development of their employees; by contrast, British companies take a short-term view, and the result is disastrous, both in terms of the survival of companies and of employee job-satisfaction.

Absolutely crucial in the Japanese approach, as has been emphasized already, is the personal responsibility accepted by managers for the development of skills in their staff. This can be summarized in the way shown in Table 6.5.

The individual's responsibility for self-development

There needs to be increasing recognition of the importance of structuring the learning of individuals and giving them support in taking responsibility for their own self-development.

In Mitsubishi Heavy Industries, for example, all managers have for many years prepared self-development plans which include sections such as:

- Review of previous year's effort.
- Description of its focus, and whether satisfied.
- Description of present job.

Table 6.2. Utility of knowledge/skills acquired through On-the-Job Training (OJT). (Figures extracted from Table 6.1; technical skills only)

	Japan	UK
For present tasks (%)	28.0	58.2
For future tasks (%)	45.2	25.4
Total number of OJT incidents	83	67

- Own views of present job. Is he or she satisfied? Is he or she stretched? Is he or she seeking something different?
- Description of future objectives.
  What is the focus?
  What needs to be accomplished?
  Where does he or she wish to work, in Japan or overseas?
  What type of job is he or she looking for?
  What does he or she want to do to develop himself/herself?

In a paper presented at a Symposium in Malaysia in 1991, Dr Kaneichirō Imai, Vice-President of the Japanese Society of Engineering Education, and former Member of the Science Council of Japan, Senior Managing Director of IHI, and winner of the highly prestigious Deming Prize for Quality, showed the striking difference in productivity between large enterprises in Japan and the small to medium-sized ones (Table 6.6).

Table 6.3. Methods of On-the-Job Training

	Japan (%)	UK (%)
Formal		
Individual	–	–
With one another	2.5	1.5
Group	38.8	3.0
Spontaneous		
Individual	21.1	79.1
With one another	15.0	8.9
Group	22.5	7.5
TOTAL	100%	100%

Table 6.4. Methods of Off-the-Job Training

	Japan (%)	UK (%)
Internal seminar	53.6	52.2
Internal course	10.7	17.4
External seminar	28.6	13.0
External course	7.1	17.4

Table 6.5. Comparing the role of managers in the UK and Japan

	Japan	UK
Cognitive framework	System perspective	Narrow
Motivation for learning	Student-based Future-orientated	Pragmatic, for immediate specific purposes
Approach to learning	Group-based	*Ad-hoc* individualistic
Role of supervisor	Crucial	Unimportant

Table 6.6. Comparison of productivity of Japanese enterprises[3]

	Number of establishments	Number of people employed	Value added
Small to medium-sized enterprises*	870 262 (99.5%)	9 955 000 (74.4%)	55.5%
Large-sized enterprises	4 209 (0.5%)	3 421 000 (25.6%)	44.5%

* <300 employees, <100 million yen capital

Dr Imai explained that this 2.3 to 1 advantage in productivity of larger Japanese companies in relation to their smaller and medium-sized counterparts is largely due to the much greater structure of training and career development in the former. He also confirmed that there is much greater use of self-development planning documentation, of a very similar nature to that with which the British author has been involved in the UK, in the larger companies.

What, one may ask, would be the real potential of Japanese industry if these smaller and medium-sized enterprises achieved the productivity of the large ones? And what would be the real potential of their Western competitors if they too released the true potential of their employees?

Giving time and structure to self-development

There is considerable emphasis in Japan on self-development through formal study, largely in the employee's own time. A typical example was the case of six engineers interviewed at Hitachi. All had attended on-site courses organized by their Training Department. These had been for two or three hours each night at the end of normal hours, once or twice a week for, typically, 4 to 12 weeks. Topics covered were:

Course	Length	Lecturer
English conversation	Once a week for one year	Hitachi lecturer
Physics, Maths, and English	Once a week for six weeks	Hitachi lecturer
Semiconductors	Twice a week for 11 lectures	Manager of the Semiconductor Department
Cost calculation	Once a week for three weeks	Accounting staff in the Technical Division
General self-development course (e.g. logic design of VLSI, INS, etc.)	Every two months for two or three hours each	Outside lecturers, for example from NTT
Technical lectures for higher-level engineers (e.g. Power supply, LSI technology)	Each subject for two hours a week for four or five weeks	Senior Hitachi managers
Software	Once a month for five months	Hitachi manager

In all these cases the engineers attended voluntarily and were unpaid.

There is, in fact, a very great commitment in Japan to self-improvement and continuous learning. One illustration of this comes from a survey carried out in March 1987 by Denki Rōren, the federation of enterprise unions in large electrical companies. This union has some 570 000 members, about 120 000 of them university graduates. Like many Japanese trade unions they have a very sophisticated research department which regularly surveys their members' views. This particular survey received 2415 replies from 2800 questionnaires sent out. The analysis of one of the many questions asked commented that:

Self-education also is carried on for an average of two to three hours a week, other than during office hours. The item of 'none' was checked off by as many as 30% of employees in the section described as 'Product development/design/improvement'. Although this is an important aspect of employee development, the fact that this proportion admitted to not giving their time to self-education needs to take into account that the average overtime worked is more than 40 hours a month.

Put another way, given the fact that on top of this considerable amount of overtime these engineers would have a journey home of between one and two hours, it is surely an enormous tribute to Japanese engineers that they appear to devote an *average* of between two and three hours a week of their own time to self-development activities.

Plenty of opportunity for distance learning

Distance learning is another important aspect of self-development in Japan. The Japan Industrial and Vocational Training Association have a directory of 900 correspondence courses available at 88 colleges. Typically these courses range in length from three to twelve months, and the price from £15 for a simple technology course over three months to £550 for a financial course over six months. Company policies on reimbursement for correspondence courses vary; Toshiba pays one-third of the course fees, while Mitsubishi Electric pays nothing. On occasions companies devise their own self-study courses, as with the Seiko Instruments and Electronics course in Quality Control mentioned in Chapter 5.

Reading – an important form of self-development

As any traveller on public transport in Japan will soon observe, reading of books and articles in the employees' own time is a widespread activity. One aspect of this is that the subject-matter is often recommended by managers or colleagues. For example, the Managing Director of Toshiba Kikai explains that books in his company are only recommended in the early stages of an engineer's career. One interesting approach he uses, combining both technical and language training, is to give an English technical book to a team of engineers, who each translate a section (for example, 10 pages) into Japanese; the result is then published within the company. Another similar method used is for a section manager to give a young engineer, with two or three years' experience in the company, an article in English and ask for a summary in Japanese; there is a standard form for these summaries, and good ones are circulated to senior managers, who note the engineer's name, thus providing a direct incentive to the engineer and talent-spotting for senior management at the same time – quite apart from obtaining free translation!

Engineers are also expected in Toshiba Kikai to present lectures to their colleagues on technical books or articles they have read. The Managing Director's view is that, 'Toshiba pays you to work, so you should study at home and not at work.'

Why, one wonders, are such cost-effective and fundamentally obvious methods of developing company expertise not more universally used around the world?

A structured approach to off-the-job training

It will by now be abundantly clear that the philosophy in Japan is continuous self-improvement through the job itself, together with self-study.

Nevertheless, all this is backed up by systematic Off-the-Job Training on a more effective and larger scale than is generally seen in Western companies. Two aspects of this are very important. The first is that the OffJT activities are built on the solid learning environment of OJT. The second is that OffJT learning is very definitely integrated into applications in the job itself. In both these key respects Japan has for long realized that, without these two preconditions, much of the potential benefit from formal and expensive training is often wasted.

Mitsubishi Electric – a case study

Mitsubishi Electric has 48 000 employees and net sales of $20 billion p.a. in electronic systems and devices, heavy electrical machinery, industrial and automotive products, and consumer products. On 31 March 1991 they had 33 factory sites and 13 laboratories. Their corporate philosophy states: 'Training and education, combined with judicious promotion of the talented, is the source of industrial development; training and education is the essential activity of the company upon which management foundations are established.'

One Mitsubishi Electric example is their Engineering School ('Kōgaku-Juku'), started in 1983. Every six months some 20 high-flying engineers in their early thirties start an intensive series of inputs for one week each month at their Kobe Training Centre, over a period of a year (a number of these participated in the International Research Project described earlier in this chapter). In total these 12 one-week courses cover all the company's major technologies listed in Table 6.7. The lecturers are mainly the company's own practising expert technologists, and the course is aimed at giving the participants broadening

Table 6.7. The 12 one-week courses run at Mitsubishi Electric's Engineering School

1	Energy Engineering
2	Mechanical Engineering
3	Materials Engineering
4	Semiconductor Devices Engineering
5	Computer Engineering
6	Software Engineering
7	Control Systems Engineering
8	Communication Engineering
9	Manufacturing Engineering
10	Reliability Engineering
11	Systems Engineering
12	Short Management Course

expertise outside their own existing specialisms. The way they describe this is as 'creating Fuji Mountain Engineers' (*Fujiyama-gata Jinzai*), and is illustrated in Figure 6.2. The objective is to develop a number of multiskilled engineers who will help to spearhead the company's future technical developments either as project managers or as innovators. An important objective is to create a cadre of highly competent development-oriented engineers (over 300 have now graduated) who will in future years maintain their personal and technical links with each other and help to develop and implement the company's corporate strategy. To this end up to 50 per cent of the time is discussion-oriented, and the course includes projects on which papers have to be presented by the students.

Mitsubishi Electric has many other important ways of developing technical competence. Each engineer, for example, typically selects one or two corporate engineering seminars each year; these cover all levels from basic to advanced in all engineering fields, with the objective of 'enhancing an engineer's practical ability and basic knowledge of technology'. There are four categories of engineering seminars:

- Basic courses using satellite communications.
- Classroom-based lectures and discussions.
- Computer-based 'skill' training and education.
- Advanced courses.

In addition, there is a Corporate Engineering Society, with 14 sections, each specializing in a particular business area. The objectives are to encourage engineers' self-motivation and to support voluntary activities for mutual and self-development. Of the company's 20 000 engineers, over 80 per cent are active members.

In July 1990 the company established an Institute of Technology with the aim of further improving technical education. There are ten engineering departments and two management groups. Of the 50 staff members, over 30 are engineering experts, including 12 with PhDs.

In Mitsubishi Electric it is notable that promotion between grades is dependent on success in paper tests, for which employees are prepared with Off-the-Job Training. These tests are backed up by interviews by the Personnel Affairs Manager and the candidate's manager.

Mitsubishi Electric also organizes an annual Foreman's Convention. This is aimed at updating them on new technical developments, for example in electronics. This is just one aspect of a phenomenon common in Japan – lectures given by experts in one of a company's divisions to employees in other divisions or departments.

It is this comprehensive and well thought out approach to technical

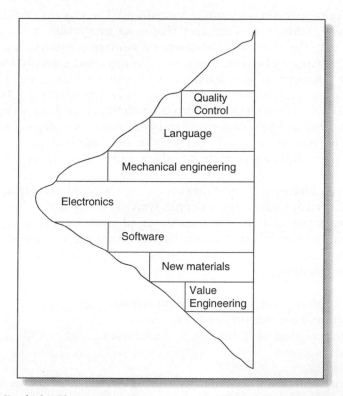

Fig. 6.2 Mitsubishi Electric Corporation's concept of a 'Fuji Mountain engineer' (example for a mechatronics engineer).

education and training which is so effective in Japanese companies. It is a battle-winning strategy.

Hitachi – another typical example

One of the largest providers of OffJT in Hitachi is the Hitachi Institute of Technology, which provides an Integrated Engineering Development Programme (IED) and a Specialized Engineering Development Programme (SED). The former consists of short intensive courses, lasting for between one and five weeks, designed to broaden and update some 800 staff each year, who are typically in their early thirties; 75 per cent of the lecturers are Hitachi experts, with the rest brought in from universities. There is usually a two-day follow-up course a year later. The IED is designed more for university graduates in their late twenties, with half the 90 students each year having masters' degrees; it is part-time, with two days every fortnight for 18 months. There are 400 hours of lectures plus 1000 hours of private study.

A detailed study – the NEC Technology Training Centre

Another Japanese company with a similar Institute of Technology of its own is NEC. Interestingly, both NEC and Hitachi are seen as probably amongst the most aggressive electronic companies from a commercial point of view.

It is instructive to look at the systematic way in which the NEC Technology Training Centre came to be founded in 1979. Two thousand technical personnel were surveyed by questionnaire in 1977, and revealed that there was increasing difficulty amongst engineers in keeping abreast of new technology. A special project team was formed, consisting of 17 Executive Directors under the leadership of a Vice-President; when the Technology Training Centre was founded, the latter became the Centre's Vice General Manager, and one of the former group became Education Manager.

Three levels of course are run. The lowest level is the Relevant Technology Training Programme, which is aimed at converting the skills of experienced engineers to enable them to move into new fields such as software. These courses are run whenever requested over 10 or 20 days per course, depending on the subject. In view of the difficulties experienced in cross-training experienced personnel, the lecturers are experienced instructors. Typical courses are the use of microprocessors, the operation of computers, project management, technical writing, and marketing for technical personnel.

The middle-level course is called the Integrated Technology Study Programme, and has a range of five courses; these are in communication technology, devices technology, production technology, and information-processing, with hardware and software variations. These are aimed at staff of graduate calibre with at least two years' company experience, and are lecture-type courses run once a week for 40 weeks. There are 40 trainees per course, with all trainees studying all five topics. There are 300 instructors (in other words far more instructors than students), 85 per cent being experienced NEC personnel at the forefront of their specialist topics who are released from their jobs specifically to provide a lecture and for whom the task of sorting out and systematizing their knowledge is considered additionally beneficial; the other 15 per cent of instructors are mainly from universities, the rest being from public research laboratories. Between 5 p.m. and 6 p.m. each evening they have a 'mutual study hour' in five groups of eight students in which they discuss the day's learning. Question memos can be submitted by the group for answering the following week by the course tutors. This one-hour session is also intended to develop human relations; in fact a major aim of the whole course is for future senior managers to establish and maintain contacts with each other; this has important implications for the capability of NEC to marshal its expertise in future years to its strategic advantage. Test questions are also provided, and the Centre is open until midnight for students who wish to remain. There is an exam at the end of each half year covering all subjects studied, with open reference to any study materials.

The final, and most senior, course is the Key Technology Training Programme. This is aimed as a continuing technology programme for high-level engineers who are enthusiatic and energetic. They attend seminars, rather than lectures, for half-days every two weeks in groups of about ten. Six to eight topics are covered in the first half of the one-year course, the subjects depending on technological strategies directly related to the company's business objectives, covering such themes as digital signal processing, software engineering, and pattern-recognition; for the second half of the year each student prepares a thesis on a chosen subject. A new course starts every six months, so at any one time there is one seminar-based course and one thesis-based one. Each year the course is run by 150 instructors, who act as group discussion seminar leaders; as with the Integrated Technology Study Programme, the bulk of these are senior practising engineers seconded from their everyday jobs.

All these courses should be seen in the context of the fact that the 35 per cent of NEC's 38 000 employees who are university graduates get an average of eight to ten days OffJT each year on average, some of them on Saturdays and thus unpaid. The 65 per cent of employees who are senior high school graduates have an average of one or two days p.a. each of OffJT.

And Toshiba too!

Toshiba, too, has advanced courses for technical specialists. These are for newly appointed specialists, senior specialists, and senior researchers. Most of the teachers are company employees in the divisions, who pass on their personal experiences. There are also panel discussions chaired by the Chief Engineer, lectures by senior executives, and group discussions.

A practical approach to management training

All the large Japanese companies have extensive OffJT management training programmes, but their emphasis is very different from that of those found in the West.

A typical syllabus soon illustrates the fundamental difference. The lecturers are not full-time 'management' experts, but instead are senior managers and experts passing on the benefits of their experiences. *Surely this is a much more effective method of developing management skills than the West's typical MBA case-study approach?* In Japan the students learn from real tales of success or failure *in their own company.* One of the authors, for example, knows of one recent Fellow in Management Development in a prestigious British Business School who has never had any management experience, and whose career has almost entirely been in academia. In recognition of the severe limitations of MBA courses staffed by such academics, there are only four of them in Japan; the oldest, at Keio University, has been run since the mid-1970s, with other more recently started ones at the Aoyama Gakuin University in Tokyo and the International University of Japan in Niigata (both private universities), and at the University of Tsukuba, a National University north of Tokyo. None of these is particularly highly regarded, although it needs to be said that a number of Japanese are sent overseas each year to do MBAs overseas, particularly in the USA.

Perhaps most remarkable, in contrast, is Fujitsu's FIMAT programme. FIMAT (Fujitsu Institute of Management) has provided an intensive training programme (originally three months long, now one and a half months long) for all 45-year-old Fujitsu white-collar employees since 1979. The investment per employee in this programme is £10 000 (one third being the tuition fees and two-thirds the employee's salary). The increasing numbers of employees attending this programme is shown in Figure 6.3.

This level of commitment to the development of employees is particularly notable in a company of 80 000 employees, of whom about 30 000 are white-collar and therefore eligible for FIMAT on reaching the age of 45. Between 1981 and 1985, for example, Fujitsu more than doubled sales and increased employees by over 50 per cent. The rate of expansion of this company is also illustrated by the fact that there are 81 Fujitsu subsidiaries with more than 51 per cent of Fujitsu capital, with 80 per cent of these established since 1979. The purpose of FIMAT is to refresh and stimulate employees in the middle of their working lives, at a point where they still have 15 to 20 years to go to retirement. Fujitsu argue that an extra benefit of this programme is that the 45-year-old's subordinate stands in for him for the three months, and that is excellent training for the subordinates, who tend to be promoted elsewhere on their manager's return.

Another remarkable aspect of FIMAT is that during the three months programme every participant is personally interviewed by every Fujitsu Director – a mammoth talent-spotting exercise! How many Western companies show anything like this commitment to employee development?

Typically for a Japanese company, Fujitsu are now looking forwards to identify the types of courses best suited to their future needs; the Japanese are never satisfied, and are forever seeking even better solutions to everything.

The impressive availability of external training

There are over a hundred companies in Japan involved in post-school education; if English-language education is included then the number is much larger. The total size of this post-school education market is said to be over £1.5 billion p.a.

Kōgaku Kenkyūsha runs 150 courses for 30 000 engineers each year. While they have 45 employees, the courses are actually run by lecturers selected from a database of a thousand experts. Since Japanese engineers do not like others to repeat their own mistakes, they are quite happy to pass on the benefits of

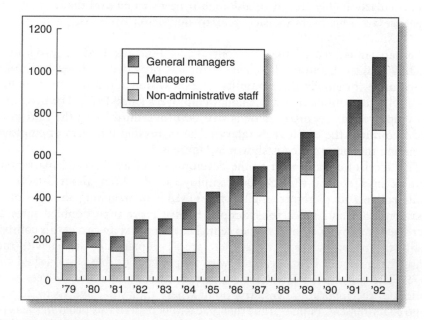

Fig. 6.3 Numbers of employees attending Fujitsu's FIMAT programme.

their experience. It appears that their companies have no objection to this in the greater interests of Japan!

In December 1987 an association of non-governmental education organizations was formed to promote the skills development of those working in industry. Zenkoku Sangyōjin Nōryoku Kaihatsu Dantai Rengōkai (The All-Nihon Industrial People's Capability Development Association), known as Zensan Nōren for short, has 49 members. In January 1988 this Association was granted corporate legal status by the Ministry of Labour. Government subsidies are available towards the costs of selected courses (574 in August 1991).

The largest organization in the correspondence course business is Sanno College, which has 500 000 students each year, while the second largest is the Japan Management Association, with 250 000. Another large organization in this sector is JEDECS (The Japan Education Development Centre for Skilled Workers), providing courses for 100 000 technicians every year.

Organizations providing a wide variety of supervisory and management courses include the Japan Management Association and the Japan Industrial and Vocational Training Association (JIVTA). One of the authors was shown, for example, numerous charts by the Executive Director of JIVTA, Mr T. Yashiro, with the analysis of a survey conducted among 628 member companies; these were typical of the enormously systematic approach to identifying training needs which is widely evident in Japan.

Systematic analysis of, and response to, training needs is the key

Toyota is a very good example of the benefits that will arise for any company which systematically analyses the training needs of its employees and implements suitable responses.

A paper by Professor Shōyū Kishida of the Toyota Technological Institute explains:

At the beginning of every calendar year, a questionnaire is distributed to engineers, and they self-appraise their levels of technology and fill in the questionnaire. A superior reviews the completed questionnaire and discusses it with his engineers. As a result of discussion, an objective assessment of levels of technology for each engineer is obtained. Based upon this objective assessment, each engineer is expected to plan a year-long self-tutoring schedule and to report the results to a superior at the end of the year. Under this system, an engineer is urged to become an engineer with balanced technological knowledge.

The technology for stamping dies consists of 15 items, each of which has four or five important components. In filling in a questionnaire, an engineer should self-appraise his own level of technical skill and knowledge in terms of those items and the components of each item. In order to appraise the level of technology, a five-point scale is used.[4]

The highly visual system used is shown in Figure 6.4. The effect of this highly systematic approach to the skills development of employees is reflected in Table 6.8, showing the remarkable reduction in set-up times and batch sizes in Toyota during the 1970s. It cannot be emphasized too strongly that this is the basis of the *kanban* and Just-In-Time systems, which otherwise could not be implemented in the way in which they have been.

Another illustration of this point is in the Nissan plant at Washington in England. There the competencies of each team member, together with the level of those competencies, are shown on charts for each team that are displayed prominently throughout the factory. An equally thorough analysis and monitoring of skills development is carried out for all technical staff. All 3500 employees had Personal Development Plans by the end of 1991. As a result, in a factory where almost all employees are British, the quality of cars produced is higher than in any other Japanese-owned car factory in the world.

The financial investment in training

It is significant that Japanese companies actually spend far less on training in cash terms than their Western competitors. When asked about the level of their financial investment in training, Japanese companies will give replies ranging typically from 0.02 per cent to 0.5 per cent of sales. In the case of the former figure it will probably represent only the cost of head-office training staff, while in a company such as Hitachi the 0.5 per cent will be more realistic, including the salaries of trainees as well as other associated costs. However, it will always be emphasized that these costs exclude OJT, which it will by now be realized is the predominant approach to training. If the indirect financial investment of OJT were to be measured, then it would be much higher than the other training costs more usually measured in the West.

In comparison, the annual investment in training in a good Western company might well be 2 per cent of sales, or in North America even 3 per cent of sales. While these companies deserve commendation for giving such importance to training, their inability to compete with Japanese companies demonstrates the folly of seeing training as being about throwing money at the problem. Training, as the Japanese see it, is about those with the skills and knowledge giving the *time* to passing them on to others. They are right; and the prime purpose of this book is to explain that vitally important truth to the West.

Another question concerns the level of public funding for training carried out in industry. There is a payroll levy of 0.35 per cent of emoluments for all companies; but the majority of this is utilized to fund the Polytechnic University of Japan and hundreds of vocational training colleges and schools, which will be described in the next chapter. However, some grants from public funds are available to companies for employee development.

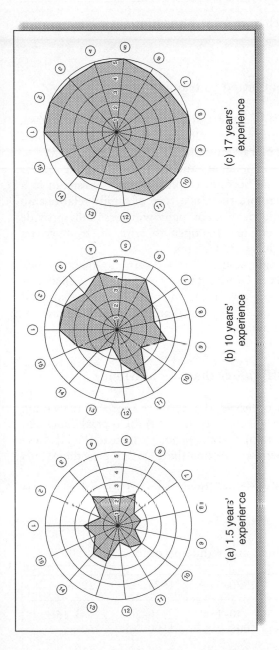

(a) 1.5 years' experience

(b) 10 years' experience

(c) 17 years' experience

Fig. 6.4 Skill level analysis in Toyota.

Level 5: indicates 'I have enough technical ability and knowledge, and have the ability to make improvements.'

Level 4: 'I have technical ability and knowledge to a certain degree, and can perform the work by myself.'

Level 3: 'I can perform the work under guidance of an assistant manager or senior engineers.'

Level 2: 'I can perform the work only under the detailed instructions of senior engineers.'

Level 1: 'I have no knowledge at all.'

A significant sum is available each year as a subsidy for vocational training provided by employers.

So why are the Japanese so committed to training others?

The British author recalls asking Mr T. Izumi, at the time Director of the Basic Research Department at the Research and Development Institute of Vocational Training (and now a professor at Nara University), this question in 1985.

'First', he said, 'jobs are done in a team, and therefore teaching others produces better results for the team. Second, employees tend to remain in a company for a long time, and therefore there is a type of family relationship between employees. Even the President of a company will personally provide training for his staff. Third, supervisors are open to criticism from young employees if they do not provide adequate training.'

Supervisors and managers throughout the West are certainly open to such criticism! The employees of the Fort Dunlop factory in England, which was taken over by the Japanese company Sumitomo in the 1980s, were stunned by the seniority of the Japanese managers who personally tutored them when they were seconded to Japan for training.

Effective training is about TIME rather than about Money

As the late Professor Keith Thurley observed, the Japanese approach to training is essentially that of a poor nation; this is in contrast to the typical American approach of training by 'throwing money' at the problem. Instead the Japanese concentrate on those with the expertise investing the TIME to pass their skills and knowledge on to others.

A telling story is told by Dr Kaneichirō Imai, referred to earlier in this chapter. In 1957, he explains, IHI (a major Japanese engineering company

Table 6.8. Shortening of set-up times and reduction of lot size: 1970–80

		1970	1975	1980
Stamping	Set-up time (minutes)	40–150	20–30	5–15
	Lot size (no. of items)	5000	1500	500
Forging	Set-up time (minutes)	100–200	20–50	10
Casting	Set-up time (minutes)	60	20	4

Source: Toyota Motor Corporation – Company Report, January 1984.

in which he ended as Senior Managing Director) bought advanced technology from a US manufacturer considered to be the world's number one in a particularly important field; as part of this contract they paid more than the equivalent of a month's salary for IHI's President at the time to have their IHI employees given one week of training in this technology. 'What we were buying was *TIME*', says Dr Imai. 'We wanted to know *HOW* the technology worked, *WHY* it worked that way and *WHO* the key people were in the American supplier. Our next step then was to overtake the Americans technically in as short a time as possible.'

This dedication to detail later led to the company, when headed by Dr Imai, obtaining the highly prestigious Deming Prize for Implementation – Japan's top award for quality.

Therefore if companies do not rapidly learn the crucial and simple lessons on how to develop the inherent abilities of their employees which are described in this chapter, then they will in turn become the impoverished of the world – and will fully deserve their fate!

References

1 Research and Development Institute of Vocational Training, Employment Promotion Projects Corporation, Bulletin No.59, *Problems and prospects of in-company human resources development in a new era – towards the new concept of "learning company"*, Sagamihara, November 1984, p. 23.

2 Research and Development Institute of Vocational Training, Employment Promotion Projects Corporation, *Country report on the planning, programming and education of vocational training – Japan*, Sagamihara, December 1984, p. 26.

3 Dr Kaneichiro Imai, *Engineering education – current state and future trends mainly from the manufacturer standpoint (in Japan)*, AEESEAP (Association for Engineers Education in Southeast Asia and the Pacific) Symposium, August 1991, Kuala Lumpur, p. 11.

4 Masumi Tsuda, Shōyū Kishida, and Michio Fujiwara, *Human resource development and new technology in the automobile industry: the Japanese case*, Centre for Educational Research and Innovation, Organization for Economic Co-operation and Development, Paris, June 1984, pp. 127–32.

7

The Japanese emphasis on technicians

'If Western industry succeeds in matching Japanese productivity, life could be very tough indeed for Japanese industry. This is a bigger problem (for Japan) than the rise of the newly industrialized countries, which are only strong in certain sectors.'
– Takashi Ishihara, Chairman of Nissan

Introduction

What are the lessons from Japan in the recruitment and training of supporting staff – the technicians and equivalents below the university graduates?

Could, for example, the severe shortage of technology graduates in the West be alleviated by the better use of supporting staff, so that the graduates' efforts are not dissipated in doing lower-level technical and administrative work? Would there not then be greater job-satisfaction for those expensively educated and trained graduates as a result, thus reducing staff turnover and improving productivity?

This chapter shows how this is indeed a very important aspect of Japan's success.

Whither the technicians?

In Britain there was historically a tradition of developing engineering competence through practical experience, with a large proportion of engineers, for example, achieving degree-equivalent recognition from their Professional Institutions via a practical technician apprenticeship route. In the 1960s this route to Institution membership was largely closed, and the result has been a steady decline in the numbers seeing such practical apprenticeships as being attractive career paths. At the same time British companies have systematically reduced the numbers of craft and technician apprentices, as is shown in Figure 7.1.

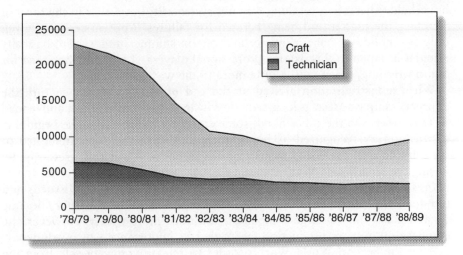

Fig. 7.1 First year engineering craft and technician trainees in the UK. *Source: IDS Report 560*, January 1990.

Support staff are a vital ingredient in Japan's success

Visitors to development laboratories in large Japanese companies will be told that the technical staff are recruited equally from senior high schools and universities. Indeed, as was explained in Chapter 4, the importance of technicians is such that large companies recruit on a national, rather than a local, basis from the senior high schools.

Small companies generally have a preference for the more specialized output of technical senior high schools and technical colleges. It is also arguable that the calibre of the graduates from the lower-ranking private universities, from whose ranks smaller companies are perforce only able to recruit, is more akin to the output of technical colleges in the UK.

A disappearing tradition of apprenticeship

In general, in Japan unlike much of Europe, there is now no system of apprenticeships. Furthermore, in contrast to, say, Britain and Germany, there is no system of release from work to attend study at publically funded technical colleges either.

In feudal times Japanese apprenticeship was seen in the form of *nenkibōkō*. *Nenki* means 'a certain period of years', and *bōkō* is 'service'. It involved living for a number of years in the master's house, and for the first one or two years doing duties such as cleaning, cooking, and taking care of the children of the household. Thereafter, teaching was not systematic, but rather in the form of watching the master and being berated for failures. Apprentices were given only two holidays – one in winter and one in summer; this system basically remains in Japan to this day for professional players of Go and Shōgi and for Sumo wrestling, albeit with a little more in the way of holidays!

When industrialization arrived at the end of the nineteenth century the apprenticeship was seen as long-term, low-waged, and exploitative, and tended to fade away. On the other hand, some emerging industries at the beginning of this century recognized its importance, and some factories attempted to organize an apprenticeship system on an in-house basis; this grew rapidly during the First World War.

In 1939 the In-plant Training Act for Skilled Workers was issued, and the apprenticeship system, which until then had developed *ad hoc*, became organized not only in large companies, but much more widely. However, the emphasis on military production meant that its importance was overlooked.

After the Second World War, in order to release young people from the feudal labour system and also to organize traditional vocational training more efficiently, the Labour Standards Act provided guidance on skills training. Then the Vocational Training Law was promulgated in 1958, and was radically revised in 1969.

Japan's strategic approach to skills development

The detailed strategic planning by the Japanese Government to ensure that there have been sufficient skills available to support the expansion of the Japanese economy is illustrated in this excerpt from a report by the Research and Development Institute of Vocational Training:

In the National Income-Doubling Plan of 1960–1970, in order to attain an economic growth of 7.2 per cent annually, the shortage of supply of:
  '170,000 university-graduate-level scientists and engineers, 440,000 technical high school graduate-level technicians, and 1.55 million skilled workers trained through public vocational and authorized vocational training'
is identified, requiring an increase in the number of trainees.

Although both public vocational training and authorized vocational training tried to increase considerably the number of trainees, the annual economic growth rate during the above-mentioned programme period reached 11 per cent, and by the late 1960s the shortage of skilled workers exceeded 1.8 million.

Therefore, in the first-phase vocational training basic plan drawn up by the Ministry of Labour in 1971, a plan was set up to triple the number of trainees in initial training for the five years starting from 1971, mainly by expanding authorized vocational training.

However, after the oil crisis in 1973, Japan's economy changed from that of high growth, and the demand – supply relationship in the labour market was relaxed, and the demand of industry for securing skilled workers rapidly weakened.

The expansion plan for trainees in initial training courses of public vocational training went almost unchanged in the early half of the 1970s, but that of authorized vocational training decreased, with 1971 as its peak.

A decrease in employment demand in the labour market tends to increase unemployment in the young generation in the US and Europe, but in Japan, on the other hand, there is a tendency for older workers to become the unemployed. Partly because of ageing of the labour force, which began from 1975, the unemployment rate of older workers increased. Therefore, it became necessary for public vocational training facilities to expand their occupational capability redevelopment training for the older unemployed.

The planned number of redevelopment training courses conducted by public vocational training facilities increased from 64,000 people in 1976 to 82,000 in 1983. The ratio of trainees over 45 years old rose during the same period from 33 per cent to 41 per cent.

The number of trainees for initial training, on the other hand, decreased from 61,000 in 1975 to 38,000 in 1983.[1]

Contrasts with Europe

All this contrasts with Britain, for example, where no government has ever made even the remotest attempt to quantify, let alone plan the development of, the overall skills pool. The comparison, instead, can be made with the other supremely successful national economy, Germany, which has some 330 occupations covered by the 'dual system' of in-company training linked with vocational education at a local college, usually for one or two days each week. A Skilled Workers Certificate is awarded in Germany to trainees successfully passing examinations which test practical skills and theoretical knowledge, including subject-matter taught at vocational schools. This system is immeasurably strengthened by the German *Meister* system, whereby skilled workers are able to obtain the higher qualification of Master Craftsman (*Meister*), study for which includes both pedagogical and higher technical skills. These *Meisters* are then given the responsibility for the skills development of employees, which they achieve in a highly structured and professional way, quite unlike the haphazard and largely ineffective methods usually seen in Britain.

Unfortunately, Britain has adopted a competence-based approach, called National Vocational Qualifications (NVQs), which no other country had ever attempted. There was, until 1993, no direct link required between academic attainment and work-based competence, there is no clear and cost-effective system for accrediting competences at work, and the system purports to achieve both portability between different types of occupation and to provide useful detailed analysis of the skills required for a particular job – objectives which are mutually incompatible. The definition of competencies has been given to a very large number of so-called Industry Lead Bodies, which in many cases overlap, and which have taken over six years to produce relatively few national specifications of competencies, some at vast expense. Worst of all, hardly any British managers have the remotest idea of what NVQs are, and even most British training managers do not understand them – and many of those who do are great critics of the system, being very uncomfortable, for example, with pseudo-academic concepts such as 'Range Statements' and 'Performance Indicators'! So yet again Britain has shot itself in the foot. Australia, New Zealand and the USA are now trying to emulate this competence based approach – whether with any success remains to be seen.

Japan has licensed instructors

In comparison, by 1992 there were 158 different occupations in Japan requiring licensed instructors.[2] The Human Resources Development Promotion Law requires that instructors in charge of statutory programmes of initial training and occupational capability redevelopment training possess a teaching licence for the relevant trades. The licence is issued to individuals who meet one of the following criteria:

(a) those who have completed instructor training courses designated by the Minister of Labour;
(b) those who have passed the qualifying examination by the Ministry of Labour; or
(c) those who are acknowledged by the Ministry of Labour as having equivalent competence to (a) and (b) above.

A post-war shift from apprenticeships to senior high school recruitment

Looking back historically, after the second World War the major companies all had their own technical training schools. For a time before 1960 many pupils left school at the age of 15, and followed three-year courses at company high schools. Others went from junior high schools to one-year courses in Industrial Training Schools. As the general level of education in Japan improved, companies started dropping their company high schools, and the Industrial Training Schools changed to taking in trainees from senior high schools at the age of 18. After 1965 companies introduced Training Schools with OffJT facilities, mainly available as night schools, and encouraged Open Learning for employees.

After a revision of the Vocational Training Law in 1985, the Ministry of Labour gave guidance for companies to establish two-year vocational training colleges. Between 1986 and 1991 twelve companies established their own colleges for training technicians.

No interest in post-school national qualifications

It is worth emphasizing that, unlike what happens in Europe, there is no interest in national qualifications for technician staff in Japan, for two reasons. The first is that there is an assumption of lifetime employment in the larger companies which provide the bulk of the formal technician-level training schemes, and therefore nationally transferable qualifications are irrelevant. The second is that the emphasis is on OJT, rather than further education to national standards; Japanese industry leaves it to the schools to educate pupils to a high level of numeracy and literacy, and concentrates itself on providing new recruits at all levels with practical skills and competence.

Two specialist technical educational routes

Before describing the Japanese counterparts to European apprenticeships, it needs to be remembered (see Chapter 3) that there are two specialist technical educational routes of study prior to employment in industry.

The first is at a technical high school, which is a vocational alternative to a senior high school. Technical high schools were initiated in the 1960s as a specialist route for those students with more practical than academic abilities, although many of the better students prefer their more practical syllabus.

The other technical education route is at a technical college, where students follow a five-year course between the ages of 15 and 20. Again, the numbers produced are relatively small, being about 10 per cent of the numbers of university technological graduates. Statistics on these numbers are provided in Table 7.1, which also provides a comparison of those studying at junior colleges and universities.

These technical colleges (known as *kōsen* in Japan) have traditionally attracted students from a family background where the parents were insufficiently wealthy to afford to finance their sons through university. These five-year *kōsen* courses provide specialist technical staff who can command higher than normal starting salaries in industry. They produce, for example, welders and field engineers. Many *kōsen* are residential, giving the students more time to enjoy student life. They do not have to experience the extreme educational pressures at a senior high school in order to achieve a place at a university. According to Dr Yutaka Yoshitani from Nagaoka University (a university, to be described later, established specifically to recruit students from *kōsen*), while academically weaker than their colleagues at universities, their students are nevertheless emotionally more stable. In his view, they tend to be more independent-minded than, for example, a Tokyo University graduate, and have a much more rounded view of life and more interesting personalities.

Table 7.1. Number of engineering graduates of Japanese universities, junior colleges, and technical colleges (1994)

Specialism	First Degree	Masters'	Doctoral	Junior College	Technical College
Mechanical	18 664	3 095	138	3 500	2 485
Electrical/communication	27 346	5 010	346	4 895	4 283
Civil/architecture	18 015	2 440	159	1 028	1 476
Chemical	10 335	2 684	242	225	1 111
Applied science	1 523	422	53	—	—
Nuclear engineering	450	199	19	—	—
Mining engineering	336	107	6	—	—
Metallurgy	1 125	398	29	42	177
Textile	346	130	—	26	—
Marine	252	62	12	—	130
Aeronautics	776	134	18	—	34
Administration	4 757	239	12	276	—
Graphical/industrial	507	20	—	—	50
Art	—	—	—	80	—
Others	5 854	3 038	487	740	152
TOTAL	90 286	17 978	1 521	10 812	9 898

Source: Same as for Table 3.1

The Japanese counterparts to European apprenticeships

A limited form of apprenticeship system does exist in a few large companies.

Hitachi, for example, have a Training Centre for Apprentices providing a three-year course for 150 students each year entering from junior high school. There are also 15-month courses at the two Hitachi Technical Colleges for about 220 students each year. Entry to these two Technical Colleges is by examination, and about one-third of all senior high school entrants to Hitachi succeed in entering this course following a two-year basic programme of induction into the company.

Other large companies have equivalent courses. One hundred students each year enter Fujitsu's Academy of Industrial Technology from technical junior high schools, and follow a one-year full-time course. Fujitsu Technical School (FTS), on the other hand, enrols a minimum of 115 students each year. The students must have completed one year of initial OJT in Fujitsu, and then follow one of four types of courses over a further three years on a part-time (after working hours) basis. On graduating from FTS the students have the same qualification as pupils graduating from a *kōsen* or junior college. The top 10 per cent of FTS graduates each year, some ten people, are according to Fujitsu, allowed to continue at a normal university for one year as a 'research' student selected according to area of specialization. Another interesting aspect is that about 10 per cent of the FTS students are ex-blue-collar workers, indicating the meritocratic promotion opportunities the company offers.

NEC's Technical College for high school graduates was established in Kawasaki in 1986. This was a development out of NEC's in-house training organization, founded in 1956. Two courses were provided in 1992, one in mechatronics and the other in information technology. Each course is two years long, and sixty senior high school graduates enter each course each year. The mechatronics course began at the establishment and is, they believe, the first one in Japan at this level. The information technology course is a new programme which began in 1989. NEC's Technical College is the first corporate in-house junior college in Japan that received government recognition by the Ministry of Labour in accordance with the Vocational Training Law revised in 1985. 20 companies had such colleges approved by the Ministry of Labour by 1992. NEC explain that their Technical College aims to 'educate students to be production engineers equipped with technical skill'. Their unique programme is a well-balanced fusion of theory and practice. These students are considered to be production engineers who will possess not only in-depth knowledge and practical experience, but also integrated approaches to put their training to work on real problems.

Two universities specifically for *kōsen*

A particularly interesting development in Japan has been the establishment of two universities specifically for *kōsen* (five-year technical college) graduates.

These originated through the endeavours of a distinguished academic, Dr Matsumae, who went on to Tohoku University from being a pre-war higher technical school graduate, and personally experienced the difficulties they had to face in entering a university. At that time only Tohoku Imperial University accepted higher technical school graduates, albeit by means of a very tough examination. He put forward the idea of a special university for *kōsen* graduates in about 1960, but the Ministry of Education refused to pursue the proposal. However, the section within the Ministry responsible for *kōsen* took up the idea and pushed it. It took 15 years, and many committees, before the proposal bore fruit. In fact two such National Universities were founded in 1976, and took in their first students in 1978. Toyohashi University was sponsored by Nagoya University, while Tokyo Institute of Technology sponsored Nagaoka University, in the sense that both parent universities set up committees to plan the new ones. One-third of the lecturers were recruited from industry, and the rest from other universities. Dr Yutaka Yoshitani, mentioned earlier in this chapter, for example, himself left a well-paid job with Nippon Steel to join

Nagaoka at half the salary, simply because he felt committed to the idea. In addition, there are many specialist part-time lecturers from industry.

Figure 7.2 shows the extremely interesting structure of the Nagaoka University courses. Ten students each year enter each of six different engineering degree courses, mainly from technical high schools, a total annual entry of 60, and follow a four-year degree course, as at a normal Japanese university. The difference is that the emphasis is on accepting students from technical, rather than from general, senior high schools. The majority of undergraduates, however, enter from *kōsen* half-way through the course, and are required to study the last two years of the degree only; 240 such students enter each year, 40 into each of the six engineering degree courses. The total output from the degree course is therefore 300 p.a., and 75 per cent of these continue to do the two-year masters' degree course. A new three-year doctorate course, following on from the masters', started in 1986 with some 16 of the masters' graduates enrolled.

It should be noted that, despite the almost total absence of industrial sponsorship, all undergraduates are given five months of practical training in industry in their final year. This practical training is mainly project-based, and might involve, for example, improving a process. University tutors make three visits to each factory to assess the student's performance.

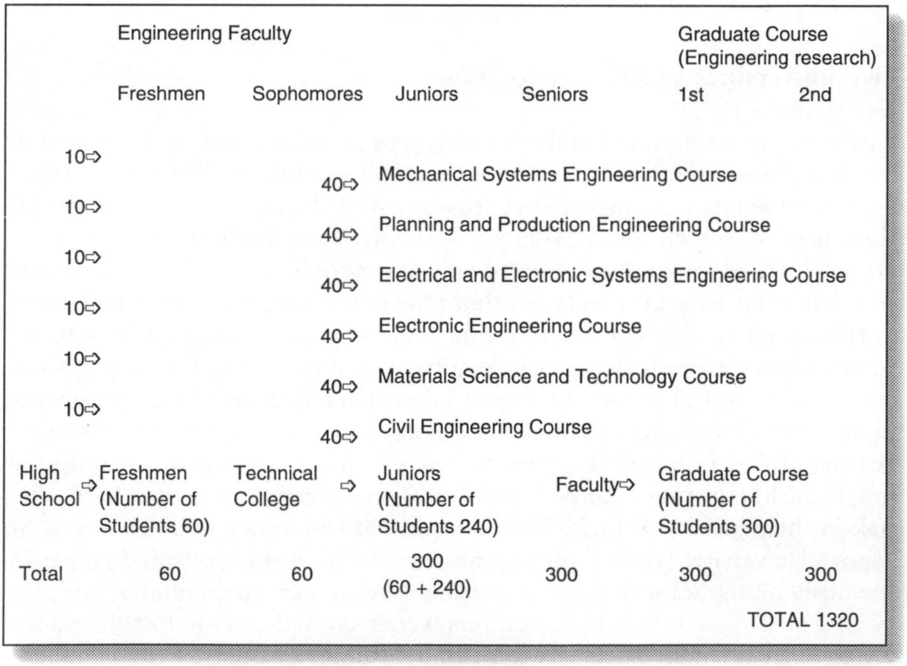

Engineering Faculty				Graduate Course (Engineering research)	
Freshmen	Sophomores	Juniors	Seniors	1st	2nd
10⇨		40⇨ Mechanical Systems Engineering Course			
10⇨		40⇨ Planning and Production Engineering Course			
10⇨		40⇨ Electrical and Electronic Systems Engineering Course			
10⇨		40⇨ Electronic Engineering Course			
10⇨		40⇨ Materials Science and Technology Course			
10⇨		40⇨ Civil Engineering Course			
High School ⇨ Freshmen (Number of Students 60)	Technical College ⇨	Juniors (Number of Students 240)	Faculty⇨	Graduate Course (Number of Students 300)	
Total 60	60	300 (60 + 240)	300	300	300
					TOTAL 1320

Fig. 7.2 Structure of courses at Nagaoka University.

Altogether, Nagaoka and Toyohashi Universities are stirring examples of the response of the academic and civil service climate in Japan to the inspiration and commitment of a few to providing a university route for the more practical students from technical high schools and technical colleges.

Toyota Technological Institute – a remarkable commitment

Another quite remarkable university in Japan is the Toyota Technological Institute (TTI) in Nagoya. This was established by Toyota in 1981, and is possibly the smallest university in Japan.

Dr M. Komai, the President, and Mr M. Miki, Secretary-General, said in 1985 that Toyota saw itself as having social responsibilities, and established TTI as a contribution towards the build-up of engineers for the benefit of society. In fact only about one-third of the undergraduates work for Toyota, and it is therefore even more remarkable that Toyota donated £140 million to establish TTI, of which one-third is for buildings and equipment and two-thirds is invested, with the income generated from the interest used for running costs. There is no Ministry of Education financial contribution, whereas a normal private university would receive about 15 per cent of its funds from Monbushō (the Ministry of Education). Toyota are concerned about the tight control that would be associated with any Monbushō funding. Student fees only cover 5 per cent of the budget, compared to the 70 per cent this source would contribute to a normal private university's budget. (In general, other private universities' fees are used not only for student tuition, but to fund research as well.)

Toyota's concept is unique. Not only is TTI open to non-Toyota employees, but, in comparison to national universities, TTI spends 3.3 times as much on educating each student, and 10 times the amount when compared to other private universities!

Preference in selecting students at TTI is given to young people who have had previous work experience. Students are recruited with at least two or three years' experience in industry, with educational backgrounds about equally split between technical colleges, technical high schools, and senior high schools. In that context, it is therefore interesting to note that help and advice in setting up TTI came from Nagaoka University, which we noted earlier is one of two universities specifically established to recruit from technical college graduates.

The average age of entry is 21, with the oldest student so far admitted being 32 on entry. Students come from all over Japan, and very few are married. Students must live in a dormitory on the campus for the first year, partly to establish a group spirit and partly to allow TTI to recruit students from distant Prefectures. There are social difficulties here, because rural families are very reluctant to send their sons to a distant university. There are no girls on the course, not because of discrimination, but because there would be problems in having girls sleeping in communal dormitories. However, it is admitted that another reason is that companies are reluctant to provide training places for female undergraduates.

Eighty students can be accepted each year on the undergraduate courses, which are equally split between a Department of Mechanical Systems Engineering and a Department of Information and Control Engineering. However, by 1992 there were only 246 undergraduates as against a capacity of 320.

The aim of the degree course is to create engineers who will contribute to society, and the structure of the degree therefore emphasizes technological problem-solving from the first year. This structure is therefore fundamentally different from that at a traditional Japanese university. The course includes lectures emphasizing the importance of engineering as a social activity. The course structure is shown in Figure 7.3. Industrial experience is provided in each of the first three years.

In addition to the undergraduate course, there is also a two-year masters' degree in Production Engineering.

The Toyota Technological Institute really is a highly impressive demonstration of the commitment by a major Japanese company to increasing the country's skill base on an unselfish basis.

The Polytechnic University of Japan

Another extraordinary example of Japan's commitment to increasing its skills base is the Polytechnic University of Japan (PUJ) at Sagamihara, in Kanagawa, just outside Tokyo. This reports to the Employment Promotion Corporation (part of Rōdōshō – the Ministry of Labour).

PUJ provides a four-year degree course for those intending to make a career in training (although many of its graduates subsequently choose a career other than in training), with an annual intake of 220 from senior and technical high schools. Many graduates from this course go on to industry, and a high proportion, after some years of industrial experience, then become instructors.

In addition, there are other courses such as:

- One-year/six-month courses for those having an instructor licence or who have passed the Grade II national trade test and subsequently had over three years' experience, or who alternatively have equivalent skill levels.
- Various upgrading courses for Japanese instructors.
- Ten-month group training courses for overseas instructors in English, with an intake of 50.
- Six-month high-tech individual courses for overseas instructors (in English).

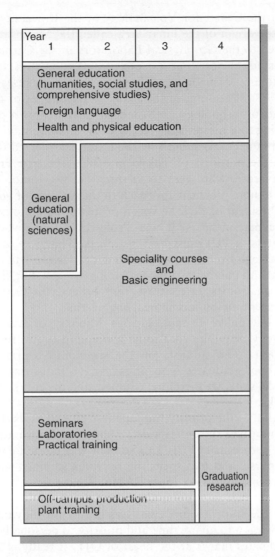

Fig. 7.3 Course structure at the Toyota Technological Institute.

The most interesting aspect of the PUJ, in the view of the British author, is that all the teaching staff also pursue research interests at the highest level. Dr Shigeru Sano, for example, is a leading mathematician who had a strong influence on young French scholars with his contribution to the Plancherel formula on symmetric spaces. This problem arose from the expansion of Schroedinger's quantum theory for explaining the behaviour of elementary particles. Another distinguished member of staff is Professor Tsutomu Murase; he was once a

Visiting Scholar at the Center for Volcanology at the University of Oregon, where he studied the origin of the lunar area called the Mare Tranquillitatis. Later he was invited to the Geophysical Laboratory at the Carnegie Institute in Washington to study the earth at a depth of 200 kilometres, including the influence on volcanoes and earthquakes. In other words, the research interests pursued by the PUJ staff are not, in the main, in techniques of training, but in the fundamentals of technology itself. Indeed there is now a postgraduate course corresponding to a master's degree, with an annual intake of 20.

The PUJ opened in a Tokyo suburb in 1961, and transferred to its present impressive site on the outskirts of Tokyo in 1973. The first President was Professor Masao Naruse, who went to Germany in his youth, and decided that Japan needed a more practical approach to the training of young people. Before becoming President of PUJ, he was a professor at Tohoku University, and was a great expert in gears. It was Professor Naruse who originated the idea that lecturers at PUJ must be researchers. The view of PUJ is that Japan has an advantage over Germany in that the former has an emphasis on both mechanical and microelectronic technologies, including the combined technologies of mechatronics. In contrast, they believe, the German *Meister* system tends to concentrate on mechanical engineering.

Like Germany, but unlike Britain, Japan's Ministry of Labour requires instructors in industry or public vocational training institutes to be licensed, with some exceptions. The students on the six-month instructors' course are senior high school graduates who already have industrial or insructor experience. Technical skills are therefore assumed, and the course concentrates on pedagogical skills.

Another illustration of the priority the Japanese give to skills development, and OJT in particular, was the description given to the British author by one of Professor Kenjo's students at PUJ. This student was in the final year of his four-year degree course, and had spent the previous summer working for a small company for two months on 256K RAMS. What particularly struck the British author was the fact that this student's supervisor in this company had spent the whole of the student's first two days in the job showing him what to do; it is this dedication to giving time and priority to personally developing the skills of subordinates that is at the heart of OJT. It really is a key lesson for the West.

A massive Japanese commitment to vocational training

Japanese vocational training is implemented in three different organizational categories. Firstly, in addition to the PUJ, the Employment Promotion Corporation (EPC), on behalf of the Ministry of Labour, runs 26 Vocational Training Colleges with two-year courses for high school graduates, and 61 Skill Development Centres (SDCs) for high-tech upgrading training for company employees and job-conversion training for the unemployed. Basic training for high school leavers is done at several SDCs. Secondly, prefectural governments run 270 public centres. (The 19 Vocational Training Centres for the physically handicapped across Japan are national or prefectural.) Thirdly, there is the group of company training schools authorized by the Ministry of Labour.

As a result of the Human Resources Development Promotion Law in 1992, the Ministry of Labour decided to provide local governments with funds to build a vocational education college, and the first opened in Yamagata in 1993.

EPC was established in 1961 to assist skilled workers and the private sector by setting up and managing various kinds of vocational training facilities to provide opportunities to workers for skill development throughout their careers. It also provides services such as advising employers on how to recruit and train employees, as well as retraining and finding employment for the unemployed.

Some 30 000 junior and senior high school graduates each year undergo one- or two-year-long courses at either the Public Vocational Training Centres or the Vocational Training Colleges. The latter were first established in 1974 from redesignated Vocational Training Centres to provide two-year courses of initial training at technician level. Some students enrol because they have failed technical college entrance exams, and others because they are looking for retraining after being unable to obtain the type of job they really want. In fact some 50 per cent of high school graduates leave their first job within three years; many find other jobs in their locality easily, but others go to a Vocational Training Centre.

In the 1960s and the 1970s many young people went to these Centres or Colleges as a cheaper alternative to going to senior high school or technical college. However, now that families have more money the quality of students enrolling is reducing, and some of the Vocational Training Centres have become Skill Development Centres catering for adults, both employed and unemployed. Some 50 000 unemployed (40 per cent of them over the age of 40) benefit from six-month to one-year-long courses. The largest number, however, are 130 000 employed workers who attend one-week to one-month-long in-service courses.

The ease with which the very well-educated and trained Japanese population find other jobs in their immediate locality is demonstrated by the fact that only 1 per cent or 2 per cent of job-seekers who apply to the Hello Work offices receive help from one of these Centres or Colleges.

At the core, therefore, of Japan's industrial might lies a thoroughly systematic approach to skills development. It is not, of course, without some faults. There is rivalry, for example, between the Ministry of Labour, which oversees vocational training and the development of skills up to and including technician level, and the Ministry of Education, which looks after vocational education, including the technical high schools and the development of engineer skills. This has become more blurred by the establishment of the technician entry-level universities at Toyohashi and Nagaoka.

Nevertheless, the total of some 340 000 people trained and retrained annually in 383 publically funded training centres is a massive investment by the Japanese government in maintaining and developing the skills base that their nation needs. There are hundreds of courses available, which change each year. The integrated system of vocational training is one in which the Prefectural Governments make detailed plans within an overall Central Government plan. The implementation is then effected in two ways; the first is through the Prefectural Governments, and the other through the EPC.

The impact of the microelectronic revolution

The appearance of the microprocessor in 1971 triggered a major change in industrial training. Numerically controlled (NC) machines changed the conventional concept of occupation. When the structured accumulation of experiences on conventional machines was the means of developing skilled technicians, On-the-Job Training was essential, and that is why Japan has historically placed great emphasis on OJT in skills development – which is also strongly linked with the seniority system of promotion. But a young technician well-trained in using NC technology can produce better products than a well-trained conventional technician, and it was also found that Off-the-Job Training is more effective for machines with microelectronic devices.

The revision of the Vocational Training Law on 1 October 1985, and its replacement with the Human Resources Development Promotion Law, was much influenced by the microelectronics revolution. The mainstream of vocational training departed from the system focusing on craft skills training, and moved towards a diversified approach to the development of human capability for a lifetime of work. Public training centres became the places for high-tech training for company employees. Thus Redevelopment Training and Upgrading Training became the mainstream of emphasis, rather than the basic training of high school students. Around half the 47 prefectures had two or three Skill Development Centres (SDCs) run by the EPC. One of each of these SDCs in each prefecture is being rebuilt as a vocational training college, providing two-year basic training for senior high school graduates, and there are now 25 in all so far. It is obvious that these colleges will also be high-tech retraining centres for company employees in the near future.

Another notable emphasis since 1985 has been on international co-operation. The importance that Japan attaches to all this is illustrated by the way that the Japanese government have helped the Malaysian government to establish a carbon copy of PUJ in Malaysia as part of Japan's aid to that country. This has been spearheaded by a former Vice-President of PUJ, and is a key part of Japanese industrial investment in Malaysia. A similar university is being established in China, with major financial aid from Rōdōshō; Korea, too, has started its own version of PUJ. Vocational training aid on a grand scale is an integral part of Japan's international commercial strategy.

Public funding of training

The funding for the public subsidy of vocational training that has been described is covered by the Labour Insurance Law of 1989, which originated as the Unemployment Insurance Law of 1947. T. Ishikawa, who has for long been responsible for the training of overseas vocational instructors as an official in the Ministry of Labour, summarizes the concept briefly as follows:

Establishments covered by the law must contribute 1.25% of the payroll, of which 0.9% is allocated for the payment of unemployment benefit and shared equally by the employer and employees. The remaining 0.35% is borne by the employer alone and is reserved for three governmental projects designed to promote employment and vocational training. These figures have always been adjusted in accordance with economic and industrial conditions and are a little higher for some industries such as fisheries and construction. These projects are called 'employment improvement', 'human capability development' and 'employment welfare' and are implemented by the Ministry of Labour and also a statutory body known as the Employment Promotion Corporation (EPC) established in 1961.[3]

The basis on which grants are made available to employers is shown in Table 7.2. In 1991 83.8 billion yen (£1 = 160 yen approximately) were raised through the Labour Insurance Special Account (the 0.35 per cent of payroll employers' contribution). Much of this went to fund the public vocational colleges and centres and the Skill Development Centres; it is clear, therefore, that there is relatively little public subsidy of training to employers directly.

Summary

The overall conclusions must be that for a very long time Japan has had a very high degree of commitment to the training of people at all levels, and particularly, in the context of this chapter, of the technical and equivalent categories of supporting staff. In addition to the commitment by companies and the enormous enthusiasm by employees towards their own self-development through education and training, the State has provided an overall plan, framework, and vision.

The clear argument is that in nations which thrive and prosper industrially and commercially, like Japan and Germany, all these factors are in place. In contrast, in countries which are declining in their international competitiveness, like Britain, they are not.

Table 7.2. Expenses used for training and the corresponding grants

Expense	Amount of grant					
	Vocational training is given to those of age-limit retirement before their retirement.			Otherwise		
	Large enterprise	Medium or small-sized enterprise	Maximum grant per employee	Large enterprise	Medium or small-sized enterprise	Maximum grant per employee
(1) Expenses for group training done within the business place, such as remuneration to instructors and material expenses	1/3	1/2	¥70 000	1/4	1/3	¥50 000
(2) Registration fee and tuition for educational training received at facilities outside the business place	1/2	2/3	¥100 000	1/4	1/3	¥50 000
(3) Wages during the period of training (for days of whole-day absence while wages more than the normal wages are paid)	1/4	1/3	150 days (¥7 330 per per day)	1/4	1/3	150 days (¥7 330 per day)
(4) Expenses for the training of those of age-limit retirement (bounties for training)	¥860 per day (or ¥590)		150 days			—

Note: The amount in ( ) of (4) is for group training done within the business place of (1) or for correspondence training.
Source: Ministry of Labour, *Human Resources Development Administration*, Tokyo, March 1989, p. 39.

References

1 Research and Development Institute of Vocational Training, Employment Promotion Projects Corporation, *Country report on the planning, programming and education of vocational training – Japan*, Sagamihara, December 1984, pp. 15–17.
2 Ibid., p. 49.
3 Toshio Ishikawa, *Vocational training*, Japanese industrial relations series No. 7, The Japan Institute of Labour, Tokyo, 1991, p. 13.

Career development in Japan

'If you don't know where you're going, you'll probably end up somewhere else'.
– British proverb

Introduction

There are many lessons from the ways in which the Japanese go about the career development of employees which are universally transferable; these include the systematic identification of the capabilities of each individual and the provision of suitable experience on a planned basis. Equally there are other aspects, including the highly autocratic approach to directing the careers of staff, which it would be very surprising if other nations decide to emulate; rather they are described both to give a better understanding of how Japanese companies operate and, hopefully, to provide some food for thought to Japanese companies on aspects which many of their employees would like to see changed.

Lifetime employment – is it a myth?

If there is one thing that most people 'know' about Japan, it is that everyone there benefits from the security of Lifetime Employment. But is that true? Certainly it is not for many of those of the three-quarters of the working population employed in companies with less than 300 people. Nor is it true of the part-time, subsidiary company, or subcontractor employees who often make up, between them, the majority of employees on a large company's site. Even in many of Japan's largest and best-known companies, the continuing recession of the 1990s has forced the implementation of compulsory early retirements.

Nevertheless, Lifetime Employment is certainly an objective which, given a favourable commercial wind, most companies and employees aspire to in Japan. The fact that it does not actually apply in practice to the majority of them does not alter its importance in the value system of all Japanese companies.

On the whole, Japanese companies can count on the long-term loyalty of their employees. It is true that there has been a degree of breakdown in this loyalty, with some large companies losing up to 30 per cent of their staff within four years of their joining. There has also been an increasing amount of headhunting of senior specialists from the larger companies, taking advantage of their rigid salary structures by offering attractive alternative emolument packages, usually either by smaller or foreign companies. Nevertheless, a company like Toshiba will lose only 3 or 4 per cent of its employees during their initial few years, and can therefore take a very long-term view of their investment in the skills and career development of their staff.

One of the lesser known facts about Japan is that there are in effect 'no-poaching agreements' between the large companies. One of the delightful phrases used by a professor at Tokyo Institute of Technology when speaking to the British author was that 'it is perfectly difficult to change companies' in Japan. By that he meant that Fujitsu, for example, would rarely or never recruit someone who was so disloyal as to leave Toshiba, NEC, Hitachi, etc., and vice versa. This tradition came about historically as a result of the agreements in past centuries between the merchant houses, which were organized into regulatory guilds, that they would 'refuse employment to apprentices or clerks who left the employ of other houses in the same guild'.[1]

Given that the better graduates are effectively allocated to their companies by a professor at their University (see Chapter 4), one can understand why there is every evidence that employees are not generally happy that they are tied for life to large companies in those cases where lifetime employment is in operation. It is in fact a double-edged sword. Employees are of course free to leave, but the only realistic alternative employment will in most cases be in smaller or foreign-owned companies, with lower salaries, less security, and, most important of all, a drop in status. A survey in 1988, for example, by Fukoku Mutual Life Insurance asked male employees aged between 20 and 59 what they most wanted to do but knew they would never achieve; 36.2 per cent replied that they would ideally like to find a job in another company (and 34.2 per cent fantasized about divorcing their wives!).

Those with the benefit of Lifetime Employment are undoubtedly grateful for the job security, and in almost every case genuinely proud to be working for a large, prestigious, and successful company. But they also know that they will be exploited in many ways. They will be expected to work a considerable amount of overtime, some of it unpaid; to dedicate themselves completely to the company at the expense of their family life; and to be prepared to be transferred anywhere, not only in Japan but in the world, sometimes without their families, at the company's behest. On the other hand it is very common in Japanese companies for new employees to be 'adopted' by a more senior employee who then mentors them for the whole of their career; the mentor provides advice and guidance, both professionally and personally, and in return the mentee does everything to support the mentor. One confidential Japanese study has shown that the major factor in career success has been having a mentor whose own career has been successful; the mentor and mentee rise up the organisation together.

A strategic approach to career development

It is often said in Japan that their promotion system is like Shogi (Japanese chess). All the players start at the same point, adopting similar initial moves; but there is an overall well-thought-out strategy.

Given that the vast majority of their male staff will be with the company for the duration of their careers, large companies can assume that most OJT and OffJT given to their staff will eventually be beneficial to the company. Since they are taking a very long-term view of career development, they normally provide a much slower career progression for their employees than would generally be the case in the West; the emphasis is on giving them a broad and detailed understanding of the basic aspects of the company's business.

A typical career path for a university graduate in a development laboratory might be as follows. He would join at the age of 22 or 23 (or two to five years later if he has a master's or a doctorate degree), and then undergoes the type of induction programme over one or two years outlined in Chapter 6. This culminates in the 'Conference', at which he makes a presentation on what he has achieved and learnt to the others in his cohort of graduates and to senior management. At this point the senior management will be beginning to distinguish the future high-flyers from the rest, and the future managers from the future technical specialists.

The young engineer then receives, typically, five or six years OJT, while remaining in the same laboratory. At the age of 29 to 31 the engineer is likely to be appointed as Assistant to a *Kakarichō* (Section Supervisor). The Japanese ethos requires that all graduates from a particular annual entry cohort are promoted together, at least in the early years. Indeed, up to the age of about 45 all university graduates will be paid much the same salary as the rest of their entry-cohort colleagues. The better ones, however, know they have been marked out; they may receive slightly higher bonuses or be promoted one or two years earlier than their colleagues.

Interestingly, one of the effects of the 1990s recession has been to encourage companies in Japan to start moving to more performance-related pay systems – a significant change from the traditional *nenkō* (seniority) payment system. Fujitsu, for example, have modified their annual salary contract system for administrative staff with effect from 1994; their new system retains the conventional concept of steady increases each year in the monthly pay element of the salaries, but differentiates much more sharply in the discretionary bonus element. Thus before the new scheme was introduced the differential total pay between 45-year-olds might be ¥2 million between the best and worst performers. By 1997, the intention is that this might increase to ¥5 million, with salaries ranging between ¥12 million and ¥17 million.

At the age of 35 the engineer is likely to be promoted to *kakarichō*, and to *kachō* (Manager) between the ages of 35 and 40. By 45 he is quite likely to have reached the position of *buchō* (Divisional Manager). Titles after that vary between companies, but he may well become a General Manager by the time he is 50, rising to be Assistant Head of a factory or research centre at about 55, followed by Head, often at Director level.

Normally all employees will retire at about the age of 58 or 60, depending on the company's compulsory age of retirement, with the exception of directors, who effectively have a job for life. Many senior managers will become managers or directors of subsidiaries or subcontractors, thus strengthening the bonds with the parent company and bringing the benefits of their years of experience into the smaller company. The system is open to abuse, of course, particularly where senior government employees take up well-paid positions in companies over which they used to have influential powers.

About 10 per cent of civil servants retiring as department heads and above take up well-paid positions in industry – a heavily criticized practice known as *amakudari* ('Descent from Heaven'), particularly since most retire from the so-called 'honeypot' ministries which award major contracts and licences. On the other hand, the practice of senior managers in large companies moving into positions in their smaller associated companies is surely of great benefit to Japanese industry.

The differentiation of management position from status

As has been explained, the Japanese ethic of team spirit and 'the nail not sticking out' requires that all university graduates joining a company in a particular year are promoted together for the first decade or two of their careers. Clearly, however, not all will be of equal ability, so this could be a major limitation in maximizing the contribution of the high-flyers.

Remember, however, that this is Japan, a nation of great subtlety and not a little inventiveness. The Japanese solution is typically elegant – the separation of an individual's status-ranking from that individual's management position in the company. Therefore the whole of a cohort of graduates will be given the same status-ranking at any one time, but their management seniority and real responsibilities will vary considerably, with the latter reflecting their real ability and contribution to the company.

The intriguing way in which this is arranged in three different companies

– Toshiba, Matsushita, and Fujitsu – is shown in Figures 8.1, 8.2, and 8.3, provided by Denki Rōren (the Federation of Electrical Machine Workers' Unions).

It will also be clear from these figures that senior high school graduates generally have the same career opportunities open to them as university graduates, but with two important differences; first, they will be promoted

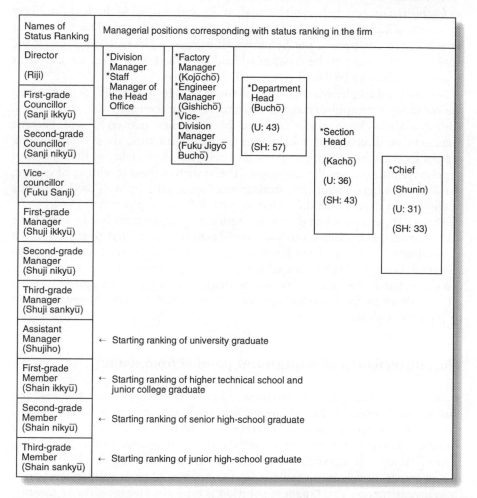

Fig. 8.1 Diagram of the status – ranking system in Toshiba and how the status rankings correspond with managerial positions within the firm, with a promotion model for an employee who has worked for the firm continuously since leaving full-time education (the Japanese names for status rankings and managerial positions, of which each firm has its own individual hierarchy, are given in brackets). The figures given in parentheses for each managerial position are those for promotion to the position, U: for university graduates, and SH: for senior high-school graduates.

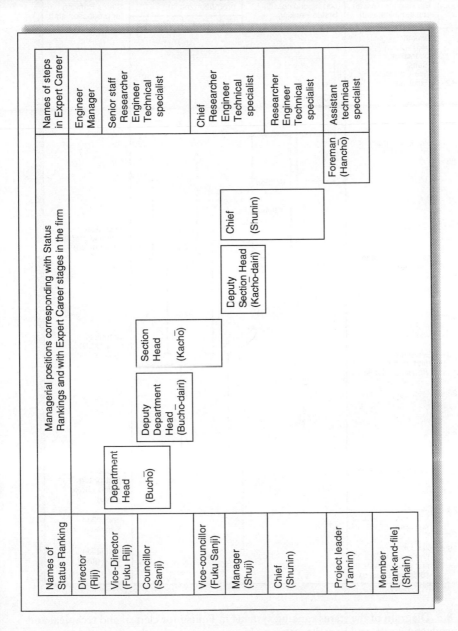

Fig. 8.2 Diagram of the status – ranking system in Matsushita Electric and how the status rankings correspond with managerial positions and 'expert career' (specialist technical) positions within the firm (the Japanese names for status rankings and managerial positions, of which each firm has its own individual hierarchy, are given in brackets).

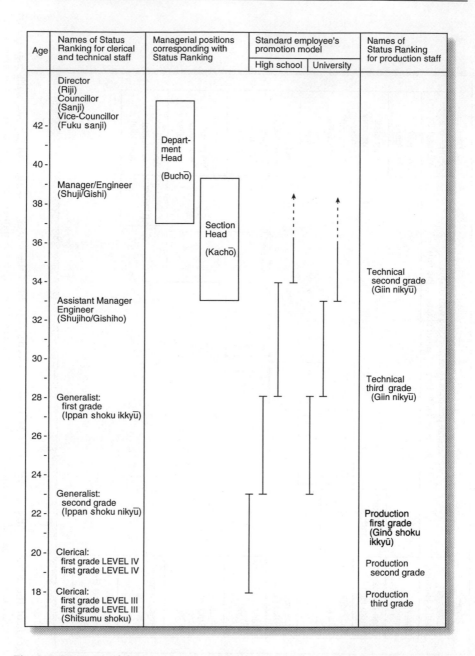

Age	Names of Status Ranking for clerical and technical staff	Managerial positions corresponding with Status Ranking	Standard employee's promotion model		Names of Status Ranking for production staff
			High school	University	

Fig. 8.3 Diagram of the status-ranking systems in Fujitsu for clerical and technical and for productive staff, and how the status rankings correspond with managerial positions within the firm (the Japanese names for status rankings and managerial positions, of which each firm has its own individual hierarchy, are given in brackets).

to an equivalent level a number of years later than their university colleagues, despite their four to nine years longer service; and second, they will be very unlikely to rise to as senior a position in the company.

A highly systematic approach to skills development

A university graduate, therefore, will generally remain in the same department until about the age of 30, and beyond that will probably be moved every two or three years. Often these job moves involve a large proportion of the staff in an organization, and take place on the same day. These moves would appear invariably to be either sideways (between functions) or upwards (promotion), but never both at the same time.

Having outlined the type of career path that is typically followed, let us look in more detail at how the underlying skills development is implemented. For example, despite the apparently static career development in one function for the first few years, there is also considerable fluidity in the tasks tackled by engineers during that period. They are transferred to help solve problems in other departments in which they have particular expertise, often at very short notice, and sometimes for very long periods of time.

This flexibility is considerably facilitated by the use by Japanese companies of centralized computer databases listing the areas of expertise of all their engineers; this is undoubtedly a major reason why they are able to adopt such a flexible approach to moving staff around as technical problems arise. Furthermore, it is also clear that senior managers in Japan generally have a far better idea of the abilities of their staff than is the case in the UK. This fluidity in staff movement also depends, it must be said, on the much greater willingness of Japanese employees to accept such flexibility in their tasks and locations than could be expected in the West.

Moving staff with the product

Another important reason why the Japanese both develop well-engineered products and well-rounded employees is that they tend to move engineering staff with the product. In other words, as a new design moves from the development laboratory to production and on through to marketing, so the team of engineers moves with it. On the way they develop new skills, and there is no danger of the sorts of misunderstandings between departments which cause so many of the extra costs and delays so often bedevilling Western companies. After all, what better incentive is there for engineers to ensure that a design can be cost-effectively and efficiently manufactured and marketed than if they know that they will be implementing those stages themselves?

One British engineer seconded to a Japanese company started by working in the research and development centre in Kawasaki (30 kilometres south-east of the centre of Tokyo). In December his entire group was told that they would be required to transfer to a manufacturing plant 150 kilometres north-east of Tokyo for two years as from the next month. The product they were designing had reached the manufacturing stage, and they were expected to assist with the production engineering and debugging.

Such relocation of employees is accepted as a normal requirement of an engineer's terms of employment, and may or may not take place with their families accompanying them. In fact the British engineer in question had a *kachō* who only went home to see his family in Tokyo from the manufacturing plant once a month, despite the factory being only one and a half hours by train from Tokyo!

Considerable mobility is expected of Japanese employees

This power of the decision-makers, whether line managers or personnel staff, to relocate staff is almost absolute. A comparison with the British military, and a reminder that Japanese industry sees itself as waging commercial war, is appropriate at this point. When Britain sent a Task Force to recover the Falkland Islands from Argentina in 1982 it no more asked the Guards, the Marines, the pilots, or the sailors whether they wished to go than most Japanese companies consult on job moves with their staff.

If an engineer does not wish to be relocated several hundred kilometres away he is usually able to express his preference for not moving; his manager will then try to find someone else who will be prepared to move instead. However, if no one else can be found to take his place, the engineer is forced to move against his wishes. One senior Japanese manager described the situation this way: 'In the past if you were asked to relocate there was only one possible reply – "Yes". Now there are two possible answers: "Yes" and "Yes, but can I tell my wife first"!'

One British engineer lecturing in the Training Department of a large Japanese electronics company told of how many of his fellow lecturers were Tokyo University graduates (in other words, the élite); however, much more interestingly, none of them wished to be in that job – they had all been allocated to that position for a period as part of their career development, much against their wishes.

Career development in Japan is therefore highly autocratic; but there is a surprisingly high degree of preparedness by the Japanese to accept such a state of affairs. This is partly because they are prepared to sacrifice their own interests for those of Japan or their company as a whole; partly because the Lifetime Employment system gives them little choice but to do what they are told; partly because their upbringing teaches them to do what they are told; and partly because the family relationship is different from that in the West.

One Personnel Officer described how, for example, his father had been transferred twenty years earlier from Tokyo to Kobe, about four hours away by Shinkansen train. Since he and his sister were at good schools in Tokyo, and because they did not want to lose their family house in Tokyo, his mother remained in Tokyo with the children. This state of affairs continued, so that his parents, for the previous twenty years, had normally only seen each other just once a month! In fact this Personnel Officer and his wife live with his mother, which is relatively unusual these days.

This practice of transferring employees to new work locations for a specific period of time is known as *Tanshin-funin*. It involves a secondment to another location for between three and five years for 90 per cent of the 180 000 Japanese in this position at any one time. One survey suggested that a typical 35-year-old *kakarichō* has been moved in this way 2.7 times, a 45-year-old *kachō* 4.6 times, and a 55-year-old *buchō* 6.2 times. In some cases they have been moved 7, 10, and 12 times respectively. Again, there is a long history of Japanese employees being expected to be highly mobile; one classic example was the practice of *sankin-kōtai*, under which feudal lords alternated their residences by law between Tokyo (where the Shogun could monitor their loyalty) and their territories. As some Japanese industries, like steel and shipbuilding, have declined, many employees have found themselves 'loaned' to quite different sectors of employment as an alternative to facing unemployment. Sometimes this involves secondment from, say, a steel company to a customer car company; in other cases companies like Nippon Steel have diversified into completely new fields, including carbon fibre, fine ceramics, and even mushroom-growing.

The British author recalls visiting the computer factory of one of the large electronic companies. on the outskirts of Tokyo in 1985. He remarked to the Engineering Administration and Technical Training Managers who had conducted Professor Keith Thurley and himself around the site that, of the 3000 software engineers, hardware engineers, production staff, marketing department employees, etc., they appeared to be the only ones over the age of 35. They agreed that that was correct. The next question was, obviously, what happened to employees who reached that age! The reply was non-committal, but indicated that they were moved to other sites. The conclusion afterwards was that this could only mean that above that age employees were considered too old to give of their best to the latest technologies, and were transferred to other sites involved with older technologies.

Not long afterwards this aspect was discussed with Denki Rōren, the federation of enterprise trade unions in large Japanese electrical and electrical engineering companies. They confirmed that Japanese engineers generally have no say about their career moves. Their members in Research Centres, for example, expressed a desire to have a greater say in their areas of research, and indeed there is an increasing tendency for companies to give greater choice to research staff. At factory level, however, the range of freedom is limited. Engineers have no choice about being moved from research and development to production and vice versa. When challenged on whether their union therefore gets involved in the subject of compulsory relocation, the surprising answer is that this is not the case. Instead, it campaigns to improve the working environment through such events as a national conference of its members at Matsushita, with delegates from various research and development centres making joint recommendations to management. In the past university graduates used to be a minority in the union, which was heavily influenced by the views of blue-collar workers. Denki Rōren, however, now has an increasing proportion of university graduates among its members, and admits that they are strongly critical of it as a union; therefore perhaps it is possible that this issue of compulsory relocation will one day become a matter for negotiation.

On the other hand it must be admitted that Japanese trade unions are unlikely to see this issue as one over which they should take up arms. They are, on the whole, very close to the company's management when it comes to the value system they advocate. They see their role predominantly as supporting the company in its highly competitive endeavours. The unity of purpose between Japanese unions and management is such that many company directors earned their spurs by acting as union officials earlier in their careers, using it as an opportunity to show leadership, and organizational and communication skills which were developed further when they moved into management responsibilities in the company.

The importance of powerful personnel functions

The weakness of Japanese trade unions, as it is seen in Western eyes, is in contrast to the strength of Japanese personnel functions, which are often very powerful.

The recruitment targets for all Divisions are usually determined by Head Office, and there is also generally centralized career progression, training records, and, sometimes, career-preference monitoring.

The importance attached to the skills development of employees is such that the General Managers make it their business to know the detailed career plans of their staff, working closely with the Personnel Director and his department. The Personnel Director himself often ranks number three or four in the management hierarchy, co-ordinating, among other things, the annual job moves. These take place on a fixed date, for example in January or July, involving perhaps 10 per cent of all staff, and are controlled directly from the Head Office Personnel Department, taking into account the recommendations of the *kachōs* and *buchōs*. These in turn see it as being of supreme importance that they know the real competencies and potential of every member of their team, which they pass on both formally and informally to the Personnel Department.

A union viewpoint

The sophistication of Japanese trade unions is such that it is valuable to hear the views of one such as Denki Rōren.

This confirms that almost all university graduates become *kachōs* at the age of 40, with about half of senior high school graduates also eventually reaching that level. However there are increasing signs of problems with this. For example, they say, there has been a conspicuous increase in the numbers of software engineers since 1970, when Fujitsu, for one, began to recruit 1000 university graduates (100 of them women) for this function each year. Another source of recruitment is of senior high school graduates who have then gone on to Software Colleges, while many junior colleges, providing two-year courses predominantly for women, have switched their courses from flower-arranging to software.

Now all these software engineers (not the women, though, who will have married and left) are reaching the position of *kachō*, and a major management problem is how to solve the problem of promoting such a large number to that level, for which there are enormous cultural pressures. This is particularly critical because inevitably becoming a *kachō* brings with it social status as well as job function, and the problem is not entirely solved by the status-ranking system. This problem becomes increasingly difficult in all functions, as Japan's economy expands less rapidly and there is a general reduction in the rates of expansion of large companies.

Two solutions are being effected, according to Denki Rōren. The first has been to establish new companies with external clients, for example specializing in software or computer services for banks, and moving staff out to be managers of these companies. The other has been to establish a new system of promotion for engineers above the age of 30, with a Specialist route paralleling the Management route; in the UK these two paths would be described as Technical and Managerial. In their surveys of their members the union finds that the majority prefer to be promoted as Specialists rather than as Managers. Fortunately this suits companies well, since the number of management positions is necessarily limited.

It is also important to recall that selection for promotion in Japanese companies is rigorous, with Mitsubishi Electric's promotion system for skilled and managerial staff, for example, being closely tied to passing a paper test and interview, followed by a training course between one day and one week long.

Some specific company examples

Matsushita

Promotion paths are very similar between large companies, but the approach to job-rotation necessarily varies.

At Matsushita (the parent company of brands such as Panasonic, Technics, and JVC) there was only limited job-rotation until the late 1970s. Then the new President, Mr Yamashita, insisted on job-rotation, expressing the view that it is bad for anyone to hold the same job for more than five years. Rotation therefore now occurs every five to seven years. The company has found this relatively difficult to achieve in technical departments, but much easier in functions such as accountancy and personnel. There is a human-relationship problem between the manager and the subordinate where a manager is reluctant to release a good engineer (a problem all too familiar in the UK!). Matsushita's solution to this has been to insist that engineers can only progress from Co-ordinator to Senior Co-ordinator, for example, after having had a job-rotation. In order to sweeten the pill for the manager, secondments are often arranged to a different plant for a limited period of about a year, so that the manager knows that the subordinate will return.

In Matsushita the controlling power of the Personnel Department is relatively weak, because of the company's divisional decentralization, and the pressure to ensure that job-rotation is implemented therefore comes from the General Managers.

NTT

This is an interesting organization, facing the same problems as other telecommunication network operators, like its equivalent British Telecom, in having moved rapidly from electromechanical and analogue to digital electronic and software-controlled technology.

It is possible for a university graduate to become a kachō after eight or nine years, with a senior high school graduate perhaps taking twice as long. The former will typically spend two or three years in his first job, with a longer period for the latter. Someone recruited as a specialist will stay in one job, while those identified as having managerial talent will rotate between jobs.

For the first ten years they are assessed on aptitude, attitude, and performance to decide which route they will follow. There is a formalized annual assessment procedure, with the appraisal carried out by the individual's manager and co-ordinated with detailed policy planning by the Personnel Department. Employees are given the opportunity to voice their opinion on whether they stay or move, using a self-reporting system; but the final decision rests with the policy planning department in that area.

NTT has 230 000 employees, and the personnel function is located both at

Head Office and locally. For university graduates, the Personnel Department at Head Office has quite strong powers in moving them between jobs, but cannot ignore the views of the *kachōs*. More specifically, when a sideways move takes place within a department, then the departmental manager has a very strong say in it; but when moves are effected between departments then the Personnel Department has a strong influence on the decision. In most cases the Personnel Department listens to the views of the departmental heads. In the case of interdepartmental moves the Personnel Department effects a so-called 'adjustment'; this 'adjustment' is an informal persuasion in order to implement a formal agreement on an engineer's move between departments.

Seiko Instruments and Electronics

Here engineers are provided with two alternative career paths. The first option is to move between the same type of job, but in different divisions, such as Integrated Circuit design in the Research and Development Division, followed by the same job in the Electronics Division. The other route is inter-functional, with a job in R&D, say, followed by one in sales. The route followed depends on the engineer's abilities.

Opportunities for job moves are given three or four times up to the age of 40. Appraisals are every six months, with the engineer indicating whether he or she wishes to change jobs.

Seiko implemented a Manpower Information System in the mid-1970s, with the information on it updated annually. An engineer indicating a preference for a job move rings option number eight on the appraisal form, and is referred to as an 'eight-man'. In such cases the 'eight-man's appraisal is checked by his manager and the Personnel Department. The importance of the job then decides where the final decision lies. For example, if the engineer is wanted by the Corporate Strategy Division and he wants to move, then the Personnel Department will press strongly for him to be released, and his manager cannot stand in his way.

Yokogawa Digital Computers Limited

This company employs 350 staff, almost all university graduates.

Mr T. Yamada, the President and Chief Executive, also implements an annual appraisal system, including self-appraisal, where the engineer indicates a preference for his next job, which is not necessarily granted.

Mr Yamada makes the decision personally before any engineer is moved, and, while keen to move staff between jobs, takes the firm view that they must prove themselves competent at their current job before being moved to another. It will be recalled from Chapter 5 that, while Mr Yamada has a plush office for meetings, his normal place of work is sitting in the open-plan office in the middle of his engineers, and he is therefore exceptionally well placed to understand their abilities. How many equivalent Western managers could say the same?

Air Conditioning Services Limited

The Managing Director of this small company of 50 employees, Mr Inoue, very kindly invited one of the authors to speak to some of his employees.

One of these was aged 21 and had joined the company 15 months previously after five years at a technical college. When asked what his career ambitions were, he said that after a number of years' experience in the company he hoped to be able to set up his own little company. When questioned on how he would finance this, he explained that, after employees have been with the company for ten years, Mr Inoue makes a gift to the employee of a company service vehicle.

There had in fact been four employees who had not long before left the company and set themselves up in business. This is a very interesting example of the strong Japanese ethic of mutual obligation.

A historical sense of mutual responsibility

This last example from Air Conditioning Services Limited has strong parallel analogies with the tradition in the Merchant Houses in the Tokugawa Period (1603–1868) when Japan was sealed off from the rest of the world. This is described in Rodney Clark's *The Japanese company*:

Apprentices would enter a merchant house at about ten years of age to be taught reading and writing as well as business procedures, and to begin simple and often menial work in return for board and lodging . . . The longer he stayed and the more responsibility he was accorded in the affairs of the house the nearer his status became to that of the house member. He might be married to a daughter of the house and treated almost as one of the family – though distinctions were usually preserved between family and staff. Even if the apprentice did not rise so high within the house he could expect, after ten or more years of service, to be given the money to start a branch house under the house badge – though, again, his branch was hardly likely to be as big as that of a younger son.[2]

Japan's biggest missed opportunity – careers for women

Not everything is commendable in the Japanese approach to career-development, as has been seen from several examples earlier in this chapter. But Japan's greatest missed opportunity is surely the highly chauvinistic approach to women. The 1985 Equal Employment Opportunity Law (see Chapter 4) is undoubtedly beginning to change the severely limited career opportunities for women, but only relatively slowly.

In private, women are in charge of their households, looking after the family budgets, bringing up the children, etc. However, to most Japanese men that is the limit of the reponsibility they are prepared to concede to women. Female university graduates will rarely be given real responsibility in Japanese companies, and will even be expected to resign on marrying in order to look after their household. The only realistic career opportunities open to them are either in foreign companies (in other words, they form an important source of talent for companies investing in Japan) or as entrepreneurs. For example, recently Japan's top life-insurance agent, Kazuko Shibata, was a woman; indeed, a significant number of the best sellers of life-insurance in Japan are women.

In September 1986 Takako Doi was elected as the first woman to head a major political party, the Japan Socialist Party, lasting as leader until August 1989. However, at the time she resigned, the re-elected Liberal Democratic Prime Minister, Mr Toshiki Kaifu, did appoint two women as Cabinet Ministers. Nevertheless, there was then furious debate in January 1990 when Japan's first female Chief Cabinet Secretary, Mrs Mayumi Moriyama, announced that she would exercise the prerogative of her office by handing the Prime Minister's Trophy to the winner of the sumo wrestlers' New Year's Grand Tournament. The Tournament organizers protested that it is regarded as unlucky for a woman to tread on the sacred soil of the 'Dohyō' (Fighting Ring).

In the general election in February 1990 a dozen women were elected to the 512-seat Lower House, the highest number since 1946 – although none of them belonged to the ruling Liberal Democratic Party. In the July 1993 general election women won a record fourteen seats and Takako Doi became the first woman to be Speaker of the Lower House.

Tradition has a strong influence in Japan, and in most areas of her life serves her well. But in this underutilization of the real talents of Japanese women, surely the country does itself a gross disservice for which her overseas competitors should be extremely grateful.

The long-suffering Japanese housewife

Even when displaced from her career to become a housewife, the travails of the average Japanese woman are only just beginning. Up to now this long-suffering sector of Japan's population has accepted its situation stoically, but the signs are that there are the beginnings of pressure for change.

In the 8 January 1992 issue of the *Nikkei* newspaper there was this article:

Petition by Wives

Last autumn Sotowo Tatsumi, President of Sumitomo Bank, received four letters from wives of his employees. One of them says:

'You talk about "more leisure time for bank employees". I am grateful for your words, which have never been heard before. However, in practice, these are just "words" and no changes have been seen. It is still gone midnight by the time my husband returns home on every weekday. He sleeps like a dead man on Sunday, and Monday comes before he is refreshed. As his wife I cannot do anything for him. What will be awaiting us after such a life? If he dies of overwork, I will hate the Bank.'

The sender's name and address were clearly written. Such a non-anonymous letter was the first to Mr Tatsumi. This is a 'petition' which risks her husband's position. 'Company men', who work to the detriment of their health and families, are not unusual in Japan. If executives are asked what the point is of such sacrifice, most of them will be unable to give a suitable reply, because they cannot guarantee themselves a good position and bright future at the cost of today. Does the [Japanese] company as an organization not take too much advantage of employees' diligence?

Mr Tatsumi decided not to disclose the sender's name, but instead gave instructions to the divisional heads to reduce overtime working as much as possible, giving up perfectionism. Wives' questions throw a stone at a swarm of working bees.

Summary

One of the sayings of the Japanese is that the real strength of Japan is that it has mediocrity in depth. There is a lot of truth in this observation.

The West tends to judge success by the achievements of the most talented. In contrast, the Japanese are obsessed by the fear of failure. They recognize that a chain breaks at its weakest link, and concentrate on giving *all* employees the greatest possible level of skill, and do so in the only way possible – by a thoroughly systematic and committed approach.

The benefits of this multiskilled philosophy are apparent in Figure 8.4, showing the rising proportion of Japan's civil R&D spending as a percentage of GDP in relation to her international competitors. Japan could only achieve this with a skills base that has steadily been enhanced in the ways described in this book. And it is not only in R&D that Japan is becoming the world leader. Whereas a Western company employs perhaps ten design and development engineers for each manufacturing engineer, Japan has almost equal numbers of each. As a result Japan takes half the time of her Western competitors to take a product from concept to the marketplace. According to Dr John Parnaby, a Director of Lucas, the average added value per employee in Japan is 76% higher than in the UK.

It would be very unwise for Japan's competitors not to learn two key lessons from the Japanese. First, that it is essential for success in an increasingly competitive world marketplace to identify and develop people with potential on a broad front. And, second, to ensure that companies are led by well-rounded senior managers who have been systematically developed in depth and in breadth throughout their careers.

On the other hand, there is beginning to be evidence that Japan, in its turn, is

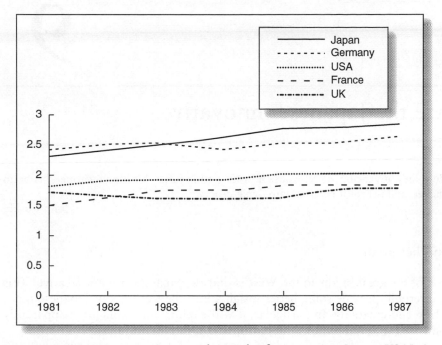

Fig. 8.4 Civil R&D as a percentage of GDP for five countries. *Source*: US National Science Foundation.

learning from the West that engineers can be given greater reponsibility earlier in their careers, and even that there are immense benefits to be obtained from giving real career opportunities to women.

References

1 Rodney Clark, *The Japanese company*, Yale University Press, New Haven, 1979, p. 17.
2 Ibid., p. 15.

9

Are the Japanese innovative?

'He is only advancing in life, whose heart is getting softer, his blood warmer, his brain quicker, and his spirit entering into living peace.'

John Ruskin

Another myth

One of the great myths in the West is that the Japanese are not creative. This chapter will provide some better insights into the truth about Japanese innovation and creativity. In particular, it will explore and explain the apparently contradictory coexistence of imitation and creativity in Japan.

Western thinking versus Japanese thinking

Western thinking is rational and analytical, dividing concepts and ideas into separate boxes. In contrast, Japanese thinking is creative; it rearranges ideas, bringing things together to provide new insights and possible solutions. The technical director of a major British engineering company, for example, commented that the pleasure of dealing with the Japanese is that they will always try out all possible reasonable engineering solutions, quite unlike his own company's cautious and conservative approach. Another British engineer, this time in Tokyo, suggests that the Japanese will not only design products aimed at specific markets, but will also cut their losses much faster if it becomes apparent that the wrong decision has been made.

The twenty-first century will be Japan's

The Japanese are highly adaptive to changing technologies. Not only do they successfully identify the best ideas and patents elsewhere in the world, using extremely powerful databases, but they are increasingly registering their own patents and developing new solutions, new products, and new markets. Their approach is much better suited to the technological challenges of the twenty-first century than the German one, which is more appropriate for more static mechanical technology. As Akio Morita, Chairman of Sony, has said, 'Anybody can get an idea. Very few people can make that idea into real industry.' More than any other nation, the Japanese are increasingly successful in doing that, so what are the key lessons?

Food replicas – innovation or imitation?

If the level of innovative ability of a nation is measured by the number of Nobel Prize winners, then Japan does not score highly; there have been just eight, as shown in Table 9.1. Most Japanese know these eight names by heart, and many suffer from an inferiority complex that the list is too short. It has long been believed, certainly since the start of the Meiji era (1868), that the Japanese have a hereditary lack of creative ability, and are instead both imitative and good at adapting. It has consequently been argued that the development of Japanese science and technology will be restricted, since there are limits to the extent to which such development can be based on imitation.

Perhaps some of the most remarkable examples of imitation are the plastic replicas of food which adorn the windows of almost all restaurants across Japan. Originally these were made of wax, a technique learnt from the West. Just as Japanese tourists are impressed by the wax replicas of great men and women in Madame Tussaud's in London, so do the Japanese food replicas fascinate Western visitors. Indeed, they are such perfect imitations that they could easily be mistaken for the real thing! However, this can be viewed from a different angle; food replicas are also an innovative industrial product, making it easy for customers to decide what they want to eat.

The Japanese debate about innovation

The whole subject of innovation is much debated in Japan, with heated argument over its classification.

Masanori Moritani, well known as the author of the book *Japanese*

Table 9.1. Japanese Nobel Prize winners

Hideki Yukawa	1949	Physics
Shin-ichirō Tomonaga	1965	Physics
Yasunari Kawabata	1968	Literature
Leo Esaki	1973	Physics
Eisaku Sato	1974	Peace
Ken-ichi Fukui	1981	Chemistry
Susumu Tonegawa	1987	Medicine
Kenzaburō Ōe	1994	Literature

technology,[1] details this discussion in another of his works.[2] Table 9.2 shows three representative classifications by two distinguished scientists and an engineer. Dr Kikuchi's classification provides a convenient explanation of Japanese innovation, arguing that the Japanese are not good at creating from nothing; rather they are best at producing things after being stimulated by ideas and information from other countries.

From imitation to creation

Moritani himself discusses in detail the characteristics of Japanese innovation, and puts forward his own classification. In contrast, Kazumasa Iinuma claims that creation is just one thing, and stands on its own. He started his study of this in 1964 when he was studying at Columbia University as a journalist working for one of the major Japanese newspapers, the *Asahi Shimbun*, collecting statistical proof that the Japanese are actually too innovative. He wrote a book[3] and several articles[4] on the theme 'From imitation to creation'. The hypothesis or assertion that he has insisted on for over twenty years can be summarized as follows:

(a) Japanese society is entering the 'creation age' and leaving the 'imitation age'.
(b) The Japanese have to create a new form of organization better suited to the creation age.
(c) This, unlike the conventional one, must be an organization in which the individual is respected, and not one based on the lifetime employment concept.
(d) A social basis is already being formed, on which such non-lifetime-employment organizations will be built.

As a result of his studies Iinuma concluded that:

1. For a nation that starts its industrialization lagging behind more advanced nations, development based on imitation is more profitable in economic terms, and this can be seen in every country. Even the USA and Germany had long periods of imitation before they entered their creation ages.
2. Japanese creativity in science and technology has been greater than is generally realized. There have been many significant examples supporting this view in the country's history since the Meiji era (1868).
3. It is indeed true that traditions and social mechanisms that have suppressed innovation have existed in Japan.
4. Moreover, there has not been the need for innovation by the Japanese, because Japan's industry has been able to develop by importing technology from abroad. However, within a century of the Meiji Restoration – just

Table 9.2. Classifications of creativity as defined by three Japanese authorities[2]

---

1 **Makoto Kikuchi**
(Graduated from Tokyo University in 1948. One of the pioneers of semiconductor studies in MITI's Electro-Technical Laboratory. From 1976 to 1990 Head of R&D Centre, Sony Corporation.)

A. Independent creativity: very new ideas generated by the inspiration of genius.

B. Adaptive creativity: a new idea is spawned from mental concentration after being given a lead and being inspired by it.

---

2 **Leo Esaki**
(Physicist, graduated from Tokyo University in 1946. Awarded Nobel Prize for the discovery of the Esaki tunnel diode. Worked for Sony and then IBM before becoming President at the University of Tsukuba.)

A. Primary invention/discovery, which contributes to the world across national frontiers.

B. Secondary invention/discovery, which contributes to Japanese technological progress across companies.

C. Third-class invention/discovery, which contributes to a company's success.

---

3 **Shinkichi Kisaka**
(Electronic engineer, graduated in 1944 from Tohoku University. From 1982 to 1987 was Vice-President of Matsushita Electric Industries.)

A. First class: creative and innovative – for example, quantum theory, or invention of the steam locomotive, radio, TV, or computer.

B. Second class: creation in a narrow sense, improvement – for example, invention of the video recorder or calculators.

C. Third and fourth class: creativity by a group or suggestion systems – for example, low-cost production of cars, or miniaturization of video cassette recorders.

---

over twenty years since the end of the second World War – the situation changed. The economic benefits of imitation (technology importation) became less. It came to be taken that domestic investment in new technologies would be more profitable. There was then a major expansion in the number of central research laboratories established.

Figure 9.1 shows the statistical data on which Iinuma bases his proof that 1968 (exactly 100 years after the Meiji Restoration) is the turning-point from imitation to creation, with 1988 as the first year of Japan's age of creativity. The index he uses in pursuing his hypothesis is the balance of trade in technical royalties. This graph presents two curves; one is based on statistics from Sōmuchō (the Management and Co-ordination Agency), which started in 1971, and the other on data from the Bank of Japan. Iinuma says that these two sets of statistics have different purposes, and that the Sōmuchō data give the more realistic figures, because the other set, does not for example, include the royalties associated with exports of plant.

The Sōmuchō index (the ratio of technical royalty exports to imports) was 10 per cent or so in 1968. Iinuma says that the figures for Britain, France, and West Germany were between 30 per cent and 40 per cent at that time. As the graph shows, the index exceeded 100 per cent in 1989. Thus Japan became a creative nation 120 years after the Meiji Restoration. The breakdown of the 1989 data is given in Table 9.3. It is the Asian countries that now provide Japan with a major part of her royalty income (as they in their turn move through the age of imitation). In comparison, Japan is still paying more royalties than it receives to most of the Western nations, with the notable exceptions of the UK, Italy, and Spain.

Iinuma says that studies by the Americans are even more striking. In 1983 the National Science Foundation surveyed the frequency of citation of existing patients in new patent applications in the USA from 1976 to 1983 by country

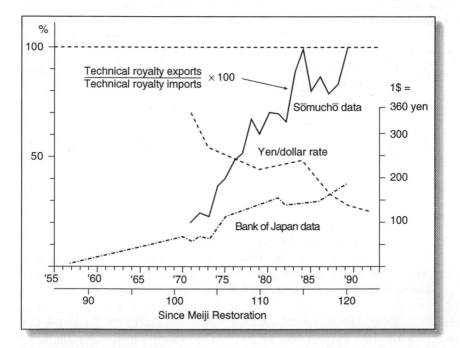

Fig. 9.1 Kazumasa Iinuma's data on Japan's balance of trade in technical royalties 1955–89[4].

of origin. An international comparison shows that Japan comes top, ahead of the USA, with the UK in third place (Figure 9.2). The result of another investigation appearing on 28 May 1991 in the *New York Times* is shown in Fig. 9.3; the associated comments say that it is not only in home appliances or automotives that Japan's technical strength is seen, but rather in every area. This strength is becoming a threat to American dominance. It is therefore a stereotype to define the Japanese as lacking creative or innovative minds.

Innovations achieved in the early days of Tohoku University

It is interesting to look at some examples of Japanese innovation in the period between the Meiji Restoration and the end of the Second World War, particularly since the common image is of a Japan which in those days was largely only capable of imitating the West. Two examples will highlight the influence of Japan's first great physicist, and in the process will illustrate how scientific and technological attitudes have developed since Japan opened her doors to the West in 1854. First let us examine the case of the third Imperial University in its early days. Tohoku Imperial University was founded in 1907, being formed by the amalgamations of the Science College in Sendai and the Agricultural College in Sapporo. In 1912, aiming to be a comprehensive university, it absorbed Sendai Higher Technical School and Medical College. (The Agricultural College became independent, as Hokkaido

Table 9.3. Japan's balance of technology royalties with various countries (1989)[4]

Country	Income	Outgoings	Income as a percentage of outgoings
USA	1077	2095	49
UK	200	108	185
W. Germany	137	243	56
France	71	255	28
Netherlands	21	211	10
Switzerland	16	190	8
Italy	39	25	156
Sweden	2	30	6
Spain	40	1	4000
Asia	1289	3	430
TOTAL	3293	3299	100

Unit: 100 Million yen

University, in 1917.) In its early days several outstanding scholars made their mark at Sendai.

The outstanding influence of Hantarō Nagaoka

Professor Hantarō Nagaoka, the father of Japan's modern science, master-minded the plan for the third Imperial University when he was at Tokyo Imperial University. His prominent contribution to science, including the Saturnine model of atomic structure, can be traced back to the influence of Professor James Ewing, who had been appointed a professor at Tokyo University at the age of 23, and started the study of magnetism and seismology in 1878. In 1911 Nagaoka chose as his main disciple Kōtarō Honda, who had just returned from four years of training in Europe, to be professor at the Science College of the new university. Nagaoka himself planned to move to Sendai later, but was prevented from doing so by the university authorities at Tokyo.

In 1917 Honda invented the KS magnet, which was four times stronger than a conventional magnet, and in 1933 discovered an even stronger permanent magnet. Honda was a unique individual; he always carried an umbrella in his

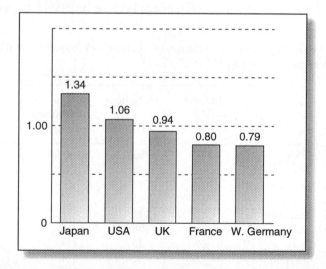

Fig. 9.2 A comparison of the nationalities of origin of important patents quoted in the USA. The preceding patents that had been quoted in patent applications between 1976 and 1983 in the USA were retrieved, and the 10 per cent of the earlier patents that were cited most frequently were classified by nationality of origin. (The vertical axis is the index, the average of the five nationalities being 1.00. The quotation frequency is normalized.) *Source: New York Times*, 3 July 1988.

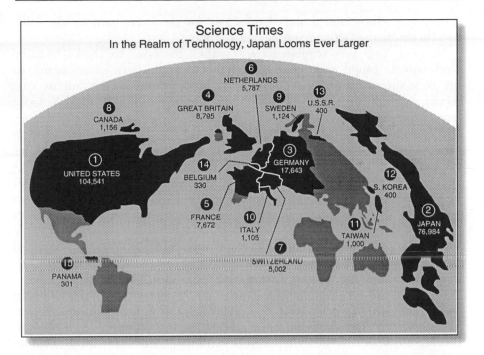

Fig. 9.3 The world of technical innovation: the relative importance of leading industrial powers in terms of new technical patents. *Source: The New York Times,* 28 May 1991.

right hand and a bag in his left hand, even on a fine day. When asked why he replied 'There are three benefits. First, I need not worry about whether it will rain or not. Second, the bag in my left hand can balance the umbrella in my right hand. And third, I can use it as a stick.'

The government emphasis on the study of metal should not be overlooked, especially in the construction of warships and weapons. This policy was very successful at Tohoku University in those early days. After the Second World War the research undertaken at the Metallurgy Research Laboratory contributed to Japan's precision industries, such as watch manufacturing. The Masumoto family in particular produced excellent scholars in this field.

Another outstanding scholar was Hidetsugu Yagi, who graduated from the Engineering College of Tokyo Imperial University in 1909 and soon became a lecturer at the Sendai Higher Technical School. From 1913 to 1916 he studied in Germany, England, and America. While he was at London University he was influenced by Professor Fleming, and committed himself to research in wireless communication. In 1926 he and his team made the notable invention of a directive antenna, thereafter known as the famous Yagi Aerial. It is interesting that the British Marconi Company took out a licence for this invention,[5] which later provided the basis for the radar used by the Allies to help defeat the German and Japanese troops.

In 1932 Yagi was requested by Nagaoka to move to Osaka Imperial University to found its Science Department. Yagi in later years considered his great success in life, much more than his invention of the famous Yagi Aerial, to be the fact that at Osaka he had recruited young Hideki Yukawa from the stuffy atmosphere at Kyoto University. Soon after making this move, Yukawa produced a theory predicting the existence of an elementary particle called a 'meson'; this eventually resulted in his becoming Japan's first Nobel Prizewinner. It is typical of the Japanese value system that even someone as eminent as Yagi should take pride not in his own achievements, but in what he had done to enable others to rise even higher! How often has this even been seen in the West? In 1939 Yukawa returned to his *alma mater* to activate its science department.

In 1942 Yagi became President of the Tokyo Institute of Technology, and two years later was appointed President of the Technical Council, but came into conflict with the Military Group, and resigned in May 1945.

Before he had become famous at Sendai, a millionaire called Saito had been so impressed by his personality that he decided to donate a enormous sum of money for electro-communication research at the university. As a result of this funding many excellent studies were carried out, leading to the foundation of the Electro-Communication Research Laboratories, which produced many very capable scholars and engineers. For example, the principle of the AC biasing technique for magnetic recording was discovered there by Professor Nagai and his colleagues.

Someone very famous in Japan, who carried out the installation of the world's first unloaded transmission cables in Manchuria and Korea between 1937 and 1939, was Shigeyoshi Matsumae, who also studied at Tohoku University. As an engineer at the Communications Ministry he opposed the Prime Minister, Hideki Tōjō. Becoming angry with him, Tōjō sent this prominent engineer to the battlefield in the Philippines, and soon after to Vietnam, as a plain soldier. After Tōjō's resignation Yagi played an important role in rescuing Matsumae from Saigon and releasing him from military status. After this miraculous return he became a post-war Socialist MP, as did Professor Yagi. He is also the founder of Tokai University, one of Japan's largest private universities.

The danger of non-innovative succession

In 1936, at the 25th anniversary of Tohoku University, Professor Nagaoka gave a so-called 'bombing' lecture. This is quoted in Kazumasa Iinuma's best seller:[6]

It is now 25 years since the foundation of Tohoku University. The original professors will soon retire and die. The problem is one of how you select their successors. The custom of succession from father to children is necessary for maintaining a family. However, is it reasonable to give the post of professor to one of his disciples with similar ideas? There may be some merits in this system for Classical Chinese studies, which do not produce new interpretations. Since in our field of engineering we are looking for new ideas, this custom needs rethinking . . . Tokyo University and Kyoto University have both filled their professorships with their alumni. But this is similar to the position of the Satsuma and Choshu parties in the early Meiji period, and is likely to be a root of evil. Tohoku University should watch this situation, and not do what will not be good for the people.

The Science faculty followed his advice to some degree, but produced no Nobel prizewinners. The Engineering faculty, in contrast, followed the normal Japanese system of placing more emphasis on the concept of continuity. Professor Jun-ichi Nishizawa, who is an admirer of Nagaoka and Yagi, has been President of Tohoku since 1991. At a co-laboratory meeting banquet he told the Japanese author that Tohoku University had been at its prime in 1926, and that since then negative ideas had loomed to discourage truly innovative scholars. He is enthusiastic about the reactivation of his university. Hiroshi Matsuo dealt with these matters in his non-fiction novel *Hidetsugu Yagi and Japanese innovators.*[7]

Riken's contribution to science

Germany became Japan's enemy in 1914 with the outbreak of the First World War, which meant a discontinuity in the import of technical products from that country. Building a research laboratory became increasingly important for Japan. This idea was originally advocated by Jōkichi Takamine, the world's first discoverer of a hormone (adrenaline). A semi-government Institute of Physical and Chemical Research called Riken was founded in 1917, with Nagaoka as the first Head of Physics. Yoshio Nishina was one of his graduate students at Tokyo Imperial University, following his first degree in electrical engineering, and played a very important role in Riken after returning from Denmark, where he had studied quantum physics. As a part-time lecturer at Kyoto Imperial University he inspired two outstanding students, Hideki Yukawa and Shin-ichirō Tomonaga, who went on to be Japan's first two Nobel Prize winners. Nishina himself changed his speciality from theory to experiment in order to build Japan's first cyclotron at Riken in 1937. Seven years later he constructed a larger one, which was destroyed by the occupation forces soon after the end of the War. Losing the Second World War was therefore a big setback for Japan's research into nuclear physics.

The most outstanding President of Riken, Masatoshi Ōkochi, was also appointed on Nagaoka's recommendation. Ōkochi attracted outstanding scholars as mobile researchers (men whose normal posts were at other organizations, such as Kōtarō Honda at Tohoku University) and provided a stimulating environment for innovative studies. Under the successful leadership of Ōkōchi, Riken produced enormous profits from its innovations. One example is the extraction of Vitamins A and C at the laboratory by Umetarō Suzuki, [6,8] who is believed by the Japanese to be the world's first discoverer of Vitamin B_1, which was originally named Oryzanin by Suzuki.

Early post-war examples of innovation

The most dramatic examples in this period are seen in semiconductor technology, which started in 1948, when Japanese industry had been almost entirely destroyed, and Japan's people were still suffering from lack of food.

How Japan's transistor technology started

On 12 July 1948 came the announcement of the invention of the germanium transistor, which had actually been discovered the year before.

Not long after, Professor Yasushi Watanabe, the Dean of the Telecommunications Research Laboratory, was summoned to GHQ. An American official whispered into the professor's ear that a device called a transistor had been invented at the Bell Telephone Laboratory. He was told that it was something made of germanium for amplifying electric signals. As the Japanese scholar had once thought about a solid-state amplifier, he quickly understood the importance of the new invention. He saw that on the official's desk lay the documents announcing the details, and asked to be allowed to read them. This was not officially allowed; but instead the official left the room, leaving the documents on his desk. The lucky scholar quickly read through them and took notes on the important points. Before returning to Sendai to give the order to his laboratory staff to start research into the transistor, the professor conveyed the news to the Head of the Electro-Technical Laboratory belonging to MITI, which later played an important role in this area. Among his staff at Sendai was Jun-ichi Nishizawa.

What if the Nobel Prize were awarded for engineering?

If it were, then without any doubt a large number of Japanese engineers and scientists would have received the Nobel Prize. As it is, however, the nearest Nobels that are available are for various branches of science. This seems a strange anomaly, and has led to a serious misperception of Japan's innovative ability in the West.

An interesting contrast is between the tunnel diode and the PIN diode. The former was discovered by Leona Esaki, the 1973 winner for Physics (while he was working for Sony), whereas the latter was the invention of Professor Nishizawa, and, in the view of many Japanese, is worthy of a Nobel Prize as well. Both diodes were created in the early stages of semiconductor studies in Japan. The tunnel diode contributed little to technology, while the PIN diode contributed a considerable amount, and led to high-speed power solid-state devices known as SITs (Static Induction Transistors).

Both inventions were dramatic. Let us quote two examples from a Japanese book[9] that was edited from a series broadcast by NHK (the Japan Broadcasting Corporation) under the title of 'Autobiography of an electronic nation – Japan':

Example 1: The tunnel diode, invented as part of Sony's development of the transistorized radio

Two methods of building a PN junction for a bipolar transistor were known: the grown junction and the alloy junction. In the US the grown junction was unsuccessful, but the alloy junction was poor in the high-frequency characteristics required for radio. Sony at that time was still a very small company, although it had been successful in tape-recorders; then they decided to develop their own transistor radio receivers as their next big project. This policy came from Masaru Ibuka, the company's first President.

The staff started by reading Shockley's *Electrons and holes*. Each member of the development team translated a part of it into Japanese at home in their own time. At the end of each day, after the company work was over, they gathered in a corner of the factory to read to each other the parts they had translated into Japanese, and to discuss the lessons to be drawn.

In 1954 K. Iwama, who later became President of Sony, travelled around America to collect the background information required to make the key decision on the manufacturing method they should use – whether alloy or grown. His 19 March report to his staff said: 'No significant new technologies have been seen that go beyond what we have studied in Shockley's book. The progress in America has been stagnant for the past year. We can catch up with the Americans in about a year.' He in fact changed his mind by deciding to go for the more risky 'grown method', despite the original intention to go for 'alloy' and the pessimism in America on the viability of 'grown'.

In 1955 Sony sold their first transistor radios. Next year came a boom in demand. However, for every 100 transistors they manufactured, they had to throw away 99; the usability rate was just 1 per cent. An important clue towards improving their productivity and towards the discovery of the tunnel diode came from a young woman operative in the factory; indeed, she had no more than the minimum qualifications accepted for joining the company, having only completed junior high school. In those days the factory operated two shifts. The morning shift started at 5 a.m., and they were provided with high school education in the afternoon, while the afternoon shift studied in the morning.

The girl decided not to attend her afternoon class, and instead spent her afternoon investigating the process to determine the correlation between the failure rate and the manufacturing method. She finally reached the conclusion that the problem lay in the crystal itself. To start with, the field engineers refused to listen to her ideas. However, when one day they adopted her advice the success rate increased from a few per cent to 20 per cent. This was kept top secret for a long time. Such vital contributions, however, by factory workers were made at every factory across Japan, and have been crucial to the astonishing success of Japanese companies.

The staff began to investigate the process for growing germanium crystals. They were using gallium for the P-layer and antimony for the N-layer. They soon found a problem in this combination. The P-type base region, which is required to be homogeneously thin, was eroded by antimony. They decided to use phosphorus as the dopant instead of antimony, and successfully produced a homogeneous base region without erosion. However, the base region was too thick to be a transistor. By controlling the process time they were not only able to make it thinner, but increased the cut-off frequency of the device by a factor of ten. In 1957 the section chief gave instructions to dope phosphorus in every crucible, expecting a major success. Instead the result was heavy damage, and the production of radios had to be stopped. They simply could not control the amount of unstable phosphorus in the production process. Sony found itself in a critical situation.

The next problem was to determine the optimum dopant concentration, and how to control it. Among the research staff was young Leo Esaki, who had been engaged in the study of the PN junction. He made a lot of test samples with various amounts of phosphorus as the N-type dopant. One day a student, who was training in the factory as part of his college curriculum, found an abnormal phenomenon in a specific sample. Most samples showed normal positive characteristics, with the current increasing with the voltage applied across the PN junction. However, in this sample the current *decreased* with an increasing voltage. Esaki at first considered this a measuring error. But when the same data were obtained with another sample, he shouted 'It's the tunnel effect!' This physical effect, whose theory maintains that an electron can penetrate a very thin voltage barrier owing to its wave behaviour, rather than its particle behaviour, had been derived theoretically from quantum physics, and physicists in those days were making efforts to provide experimental proof of it. This was found, as it happened, in Esaki's project by chance. Owing to heavy doping with phosphorus a barrier thin enough to allow the tunnel effect had been fabricated. Those first transistors doped with phosphorus did not display normal characteristics owing to the unexpected tunnel effect.

Physicist Leona Esaki was very excited by his discovery. However, engineers had to search for a suitable method of controlling the dopant in order not to produce an Esaki diode in a transistor. Eventually they were successful in producing transistors with excellent characteristics at low cost.

Example 2: Nishizawa's PIN diode

When in Sendai, in northern Japan, in 1948 Professor Watanabe told Nishizawa to research into transistors, he had no access to germanium. This essential material was simply not produced in Japan. However, the young graduate eventually came across a paper claiming that a transistor could be made using galena or pyrites, which was available. He decided to start by using pyrites and to study the characteristics of the case where only one needle is in contact with the base, rather than to build a transistor. What he first attempted was a diode. In his configuration he found, when an insulation film was formed by chance, that he had obtained rectifier characteristics with high durable reverse voltage. Later his ideas were used to fabricate a PIN diode in which an insulator layer is sandwiched by a P-region and an N-region to increase the reverse durable voltage and switching frequency. It was found afterwards that it is impossible to make a transistor from galena or pyrites.

Japan is now the archipelago of the semiconductor industry. However, at one extreme there is the view that there are no real Japanese innovative ideas; instead, it is said, they are all adapted technologies.

Japan's need for innovation for survival – and some examples

It is true that the Japanese are good at improving and adapting products. However, this is also the cause of much friction in world trade. The Americans and Europeans put great value on the principle of originality, and respect it in others. Perhaps the Japanese need fundamentally to change their attitude on this.

Professor Nishizawa is the opinion leader among those advocating the importance of innovation on the part of the Japanese. As long as they expend their energy only on improving and reducing costs, he says, the result is obviously going to be competition and overwork. This approach will never be the most profitable. At the dinner hosted by the Graduates' Society of the Nine Imperial Universities in 1986 Professor Nishizawa delivered a lecture[10] in which he explained his concerns:

I'm pessimistic about the future of Japan. Our approaches so far have not been so good. However, we need not worry provided we realize our real potential. If we can contribute to world civilization in terms of the development of good products, innovative technologies, and cultural values, we could both be respected and survive.

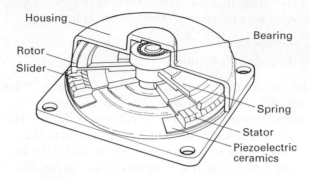

Fig. 9.4 The ultrasonic-wave motor.

Sashida's ultrasonic motor

It is also true, of course, that Japan is changing; encouraging environments are being created for Japanese innovation and creativity. Let us briefly look at the case, for example, of T. Sashida, who was born in Tokyo in 1939, and invented the ultrasonic motor.

As is seen in Fig. 9.4, unlike an electromagnetic motor, the ultrasonic-wave motor does not have coils or magnets. This tiny motor can generate a high torque at low speed that cannot be attained by a conventional motor. One of the most important applications is found in repairing robots operating in nuclear power plants.

As the autobiographical notes in the book he wrote with the Japanese author on the subject explain,[11] he had such a strong personality that he was turned down when he applied to work at a well-known large Japanese company. He resigned from his assistant post at a national university because he found that because of certain limitations placed on its functioning a university laboratory is not always a conducive environment for innovative research. After working for a very small company he started his own machine shop, and through his design work realized the need for a new motor with different characteristics from conventional electric machines. This led to his invention. By contrast to what happens in most cases in Japan, this unusual inventor was welcomed, and his invention has been studied in many company R&D centres and universities.

Another notable factor in his career is that he was given training in electrical engineering at a technical senior high school before studying physics at a private university. It is generally argued that most Japanese education programmes will not produce such an innovative and capable scientist or engineer. It is also true that the *kōsen* (the technical colleges for 15-to 20-year-olds), where students do not experience the pressures of studying for university entry examinations, have not yet produced any notable inventors, instead providing industrious technician engineers who are much in demand with commercial companies. In order to cope with the new age of innovation, the Japanese education system must invent new ways to encourage the development of individual personalities, as Iinuma says.

Kiichi Miyazawa's lecture (1969) urging that the Japanese should be creative in a wealthy society[12]

On 10 February 1969 Mr Kiichi Miyazawa, soon after resigning as Minister for the Economic Planning Agency for the second time (he was later to become Prime Minister from 1991 to 1993), gave a brilliant lecture on the subject of 'The future of Japan's economy' to a dinner of the Graduates' Society of the Nine Imperial Universities. He said:

Since we Japanese have been poor as a people, we have learnt how to cope with poverty from our parents and neighbours. However, we have not yet studied how to cope with wealth ... When Japan enters the info-society, or the third or fourth wave of industries, large investments will be made, and consumption will be seen on a large scale in these areas. In such circumstances, the concept of production will have to be different. The system of values which comes from 'producing objects' may not remain the same as our present one.

Economic prosperity or progress is not an end in itself. Rather the question is how to use it to improve the quality of human life. For an individual the objective must be to create something using his or her personality. For us as a nation, we must create a cultural environment different from that of other nations.

It is over two decades since Mr Miyazawa made this speech, and it is now believed that Japan has already entered into the age of creation. As Prime Minister he hosted a visit in 1992 from George Bush, accompanied by the American automobile industry's 'Big-Three Directors'. It is somewhat ironic that Mr Miyazawa had to resign as Prime Minister partly due to a scandal caused by a powerful LDP member who had failed to learn the skill of coping with wealth. He and his people must now create a system to maintain the prosperity of their biggest trading partner, the United States.

The real challenge faced by the West

A survey of 26 companies in seven industries in Japan by the British Chamber of Commerce in Japan in 1988[13] revealed the extraordinarily large number of research projects being pursued by Japanese companies at any one time; one of the companies surveyed, for example, had 700 in progress.

One notable aspect of the Japanese sample in the British author's Anglo-Japanese research, described in Chapter 6, was the extraordinarily high proportion of patents registered (Table 9.4). It is worth noting that of the UK sample only four engineers had registered one patent each. As Figure 8.4 (p. 169) showed, civil research and development expenditure as a percentage

Table 9.4. Number of patents registered by Japanese engineers with their present employer

Patents registered	%	Number of engineers
None	15	14
1–5	19	17
6–10	18	16
11–20	18	16
21–59	19	17
Over 60	11	11
TOTAL	100	91

of GDP is now higher in Japan than in any of her main rivals; Figure 9.5 and Table 9.5 further emphasize this point. Any competitor believing that Japan is not inventive is in for a rude shock!

Summary

The Japanese have been very good at adaptive creativity, but this does not in itself mean that the Japanese lack innovative ability, as we have seen from such early examples as Kōtarō Honda's KS magnetic steel or H. Yagi's directive antenna. These innovative scholars were, however, given their academic training in the West.

Table 9.5. International comparisons of Research and Development

Country	Year	R&D expenditure in million US$	% of national income	% financed by public funding
Japan	1988	76 249	3.35	18.4
USA	1988	126 115	2.89	48.0
West Germany	1987	35 690	3.21	37.7
France	1988	21 896	2.64	50.9
UK	1986	16 926	2.70	38.5

Source: *Japan – An International Comparison*, Japan Institute for Social and Economic Affairs, Keizai Kōhō Centre, 1991, p. 26.

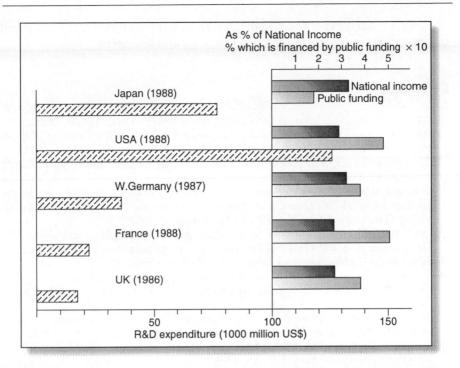

Fig. 9.5 R&D expenditure (in US$1000 million) for five large industrial economies, absolutely and as a percentage of national income, and the relative contributions of public funding in each country. *Source*: Japan Institute for Social and Economic Affairs (1991). *Japan — an international comparison*, p. 26. Keizai Kōhō Centre, Tokyo.

In Japan's post-war progress in semiconductors, though, there were many examples of innovation found among those educated entirely in Japan. Such were Professor Nishizawa (the PIN diode) or Dr Leo Esaki (the tunnel diode). However, it can be argued that these men belonged to a generation stimulated by great American innovations; and one extreme view is that there have been no real Japanese innovations in electronics.

Recent statistics nevertheless do show that Japan receives more in technical royalties than it pays to other countries, and its technical strength as indicated by patents is threatening earlier American dominance.

There have been various social factors which have encouraged adaptive creation and impeded innovation by the Japanese themselves. However, Japanese society is gradually changing in such a way that it increasingly needs to generate inventions itself. An outstanding recent example of inventiveness, which has almost no Western model, is T. Sashida's ultrasonic motor. It is increasingly realized that more Japanese innovations are needed for the survival of Japanese industry. It has also to be noted that the Japanese education system, which places too much emphasis on the entrance exams to universities rather than on beneficial experiences in the universities themselves, must be changed to produce more innovation-minded scientists and engineers.

References

1 Masanori Moritani, *Japanese technology*, Simul International, Tokyo, 1980.
2 Masanori Moritani, *Nippon wo tukuru gijutu wo tsukuru* (in Japanese; English title: *Creating Japan and technology*), Nikkankōgyō Shimbunsha, Tokyo, 1988.
3 Kazumasa Iinuma, *Mohō kara sōzō e* (in Japanese; English title: *From imitation to creation*), Tōyō Keizai, Tokyo, 1968.
4 (For example) Kazumasa Iinuma, *Mohō kara sōzō – Kono 20nen no ayumi* (in Japanese; English title: *From imitation to creation – the progress of the past 20 years*). Gakushikai Kaihō No. 794, 1992, Tokyo, pp. 60–7.
5 Jun'ichi Nishizawa, *21 seiki no kagaku-gijutsu wa dokomade shinpo suruka* (in Japanese; English title: *How will 21st century science/technology develop?*), Lecture Series No. 117, Nikkankōgyō Shimbunsha, Tokyo, 1990.
6 Kazumasa Iinuma, *Arunoka nainoka Nippon-jin no sōzōsei* (in Japanese; English title: *Is there or is there not Japanese creativity?*), Bluebacks Series, Kodansha, Tokyo, 1987.
7 Hiroshi Matsuo, *Denshirikkoku Nippon wo sodateta otoko* (in Japanese; English title: *Hidetsugu Yagi and Japanese innovators*), Bungei-shunjū, Tokyo, 1992.
8 Kazumasa Iinuma, *Ten outstanding scientists since Meiji – glimpses of Japan*, Kyōritsu Kenkyū Group, Tokyo, pp. 48–69.
9 Yutaka Aida, *Denshirikkoku Nippon no jijoden* (in Japanese; English title: *Autobiography of an electronic nation, Japan*), Vol. 1, Nippon Broadcasting Corporation, Tokyo, 1991.
10 Jun-ichi Nishizawa, *Nippon niokeru dokusō kagaku-gijutsu* (in Japanese; English title: *Innovative science and technology in Japan*), Gakushikai Kaihō No. 773, Tokyo, 1986 pp. 113–31.
11 T. Sashida and T. Kenjo, *An introduction to ultrasonic motors*, Oxford University Press, Oxford, 1993.
12 Kiichi Miyazawa, *Nippon keizai no korekara* (in Japanese; English title: *The future of Japan's economy*). Gakushikai Kaihō No. 703, Tokyo, 1969, pp. 33–43.
13 British Chamber of Commerce in Japan, *Seihin-ka: how Japan brings R&D to the market*, Tokyo, 1988.

10

Lessons for the West

'God grant me the serenity to accept the things I cannot change, the courage to change the things I can, and the wisdom to know the difference.'
– Reinhold Niebuhr

Introduction

This book has aimed to explain the fundamental reasons for Japan's astonishing commercial success in relation to its Western competitors. There are indeed aspects of Japan's approach which are unique, many of them for historical and cultural reasons. It should be equally clear, however, that the vast majority of the key lessons are applicable to any country, any organization, and every individual anywhere in the world.

The purpose of this chapter is to draw those lessons together in as simple and as structured a way as possible. The hope is that these lessons will act as a focus for action – which in many cases may be for no less a purpose than the survival of your organization.

A question of survival

If this seems in any way dramatic, it may be sobering to realize that Japan's Economic Planning Agency started a 2010 Technology Estimation Study Project in 1990. The objective was to select the 101 technologies which were thought likely to have a large impact on industries and economies between the mid-1990s and 2010, to predict the possibilities of putting them to practical use, and to analyse the nature of their probable impact.

The conclusions of this study are shown in Table 10.1. Japan predicts that, in terms of international comparison, it will by the year 2010 be exclusively top in 29 technologies, equal first in 24, second in 28, and third in 20. Furthermore, it predicts that 17 of these technologies will, by 2010, each exceed 1000 billion

Table 10.1. Conclusions of Japan's Economic Planning Agency's 2010 Technology Estimation Study Project (1990) – Japan's estimated ranking by the year 2010 in the world's 101 most important technologies

(A) *Technologies where Japan is expected to rank first or first-equal (with Japanese market-size estimations in billion [10⁹] yen where these have been estimated). Ranking is in terms of technology level, rather than market size.*

Japan is number one	Market size	Japan is first-equal	Market size
1. Terabit memories	3000	Super-intelligent chips	1000
2. Superconductor devices	1000	Self-breeding chips	3000
3. Terabit opto-files	2000	Opto-computing device equipment	1000
4. Terabit opto-communication devices	3000	Biocomputers	
5. Biosensors	2000	Super-parallel computers	2000
6. Neuro-computers	2000	Automatic translating systems	1000
7. Super-conductor materials	1000	Opto ICs	
8. New glass	1000	Molecular devices	10
9. Hydrogen-absorbing alloys		Dementia drugs	250
10. Magnetic materials		Immunity/allergy drugs	500
11. Fuel cells	200	Bioenergy	
12. Solar generators		Artificial organs	400
13. High-efficiency heat pumps	400	Videoconferencing systems	100
14. Intelligent robots	50	Videophones	10
15. AI–CNC	60	Wideband ISDN telecommunications	200
16. Hybrid machining centres	30	Opto subscription system	500
17. HDTV	3000	Opto LAN	30
18. Super-conducting linear vehicles		Next-generation automobiles	3000

Japan is number one	Market size	Japan is first-equal	Market size
19. Next-generation superconductor linear vehicles	1000	Innovative automobile manufacturing technology	500
20. Bimodal systems (hybrid transportation combining trains and trailers)	10	Ultra-high multi-storey buildings	200
21. Techno-superliners	100	Marine leisure land	10
22. Intelligent ships	100	CO_2 consolidation using catalysis	300
23. Gravitation-free underground laboratories	20	CO_2 consolidation using plants	
24. Linear-motor catapults	100	Underground water reservoirs	
25. Underground delivery networks	500		
26. Deep underground railways/roads	230		
27. Earth heat-reservoirs	15		
28. Marine stock farms	20		
29. Fluorocarbon-retrieving technology	100		

(B) *Technologies where Japan is expected to rank second or third (with Japanese market-size estimations in billion [10^9] yen).*

Japan is second	Market size	Japan is third	Market size
1. Virtual reality systems	1000	Ceramic gas turbines	
2. Self-breeding database systems	1000	Opto-chemical hole-burning memory	10
3. Semiconductor superlattice devices	500	High-performance CFRP	200

Table 10.1. *(cont.)*

Japan is second	Market size	Japan is third	Market size
4. Amorphous alloys		High-performance metal composite materials	100
5. Non-linear opto-electronic materials	10	High-performance ceramics composite	100
6. Heat-plasticity composite	10	High-performance C/C composite	10
7. Cancer drugs	400	Nuclear fusion	
8. Virus drugs	500	Ultra-super precision machines	15
9. Marrow bank		Intelligent CAD	30
10. Artificial enzymes		Product models	10
11. Modular light-water reactors	20	Concurrent engineering	30
12. High-speed breeder reactors	600	Personal communications equipment	160
13. Superconductivity power reservoirs	150	Aqua robots	10
14. Micromachines	30	Mass transportation aircraft	500
15. Self-independent distributed control	15	HST (Supersonic transportation aircraft)	500
16. YSAT/Satellite data networks	30	Small VTOL propeller aircraft	50
17. BS/CS–CATV (CS: Communications satellite; BS: Broadcasting satellite)	150	Small VTOL jet aircraft	100
18. HSST linear motor vehicles	10	Artificial islands	50
19. Advanced train-control systems	100	Floating systems	60
20. Satellite communication from cars	100	Naturally decaying plastics	500
21. Non-petrol fuel automobiles	500		
22. Surface effect vehicles	30		

Japan is second	Market size	Japan is third	Market size
23. Laboratory on the moon	500		
24. Ultra-large air dome	100		
25. High-storey building deconstruction technology	10		
26. CO_2 processing technology	100		
27. Gas replacement for fluorocarbons	80		
28. Underground scrap-treatment system	30		

yen (£6.25 billion) in market size, and another 54 will each exceed 100 billion yen (£625 million).

The need for a vision

The first, and most important, lesson is therefore the need for a very clear 'Vision' of where nations, organizations, and individuals are heading. Not only that, but such Visions need to be stated in terms which are easily understood; they need to be shared with, and communicated to, others; and they need to be real challenges that will stretch the competencies and resources of those involved. A good example of this from the past was President Kennedy's Vision of landing a man on the moon by the end of the 1960s.

An inspiring example for the future comes, not from the West, but another South-East Asian country – Malaysia. On 28 February 1991 Dr Mahathir Mohamad, the Prime Minister, set his country the objective of becoming a fully developed country by the year 2020. A number of specific targets were described, including the doubling of real gross domestic product every ten years between 1990 and 2020; allowing for a 2.5 per cent annual rate of population growth, this should lead to Malaysians being four times richer by the end of this plan. Furthermore, in order to publicize the objective, and to focus the contributions of all Malaysians, the Vision was given the catchy title of Vision 2020 (with a strong association with the pilot's term for perfect eyesight – 20–20 Vision).

At least one Japanese company is 50 years into its 250-year plan. Companies hardly need to look that far ahead; but they should certainly have a long-term business plan, extending at least 10 years forward, and ideally 20 to 25 years, within the context of which they are systematically developing their most important resource – their employees.

The importance of a cohesive system

While it is essential that nations on the one hand, and individuals at the other extreme, have such national and personal objectives clearly in mind, the hard fact is that it is organizations that actually create the key sources of wealth around the world. For it is organizations, on the whole, that co-ordinate the existing talents of their employees and that create the environment in which latent potential can be developed for the future benefit of all.

Most attempts by Western companies to emulate the successes of Japanese competitors have failed because they have tried to copy parts of the system, such as Quality Circles or Just-In-Time or Total Quality Management, and have not understood the vital need for a cohesive approach. By contrast, most attempts by Japanese companies to export their philosophies and techniques to other countries have in fact been successful. That is not to say that there have not been setbacks, or that Japan does not have many lessons still to learn in this area. But the hard fact is still there. How many failures have the Japanese moving overseas experienced? The answer is, not many. And the reason is very simple – Japanese companies have cohesive approaches which enable employees to provide quality products at competitive prices in response to customers' needs. Within such cohesive systems, mistakes may be made, but the elements still hang together and work successfully.

In his role as a consultant, the British author has had many opportunities to observe the difficulties which Western companies experience in developing the real potential contribution of employees to achieve the objectives of their businesses. A straightforward model which has helped many organizations to understand how they might do this much better is shown in Figure 10.1. This brings together the need for three essential elements which are almost invariably present in Japanese companies, but rarely in Western companies:

1. Commitment by individuals to their own self-development.
2. Competence in, and commitment to, coaching their employees by managers.
3. Organizations as a whole creating an environment in which learning at all levels really is taking place as effectively as possible.

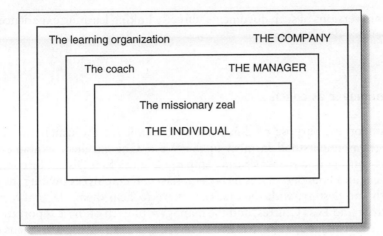

Fig. 10.1 A cohesive system of management.

The commitment of individuals

Only through systematic analysis of their learning and career development needs will individuals be able to achieve the *real* fulfilment of their abilities. In other words, everyone needs, as an absolute minimum, some form of Personal Development Plan. This should ideally include a summary of their educational and career achievements to date, together with some form of plan of how they intend to develop both of these in the future. There are many other possible contents of such documents, including:

- A record of all formal training experienced, together with the objectives agreed beforehand and the ways in which the learning has been applied and followed up afterwards.
- A summary of key lessons learnt day-to-day, including those from such sources as reading, conferences, and daily successes in the job.
- Professional activities.
- Community activities.
- Preparation for appraisals with managers, and a record of the outcomes and decisions.

One such document is The Institution of Electrical Engineers' Professional Development Record, which was originally suggested, partly designed, piloted, and launched in October 1987 by the British author in his capacity as Chairman of the Institution's Professional Development Committee. The 10 000th copy of this document was sold in 1992, with sales rising rapidly. Furthermore, this document is now also used, under licence, by the Institution of Mechanical Engineers. The British author is now developing software versions of such documents, directly linking learning experiences with competence development.

The manager as coach

One important purpose of this book is to challenge the usual concept of a manager as understood in most of the West. One excellent example of the correct concept is in the American company Digital: Ken Olsen, the company's President and Founder, places heavy emphasis on employees owning their own growth and destiny, with the manager there to help them. 'Digital has some 100 Profit and Loss Centres, and the managers of each of these report to senior managers, who internally are called "coaches". Their role is not to focus on the operation itself, but, instead, to make sure that the managers and their staff are capable of making a profit. This has been made very, very clear.'[1]

In contrast, the concept of management usually practised in North American and European companies is 'macho-management', with managers expected to achieve corporate targets themselves. They rush around making decisions themselves, when they are not involved in meetings, sending out memos, or sorting out their in-trays. The time they have left for developing the competencies and careers of their staff is minimal. They are not appointed because they are thought to be good at coaching their staff, nor are they trained to do it well; and their rewards in terms of salary reviews and promotion are largely disconnected from how well they perform in this area. No action is taken against them, for example, when all too frequently they discourage, and even prevent, their staff moving to another job within the organization (something which the British author often encountered in GEC). This often happens in Britain when employees have obtained two or three years' experience in a job, and their managers see them as indispensable.

In order to compete with the Japanese, all these faults of management must be corrected.

It is absolutely essential, too, that managers are given the skills to coach effectively. Sadly, most British managers have never learnt the skills of coaching, mainly because they have never been coached themselves. They therefore neither understand the enormous power coaching can give in releasing the real potential in their staff, nor do they feel confident enough to do coaching. Most importantly, they do not give coaching any priority and therefore *time*.

The technique that must be used **needs to start from the employee's agenda** and complement the use of Personal Development Plans. If this does not happen, then individuals will in only a minority of cases commit themselves to difficult, and often apparently impossible, objectives.

It must never be forgotten that the prime purpose of an organization, whether it be profits, market share, or anything else, can only be achieved through the combined efforts of all employees. The 'added value' of managers is to maximize this contribution. Figure 10.2 emphasizes this in graphical form – with Comfort, Stretch, and Panic zones. Ideally individuals, in concert with their managers, should be 'riding a wave' at the border between Stretch and Panic.

The challenge facing managers is how to move their employees into this Stretch zone. One technique adopted all too often is the use of fear, linked to 'Management by Objectives'. In the short run, this can undoubtedly work. Indeed, there is often an element of this approach in Japan; companies have a range of sanctions which effectively force employees to work long hours and take minimal holidays. However, the West does not usually have the same range of sanctions – employees are much freer to move to another company than is often the case in Japan. There are too many obvious negative results from managing by fear – high levels of stress and lack of real commitment by employees being just two of them. Rather than the use of authoritarian styles of management, therefore, the real lesson for Western managers is to learn the art of developing employees from their Japanese counterparts. This will most often require a change in management style and a drastic reassessment of the whole purpose of being a manager.

The results, however, which managers will find they can elicit from their staff will be quite remarkable. For a start, they will find that the respect in which they are held will rise enormously.

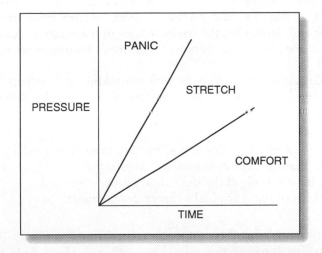

Fig. 10.2 Comfort, stretch, and panic zones. Most people in the West spend a lot of their working time in the Comfort Zone. Many more people in Japan, and high achievers in other countries, set their goals in the Stretch Zone, and grow as a consequence. The Panic Zone is where technique collapses and personal effectiveness goes to pieces.

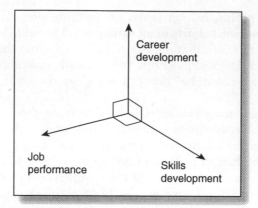

Fig. 10.3 Appraisals – the three factors.

The company as a learning organization

Most potential learning from formal training courses is much less valuable than it could be. The reason is simply that the environment at the workplace is not supportive of learning. The course is either not properly identified by the manager for its relevance to the employee or it is not effectively followed up.

These problems are merely the tip of a much more serious iceberg of a problem. As a starting-point, the value system of the organization must encompass the concept of management outlined in the previous section. **The reward, promotion, and formal training systems must be centred on encouraging and developing the competencies of managers as coaches.** In the process, of course, these managers will themselves become more rounded and experienced.

As one illustration, let us look at why most Appraisal systems fail to have any significant impact in Western companies, and rapidly degenerate into paperwork exercises. Appraisals are usually about three things:

1. Improvement in job performance, usually centred around a classic Peter Drucker 'management by objectives' approach.
2. Developing the skills of the individuals being appraised.
3. Furtherance of the individual's career development.

If we treat these as being three-dimensional, as shown in Figure 10.3, it may be instructive to compare this with Fleming's Left-Hand Rule for Motors (both authors are Electrical Engineers), shown in Figure 10.4. In the latter, the motion only takes place when a current flows in an electrical conductor placed in a magnetic field. Similarly, improvement in job performance only takes place in most cases (it is of course sometimes possible to achieve this by luck or through fear) through systematic improvement in an individual's skills development in the context of a planned development of his or her career. And yet most appraisal meetings concentrate almost exclusively on trying to improve job performance *per se*; this is no more likely to be successful than is an electric motor to turn without a source of current. Certainly in the West far fewer managers than in Japan have any real understanding of how to develop the skills and careers of their staff, and this is another major reason why the typical Appraisal meeting spends very little time on these two areas. A further analogy is that an electric motor needs to be enclosed in some kind of structure; and we can draw a parallel here with the coaching environment, which works so well in Japan, and has also been shown in many organizations to work extremely effectively in the West.

Appraisals should be a check that all is well, and an opportunity to review skills, career, and performance. There should be no surprises, and that should be because managers who coach well will discuss these matters regularly with their staff throughout the year. From the individual's point of view, furthermore, these ongoing discussions will be focused through their use of Personal Development Plans to set themselves clear targets and to maximize their learning.

Electric motors, commutation, and feedback – analogies for employee development

The whole concept of developing the skills and careers of employees is so badly flawed in the West – and it is so key a part of Japan's success – that this analogy between electromagnetism and employee development can

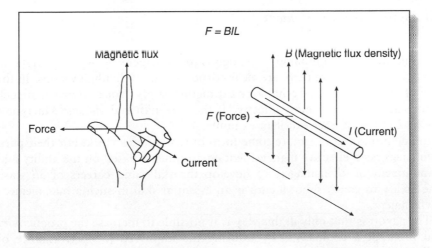

Fig. 10.4 Fleming's Left-Hand Rule for Motors.

usefully be explored further, in order to illustrate and emphasize some very important lessons.

The cohesive system

In Figure 10.4, basic physics in the form of Fleming's Left-Hand Rule for Motors shows three components – two of them are causes (Magnetic Flux,B, and Electric Current, I) and one is an effect (Force, F, which leads to movement in an electric motor).
Let us draw an analogy as follows:

Magnetic Field B >>>> Furtherance of an individual's career development.

Electric Current I >>>> Developing the skills of individuals, with continuous flow between periodic appraisals.

Force F >>>> Continuous improvement in job performance is thereby created.

The force (in a motor) only appears when a current flows in a conductor placed in a magnetic field. Similarly, improvement in job performance only takes place through systematic improvement in an individual's skills development in the context of a planned development of his or her career. This may seem very obvious, but how often does this actually happen in the West? In Japan, in contrast, it is an inherent and very effective component of everyday management values and activities.

An appropriate environment

Let us take this analogy further. An electric motor needs to be designed with a specific application in mind – analogous to 'management by objectives' – in an environment where there are clear corporate and individual visions. In the case of Japan, the 2010 Technology Estimation Study Project shows that such visions are that much more effective if they are national visions. Malaysia's Vision 2020 is another excellent example.

In addition, motors require some form of structure to work. For their part, companies need effective management environments based on the ability and commitment of *all* managers to develop the skills and careers of *all* staff. The ability to coach subordinates is an essential skill in such a management environment.

The payoff is that only in this way is it possible to increase the productivity and profit of a company – by utilizing the improved job performance of individuals.

Achieving continuity

Electric motors need some sort of mechanism for translating the incoming electric current, from a source such as a battery, into the current flowing through the coils, which in turn creates the rotation of the motor interacting with a magnetic field.

Let us take the case of a direct-current electric motor, as shown in Figure 10.5. The stationary part of the motor is called the stator, and it possesses magnets to provide magnetic flux, through which a rotor revolves. The rotor carries wires (coils) in which a current flows to create a torque by an interaction with the flux. In this model, wires are wound around the cylindrical iron core of the rotor and fixed with glue. The wires of the coil are connected via a number of terminals to a device called a 'commutator', which consists of copper blocks insulated from each other. Figure 10.6 shows the cross-section of the rotor with the current flowing into all the wires on the left-hand side and out of those on the right-hand side. Since the magnetic fields on each side of the stator are of opposite polarity, the forces creating motion on each side are complementary to each other – and the motor turns.

Each wire can be compared to an **individual** in an organization. The

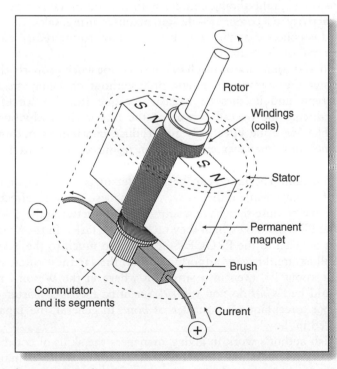

Fig. 10.5 A direct-current electric motor.

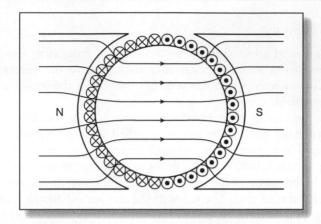

Fig. 10.6 Cross-section of the rotor in a direct-current electric motor.

mechanism which organizes the proper direction of current in each wire is the commutator (**the managers**), connected to the incoming direct current by two carbon 'brushes' (**the directors**). The current from the positive terminal of a battery is supplied through one of the two carbon brushes and *distributed* into the coils through the sliding contact with the commutator segments. The current (**the activity in a company – design, manufacturing, sales**) flows around the coils, and is collected at the other brush to flow to the return path to the negative terminal of the battery.

If the brush and commutator mechanism does not work properly then some coils may enter the opposite magnetic pole without changing the direction of their current, and in these a negative torque (turning force) will be produced, reducing the overall power of the motor. It is obvious that to exploit the Fleming Rule effectively to produce continuous output power, proper commutation (**management of human resources**) is required.

Fleming's Rule is a statement of scientific truth, while commutation is a technique or a skill. The latter can be a matter of engineering or it can be a question of management. Either way, the Japanese are very effective. And they are effective because they have a sound balance between the **TASKS** they tackle and the **PROCESS** by which they tackle those tasks. In the West far too little thought is given to the PROCESS and far too much to the TASKS. For example, to illustrate this very important point, the Japanese often say '*How* do you think about it?' even in a situation where in the Western mind the question would be '*What* do you think?' Scientific fact is a matter of *what*, while a skill or a technique is a matter of *how*. In general, the Japanese are more interested in 'how'.

In the British author's work in giving managers the skills of coaching their staff more effectively, it is the 'how' types of questions which managers tend not to ask and which they need to be shown in order to be much more effective. For example, managers with the necessary skills and confidence will be encouraged to ask 'How did you feel about that?' at the end of a meeting they have just chaired. In other words they are building not only process skills into the organization, but also feedback.

Stepping motors and dynamic performance

Let us next look at the *stepping motor*; this is a motor which is compatible with digital techniques, and is widely used in computers and other types of numerically-controlled equipment. This type of motor uses a different concept of commutation, also using semiconductors, but without feedback. Figure 10.7 shows the key parts: rotor and stator. The stator has six iron poles with a coil, and each pole has fine teeth for small precise motion or positioning control. The gear-like rotor is of iron as well. The principle is much easier than that of the DC motor. First, Poles 1 and 4 are magnetically excited by the current, and as a result the tooth surfaces are aligned under these poles. At the other poles the teeth are out of alignment. When the current is switched to Poles 2 and 5, the rotor will revolve clockwise a little (to be precise, a third of a tooth pitch). When the current is next switched to Poles 3 and 6, the rotor will make another one-third of a pitch rotation. Commutation or switching of current is implemented with transistors, and the commutation signals are supplied to the system over a frequency range which can be safely followed by the motor. The higher the motor's dynamic performance, the higher the stepping rate which can be used.

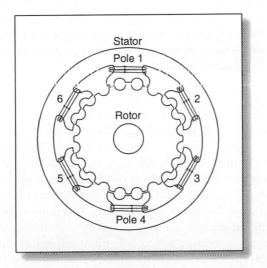

Fig. 10.7 Rotor and stator in a stepping motor. Poles 1 and 4 are in series; poles 2 and 5 are in series; poles 3 and 6 are in series.

When this analogy is applied to the administration of Japanese technical staff, the parallel is that they are thoroughly well educated, and that this is a basis for very systematic training using a combination of OJT and OffJT, with the result that they can be given quick commands with few risks of errors in their implementation.

The principle of the fine-tooth stepping motor was invented in 1919 by C.L. Walker, a Scottish civil engineer. About thirty years later in the USA an invention was made to combine this principle with a permanent magnet, to produce a small, powerful motor. This was named the hybrid stepping motor. Yet it is the Japanese who are the world's largest manufacturers of hybrid motors. This was achieved through their efforts in a combination of areas such as material development, precision techniques, manufacturing engineering, and the education and training of engineers and technicians. The British had the vision, but it was the Japanese who achieved it!

The importance of feedback for quicker fulfilment

To complete our electrical engineering analogy, let us discuss the concept of 'feedback'. Japanese management and training does indeed involve a considerable amount of feedback, supported by strong systems of control. Highly effective suggestion schemes and quality control systems, ahead of anything elsewhere in the world, are obvious examples.

A stepping motor features a positioning accuracy with a simple mechanism and electronics, but its drawback is that the safe acceleration is limited so as not to cause any step failure. However, if we employ feedback in the commutation mechanism, the motor speed can be increased considerably as its dynamic performance is maximized. For this, some means is needed to detect the rotor position in a stepping motor. If a commutation signal is applied with proper timing with reference to the rotor angle, the rotor can accelerate to its maximum speed without any motion failure.

This technique has been intensively studied by American engineers and British academics, as well as the Japanese. However, it is the Japanese who have clearly understood that **FEEDBACK** is one of the most important facets of management, just as in motor design. This is clearly understood in Japan; Japanese management is built on this principle, and it is no coincidence, surely, that Japanese technology in high-precision motors leads the world as well!

One interesting practical example of this feedback in operation concerns the Japanese author. Before the manufacture of stepping motors became significant in Japan, he wrote a book[2] on this subject. As companies in Japan decided to produce stepping motors for use in sewing machines, for example, their engineers, foremen, salesmen, and middle management all bought a copy each to read together after work each evening – the objective being to have the project up and running as fast as possible. Similar approaches must have been employed in many companies, since the engineering book concerned has attained enormous sales in the industrial sector for several years. In other words, feeding back the benefits of new knowledge as quickly as possible has been a major reason for Japan's success.

Maximizing internal expertise

Many organizations fail to maximize the use of their own expertise and know-how to grow and develop. Two key elements are necessary:

1. *TIME*. For example, allocating one hour each week for each employee for this activity.
2. *STRUCTURE*. Learning activities must be planned and controlled.

Some examples of useful practical activities are:

- Lunchtime/evening/worktime seminars
- Team group meetings structured as learning events
- Brief summary documents circulated with key information/lessons/action following training activities
- Summary sheets of activities and learning from the previous week presented and circulated to colleagues
- Planned distribution of documentation to maximize learning in the organization.
- Short-term secondments and projects
- Work-shadowing
- Mentoring, using experienced employees to accelerate the learning and development of those less experienced
- 'Conferences', as described in Chapter 6.

A structured approach to formal training

Much more thought could be given to this whole area by Western organizations, in place of the 'scatter gun' philosophy so often seen.

For example, is it not reasonable to ensure that no one is appointed to a supervisory or management position until he or she has been formally trained in the necessary skills? And why not take this a stage further, as the Japanese do, and require such promotees to pass an associated exam successfully?

How rigorous are the selection systems for appointing individuals to technical or management positions? In most Western organizations there is not only little rigour in these, but there are relatively few of them which have clearly identified the skills that are needed for such appointments.

Another simple lesson from Chapter 6 is that Management Training should be less about the theory of finance, marketing, industrial relations, and so on, and much more about those in senior positions passing on the benefits of their successes and failures to junior and middle-level managers.

Equally, technical training should be rather more along the lines of Japanese style Technical Training Institutes, where front-end practitioners are seconded to pass on their expertise to more junior colleagues.

For such management and technical training both to be successful, the organization must have an appropriate system of values. Senior staff must readily give time and priority to these activities, and so the importance of Figure 10.1 must yet again emphasized.

Skills databases

Organizations which have a detailed and accurate knowledge of the competences of all their employees will have an important strategic advantage over their competitors. How else will they win commercial battles, other than by bringing their expertise to bear in the right way and at the right time on the commercial battlefield?

The many commercial battles lost by North American and European companies to the Japanese can surely be no surprise. The Japanese make extensive use of skills databases, while few Western companies do so. And yet these are increasingly practicable, given the power of the modern generation of computers and the availability of relational databases.

Without such detailed knowledge of where the expertise lies in their organization, how do larger organizations know where to look for the people they employ who can solve the day-by-day challenges that are faced? And how can any effective forward manpower or skills development planning be implemented by companies that have only the haziest understanding of their current skills bases?

Towards the multiskilled employee

Far too few employees realize the real capacities and skills that they are capable of achieving. One of the important benefits implied in Figure 10.1 is that people developed systematically in such organizations will be much more flexible. As marketplaces become faster-changing and society becomes more complicated, with more rapid communication of information, for example, flexibility in employees will increasingly be a factor differentiating successful organizations from the rest. Indeed, it seems increasingly evident that much of Japan's relative success can be explained in this way.

Broader training and experience will remain of great importance. The Japanese approach of ensuring that all university graduates are given extensive early experience in production and marketing is a very good example of the type of lesson that must be taken to heart by both companies and individuals.

Education is a vitally important foundation

It is surely no coincidence that the most successful industrial nations, such as Germany, the Republic of Korea, and Japan also have the most effective education systems. Korea, for example, already has more students entering higher education (36 per cent) than the 33 per cent target for Britain for the year 2000.

There are at least three reasons why this should be no surprise. First, individuals who have weak educational qualifications, such as most of the British, have much weaker foundations on which to develop practical skills or their further education throughout the rest of their careers and lives. Second, those with poor qualifications have not developed, by definition, the skills to learn, which again severely handicaps them for the rest of their lives. Third, those demonstrating the ability to pass exams that are stretching have also demonstrated the degree of self-discipline and attention to detail without which they will have little chance of developing their true potential in the future.

Educationists in Britain, for example, who are strongly opposed to teaching mathematical tables by rote and correcting spelling and grammatical mistakes made by their pupils, are doing them a gross disservice. It is significant that parents readily realize this, and one must hope that common sense will eventually prevail in those many parts of Western education which have been influenced by those sociological theories advocating child-centred education at the expense of self-discipline and hard work. Germany is an excellent illustration that it is unnecessary to go to Japanese extremes to provide a sound and disciplined system of education that is highly effective.

The other common factor amongst these leading industrial nations, it must be observed, is that they also produce large numbers of technically qualified people.

Let us learn from each other internationally

This book has been written by two authors, one British and the other Japanese, who have learnt much from each other over the past few years, resulting in this joint publication. We urge all readers, wherever they may be in the world, to encourage international learning, for all nations have their own special contribution to make to improving approaches to education, training, and management.

From our standpoint, therefore, we hope that this book will further international understanding and co-operation. If the lessons we have drawn in this chapter in any way seem a little simplistic, then the reason for that is readily explained. The lessons from Japan's successes are indeed simple ones and readily transferred, contrary to popular perceptions in the West.

The great strength of Japan is that people are, on the whole, treated with individual dignity, and individuals are prepared to co-operate together for the greater good of everyone. They believe in professionalism, in paying great attention to detail, and in making the utmost effort to satisfy the needs of their customers. Should any one of us require any less than this either of ourselves or of others?

References

1 John Lorriman, *Continuing professional development – the practical guide to good practice*, The Engineering Council, London, December 1991, p. 9.
2 Takashi Kenjo, *Stepping motors and their microprocessor controls*, Oxford University Press, 1984 (English version).

11

Fifty years on from the Second World War – the implications for Japan

'To go too far is as wrong as to fall too short'
Chinese proverb

The rising yen

The 22 June 1994 was a very significant day in Japan's history – greater than perhaps most people realized. For that was the day when, for the first time, the Japanese yen became more highly valued than the United States' cent.

As it happened, that day both authors were also delegates at the first day of a conference on lifelong learning taking place on the northern outskirts of Tokyo and organized by the Organisation for Economic Co-operation and Development (OECD). The American delegate at that conference seemed unable to appreciate the magnitude of the defeat which the USA had suffered at the hands of the Japanese; this defeat has been entirely as a result of the much greater ability of Japan to implement an effective lifelong learning strategy at individual, group, corporate, and national levels.

So why had the yen appreciated so dramatically in the previous years (by two and a half times since the mid-1980s)? And why has the US dollar continued to decline so fast, as shown in Figure 11.1?

There seem to be two arguments put forward by the international economic experts. The more prevalent one argues that Japan has failed to open its markets to imports. The alternative explanation, less frequently heard, is that the USA has quite simply failed to compete commercially in world markets as effectively as has Japan. After all, is it Japan's fault if American industry and consumers are eager to buy Japanese cars, electronics, etc.? The USA's trade deficit with Japan was $41 billion in 1991, which rose to $65 billion in 1994 despite a 40 per cent fall in the value of the dollar.

No doubt there is truth in both arguments. Japan has undoubtedly made it very difficult for importers and one frequently hears stories such as the notorious one about the Japanese Government once refusing to grant an

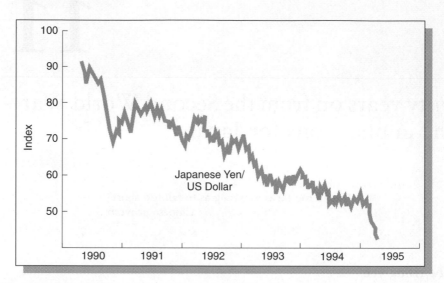

Fig. 11.1 The decline of the US dollar, 1990–1995. *Source: Daily Telegraph* 19 April 1995.

import licence to European skis with the justification that Japanese snow is different from European snow! (Nowadays there are more European ski brands on sale in Japan than Japanese ones.) Japan certainly does herself no favours by such behaviour. Equally, however, the evidence does seem to be that other countries have made less strenuous efforts to export to Japan than Japanese exporters have made. For example, US car manufacturers have only recently started exporting right-hand drive cars to Japan.

There is also a heavy penalty paid by the Japanese for the rapidly rising value of the yen. The Yamaichi Research Institute of Securities and Economics estimated in 1993 that every time the dollar's value fell by 1 yen, Japan's motor and electronics industries suffered combined losses equivalent to £333 million a year. Between June 1994 and April 1995 the dollar continued falling, from 100 yen to the dollar, to an exchange rate of less than 80 yen. The impact on Japanese industry, particularly those parts heavily reliant on exports, has been extremely painful. Using Yamaichi's estimates, that 20 per cent fall in the dollar will be costing the motor and electronics industries alone a combined loss of over £6 billion a year.

The impact on the Japanese consumer is high as well. Despite having an average household income of over $80 000 a year, the Japanese have to pay 2.3 times as much for their food than do Europeans. This is partly because of their highly inefficient distribution system in Japan, with many middle men between the producer and the consumer; this system in itself discourages importers from selling their products in Japan, reducing competition and raising prices. However, it is partly because those goods which are imported have become considerably more expensive with a rising yen.

From a psychological point of view, the Japanese have always seen themselves as poor and the rising yen will do nothing to change that or to encourage them to work less hard and to take more leisure. Even housing in Japan remains disastrously high, with a small home in Tokyo costing the equivalent of some $700 000.

Japan is facing some dramatic changes

It is not just the rapidly appreciating yen which has caused problems for the Japanese. Other changes create major opportunities for Japan, while events in Japan necessarily have significant impacts in other countries.

A 2 year chronology as follows illustrates this well.

18 June 1993	Prime Minister Miyazawa's Cabinet collapses, ending 38 years of political domination by the Liberal Democratic Party.
29 July 1993	A non-Communist coalition is formed and appoints Mr Morihiro Hosokawa as their Prime Ministerial candidate. He is elected in early August.
8 April 1994	Mr Hosokawa resigns as Prime Minister and is replaced by Mr Tsutomu Hata.
22 June 1994	The US dollar falls below 100 yen.
25 June 1994	Prime Minister Hata resigns. Socialist Prime Minister Mr T. Murayama is elected in a coalition of the Liberal Democratic Party, the Socialist Party and Sakigake.
17 January 1995	A massive earthquake devastates the city of Kobe, killing over 5000 people and leaving over a quarter of a million homeless.
26 February 1995	Barings, Britain's oldest investment bank, is bankrupted as a result of futures arbitrage trading contracts on the Nikkei 225, which plummets after the massive Kobe earthquake.
20 March 1995	Twelve die and over 5000 are injured in a sarin poison gas attack on the Tokyo metro.
30 March 1995	The merger is announced between Mitsubishi Bank and the Tokyo Bank, creating the world's largest bank. (The world's eight largest banks are all Japanese.)
16 May 1995	Aum sect leader, Shōkō Asahara, is arrested on suspicion of murder and attempted murder in connection with the nerve gas attack on 20 March.

9 June 1995	The Japanese Government adopts an anti-war resolution, which is significant in the nation's parliamentary history.
28 June 1995	Mr Ryūtarō Hashimoto and Mr Mickey Kantor reach an agreement after a long US–Japan trade dispute over automobiles.
15 August 1995	The fiftieth anniversary of Japan's surrender in the Second World War. Prime Minister Tomi-ichi Murayama acknowledges the damage and suffering inflicted upon other countries by Japan's colonial rule and aggression.
26 September 1995	Daiwa Bank, Japan's tenth largest commercial bank, announces that one of its traders in its New York office has run up 110 billion yen (£700 million) losses in bond dealing.
5 October 1995	Japan's seven trust banks agree to liquidate Jyuso, the housing loan company they founded twenty years ago, now virtually insolvent under a pile of non-performing loans. Jyuso is one of eight housing loan companies, most of which are not technically insolvent.

It is worth looking at two of these events in a balanced context.

First the earthquake in Kobe, which came as a major shock, not least because it had been predicted that such a large earthquake would be in Tokyo and certainly not in Kobe. Many of the victims survived the first shock, but died in the subsequent fires. These disastrous fires were caused by the pilot lights of the central heating systems, which readily set light to the wooden structures of the majority of houses. The Japanese had not reinforced these houses with a steel box construction, which might have survived the earthquake, nor did the central heating systems have automatic shut-off systems. Unfortunately the local gas company had no means for closing the local supply remotely, and the result was a deadly inferno. Better known is that the local government failed to make a formal request to the Self Defence Forces (Japan's army) for assistance for a crucial 2 or 3 hours. It seems that the local government was unaware that a formal request was necessary, while the Self Defence Forces were not programmed to intervene without a formal request. If the mobilization had taken place sooner, then it is thought that 2000 more lives would have been saved. In addition, the central government took 48 hours merely to grant permission to foreign rescue teams to visit Kobe, and took a week before declaring that the shattered city was a disaster zone.

The assumption made by the Japanese that their famed *Shinkansen* ('bullet train') system was earthquake-proof turned out to be wrong. Indeed, when in the early hours of 17 January 1995, Mr M. Ide, President of JR Western Japan, was awakened by the enormous sudden swaying of his house, he asked his daughter to drive him to the local Rokkomichi JR station; he found the station buildings collapsed, with the bridges' concrete-supporting iron rods exposed. As he walked along the damaged railroad, he said to himself:

'With the conventional railroads so badly damaged, we will have to use the Shinkansen to bypass them for several months.' Little did he imagine that much of the Shinkansen system, of which the Japanese have been so proud, had also been put out of action. If the earthquake had occurred just 14 minutes later, when the trains had started running, then the disaster would have been much worse.

Later it was found that waste from wooden frames had been mixed in the concrete for the railway supports, beach sand had been used for the concrete, and there had been incomplete treatment of the joints used in the construction of the Sanyo Shinkansen. The result was that the damage was many times greater than it should have been. To put these shortcomings into context, when the Sanyo Shinkansen was constructed, the total amount of concrete used across Japan equalled 100 years of use in the USA and Europe. (The Han River bridge collapse in South Korea in 1994 showed that fast growing economies can lead to contraventions of public safety elsewhere too.) Now it has been shown that there are a very large number of constructions across Japan which need reinforcement as soon as possible – but who will pay for these and when? This is an enormous problem faced by the Japanese Government and people.

Several months after this terrible disaster, the government had still not devised a comprehensive relief plan. Admittedly the government said that they would demolish earthquake-damaged buildings without charge and offered cheap loans for rebuilding homes and businesses. However, the system for applying for these benefits was so complicated that many victims had little idea of how to make claims.

Almost half of the 13 500 one-man shops affected by the earthquake were expected to stay closed permanently.

Thus, many of Japan's inherent weaknesses (such as paralysis by bureaucracy and the sacrifice by the common man for the benefit of the major industrial corporations) were exposed by this terrible natural calamity. On the other hand, despite considerable damage to the Shinkansen system, repairs were effected so efficiently and rapidly that full service across the whole system was restored by mid-April. The collapse of the Sanyo Shinkansen system was also alleviated by the provision of alternative connections by air; between 17 January and 21 March, All Nippon Airways made 1500 non-regular flights and JAL another 885.

The second disaster that needs to be seen in context is the sarin gas attack on the Tokyo metro system. This was particularly shocking to a Japanese nation which is used to seeing itself, rightly, as the most crime-free nation in the world. The massive police searches of the Aum sect buildings across Japan seemed to be the response of what is probably the world's most efficient police system, but in fact they had already been scheduled by a police force suspicious of the cult following the death of seven people by an unknown gas on the night of 27 June 1994 in Matsumoto in the Nagano prefecture. Unfortunately the sarin gas attack on the Tokyo metro took place 2 days before the date scheduled for the raids.

Mutual responsibility is of prime importance – but is being re-examined

As we have seen in earlier chapters, greater responsibility is taken by Japanese leaders for any failures in their organizations than is generally seen in the West. For example, after the Recruit Company scandal in 1989, senior executives in NTT, which was heavily implicated, agreed to cut their salaries by up to 20 per cent. The Prime Minister, Noboru Takeshita, resigned in order to take 'political and ethical responsibility' for the scandal in which many politicians and industrialists reaped large profits from shares sold cheaply by an information services conglomerate, the Recruit Company. A day later, one of Mr Takeshita's key aides, Ihei Aoki, committed suicide by slashing his wrists and hanging himself; this was seen as following in the tradition of the samurai warriors, as a way of accepting the guilt himself and preserving the honour of the master he had served for over 30 years. One of the many other examples was that of Taizō Hashida, who resigned as Chairman of Fuji Bank, one of Japan's largest banks, in October 1991, taking responsibility for a series of financial scandals; at the same time a number of other directors in the bank took salary cuts in recognition of their corporate responsibility.

In the case of the Kobe disaster, this sense of national responsibility was reflected in the cancellation of many holidays, sports, and leisure events. This is known as *jishuku* or self-restraint. Even if Japanese live far from a disaster or do not know anyone involved, they still tend to forego enjoyable events in deference to those who have suffered. For example, Keiko Kobayashi had been planning a holiday in Australia to escape the cold winter in Tokyo. However, she had doubts about doing so, saying 'I started feeling sort of guilty about taking a trip.' Mitsuru Inuta, Professor of Social Psychology at Tokai University near Tokyo, explains that Japanese tend to feel guilty about conspicuous consumption and self-restraint comes readily at times of national crisis. However, younger Japanese are becoming more individualistic and Professor Inuta says the custom of *jishuku* is losing ground. For example, the Crown Prince went ahead with a 1-week trip to the Middle East shortly after the earthquake. Another example was that sponsors of a high school spring baseball tournament at Koshien Stadium in Nishinomiya, Hyogo Prefecture, which was hit by the earthquake, decided to reject suggestions that they cancel the event entirely; however, the sponsors did decide to cut short the opening ceremony and not allow brass bands into the stadium. And in the case of Keiko Kobayashi, she had second thoughts and ended up going on her holiday to Sydney after all, although many overseas trips by the Japanese were cancelled in the aftermath of the Kobe disaster.

Another positive aspect of this ethic of mutual responsibility is illustrated by a reunion which the Japanese author attended a few years ago of his university class 20 years after graduating. During a late-night discussion among his colleagues, many of them eminent engineers and senior executives of large companies, one described his dilemma as follows:

My father died last year and my mother is living alone at the house where I was born and brought up with my brothers. Since I am the eldest son, the inheritor, I am worrying about whether or not to leave my present firm so as to return to my native place to look after my mother and the ancestral property. I hope to hear opinions from those who are in a similar situation.

Another colleague said

From the day of my birth as the eldest son of a peasant couple, I have been fated to inherit the soil of my ancestors and to take care of my old parents. As you know, I worked for a company in Tokyo for several years and designed calculators. I really enjoyed this job. A few years later, a technical junior college was built in my home town in Aomori, and I was offered a post there. Since my previous job in my company had been arranged through Professor Wada, I called on him and explained my situation. After having listened to me, he said, 'Well, do you really think that you are sufficiently qualified to be a college lecturer?' He, however, eventually understood me and allowed me to move to my present position. Now I have a favour to ask of you. In the country, there are lots of boys who were born as the eldest sons like myself. They wish to live in their birthplaces with their parents, welcoming brides from nearby villages or towns. But no good jobs are provided for these young men. So, when you have become executives in the future, please build factories in small towns in the north-east region.

It is interesting to note, as well, the need for this colleague to obtain permission from Professor Wada to move to a new job. This is illustrative of the strong influence which Japanese professors have on the careers of both their present and past pupils.

Some effects of the bursting Japanese bubble

Japan is indeed changing, although, like a great ship of state, it is often changing slowly and in ways which are sometimes difficult to detect.

One noticeable change is one which will undoubtedly please some of the colleagues of the Japanese author at the reunion mentioned above. There are definite changes in favour of smaller towns and smaller companies. For example, the cost of land in Tokyo and large towns after the economic bubble burst in the early 1990s, with the stock market plunging and land costs dropping, have been decreasing but are still excessive. In contrast there are different sights seen in the country.

Laws were enacted to implement measures to prevent over-population in large towns and to promote the development of local areas. One interesting example of people's reaction to this policy is seen in Tsuruoka, located on the Sea-of-Japan coast and which was formerly the castle town of a local lord and which has a unique culture. A central government grant of some 10 billion yen was spent on three areas of Tsuruoka: the town centre, including the castle ruins (now a park), a residential suburb, and a highway interchange area. It was expected that various developments using public capital and projects would be stimulated as a result of these governmental projects.

The construction of a 'doctor street' in this town deserves special mention. As is seen in Figure 11.2, several individual modern hospitals have been constructed, along with a street, in a paddyfield area connecting the town centre and the highway interchange. Enthusiastic bankers, real-estate agencies with foresight, and ambitious landowners have been co-operative in encouraging young medical doctors of good reputation to build hospitals, with several built even before the new governmental policy began to be enacted.

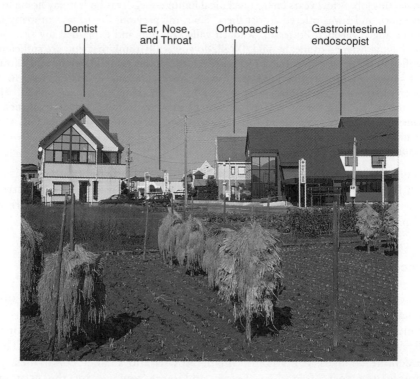

Dentist · Ear, Nose, and Throat · Orthopaedist · Gastrointestinal endoscopist

Fig. 11.2. Individual hospitals built in the Shinkai-cho area of Tsuruoka, a town with a population of 100 000 in North East Japan. The hospitals provide an orthopaedist, a dentist, a gastrointestinal endoscopist, and an ear, nose and throat specialist. The waiting rooms of these hospitals serve as community facilities for old people who come as patients from surrounding farming areas.

Because of the improved public drainage in such local towns, newly built flats are fully occupied. Office buildings are either single or two-storeys high, with plenty of parking space. As a result of progress in transportation, communication, and computers, work which used to be best suited to large towns can be done effectively remote from Tokyo. Thus, local towns have been doing their best to welcome back people who migrated to the cities in earlier years.

In contrast, the most symbolic impact in Tokyo has been the cancellation of the planned World City Expo, which had been planned in conjunction with the waterfront redevelopment of Tokyo's harbour; both of these cancellations formed part of the election platform of the newly elected Tokyo governor, Yukio Aoshima, in 1995, and were generally welcomed by a population tired of ever expanding the size of the city and its public festivals.

Another aspect of the bursting of the bubble economy concerns the recruitment of graduates. Until the early 1990s the large companies recruited most of the best graduates, as well as many of the less able ones, making it very difficult for the smaller and medium-sized companies to recruit the graduates they needed. By the mid-1990s, however, some large companies did not recruit any graduates at all – and even recognized that they had over-recruited in previous years. Nevertheless, it is still difficult for small or medium-sized firms to recruit computer science graduates from universities in the Tokyo area.

Some of the smaller companies are now pleased that they are at last able to attract the recruits they need, and there are successful and growing companies in many local towns. In the spring of 1995, the Japanese author had the opportunity to visit International Automation Industries, one such company in his home town of Shimizu. He was flattered when an engineer told him that the company staff had studied mechatronics by careful study of his books and have successfully designed a range of convenient robots. The founder of this company, Mr Shōji Ishida, retired from Hitachi in the mid-1970s at the age of 60 years and started the company as a sub-contractor to Hitachi. One of his sons, who had also worked for Hitachi for a number of years, then joined the company as well. Initially they restricted themselves to supplying Hitachi only, but real success came when, through trial and error, they developed their own designs for other markets. Since they became fully independent of Hitachi in the mid-1980s, the company has been expanding their markets as far afield as North America and Europe.

Changing Japanese personnel and wage systems

As Chapter 5 explained, most Japanese organizations have for a long time used a salary system linked strongly with the age of employees and their number of years of experience in the organization. However, the bursting of the economic bubble and the rising yen are forcing noticeable changes on this traditional system. An analysis of these changes over recent years is as follows.

1955   The pre-war status-oriented wage system changes to a guaranteed lifetime employment system. This takes into account the employee's age and family size. Suffering from poaching of skilled workers by rivals, companies introduce a seniority pay system to prevent this loss.

1965   The seniority system of pay progression is deeply embedded across Japan. Reconsideration of its merits starts. Some companies start introducing an American-style job-responsibility system.

1975   The economic high growth rate era. Increase in use of the seniority plus job-responsibility salary system.

1985   Reassessment of the assessment systems. As a result of the oil shock, there are fewer jobs available and several salary systems often run in parallel in a company.

1992   A move away from the seniority system and a movement towards an annual salary or payment-by-results system. However, this is not implemented in the same way as in the USA. Instead the typical system gives a maximum annual increase between 0 and 10 per cent, with no decreases. This is because a pure North American payment-by-results system has the following disadvantages.

1. If the payment system is based too much on short-term results, then long-range objectives cannot effectively be realized.

2. Over-hard work could damage the employees' health.

3. If employees' pay either does not increase or even falls, then they will feel uncomfortable and will leave the company, which is likely to be a loss to the company.

4. In addition, the annual contract system is thought to be inapplicable to those who are expected to work in a team, although it might be applied in jobs such as salesmen.

For all these reasons, if one asks whether payment-by-results systems will prevail in Japan, the answer is both 'yes' and 'no'.

Certainly it is true that at the start of the Heisei era (1989) too rapid expansion in the economy was halted by the bursting of the economic bubble. As a result the recruitment climate became very grim even for computer science engineers. Land prices fell in Tokyo and other large cities. Many large companies have since been having a hard time. Their responses, to give some examples, were as follows.

1. Sony, a 130 000 employee, giant employer faces the most serious crisis in the company's history due to the high yen rate and the stagnant film business in the USA. Chairman Akio Morita falls seriously ill. Norio

Ohga takes over as Chairman and gives his previous position of company President to 57 year old Nobuyuki Idei, passing over 14 of the most senior executives.

2. Nissan decide to introduce a new salary system in 1996 in which ability is the prime consideration, rather than seniority. This may influence the Japanese wage system and the annual so-called *Shunto* – the 'spring offensive', when at the beginning of spring there are large-scale national negotiations on wage increases; this is the basis on which almost identical wages are paid across a particular industry.

3. Suzuki Motor are introducing performance-related pay, initially for managers aged 55 years and over; this will be extended to all managerial staff within a few years.

4. Sanyo are starting a new flexible working system for their sales division staff. Each salesman is freed from the standard 9.00 a.m. to 5.00 p.m. working time and instead can arrange his working hours as he wishes. Another company which has introduced flexi-time has been Fuji Xerox, where all employees have to be present from 10.00 a.m. to 3.00 p.m., with flexibility at other times.

Opportunities are changing for women too!

Chikako Yokoyama is 39 years old and has just graduated from the Japanese author's Polytechnic University of Japan (PUJ) with a masters' degree in instructing at a vocational college. She is an enthusiastic learner and looks much younger than her actual age, perhaps because of her hobby – playing a swan as an amateur ballerina.

She is one of between 30 and 40 female students who enrol on this course each year. However, while most of them entered the PUJ as high school graduates, she has a more interesting background. After obtaining a masters' degree in medieval English history (the Anglo-Saxon period), with special reference to the feudal landownership system, at Tokyo Metropolitan University, she started her career working as a secretary – like many other women graduates. After 3 years she became a teacher at a technical high school teaching modern society, world history, English typing, and Japanese wordprocessor practice. She was in charge of a homeroom of third-year male students, who were absorbed with talking about motor cars. In order to understand their minds more deeply, she decided to study automobile maintenance and attended a vocational school for a year.

It was there that she learnt about the PUJ and decided to apply to study a degree majoring in automotive engineering. After completing her 4 year degree, she went on to the graduate course and studied engines (her thesis was on the two-stroke engine).

During her first year as a student at the PUJ she sent her daughter Mariko to a kindergarten. She now tells how, as Mariko grew older, she was able to help by, for example, folding washed clothes while Chikako was writing up her assignment reports after each practical session at the PUJ.

Her views on the different learning environments she has experienced are also interesting. She says that, compared with her former university, the PUJ provides a better environment in which students and teaching staff can work together closely and easily. In normal Monbusho universities students are trained to use their brains, but do not learn how to use their hands. She wanted to learn practical skills using both hands and brain and has been very satisfied with her experience at the PUJ.

One of her policies is to take a regular holiday with her husband and daughter. (When they go camping twice a year, they take their pet rabbit and duck.) Even though it is difficult in Japan to take a holiday whenever you want, they had the courage to do so; this holiday was to go near to Alaska to look at the aurora, even though her husband risked being fired by his company and her daughter had to miss a week of school. Chikako was very pleased when her daughter was highly impressed by nature's magnificent phenomenon of the aurora. She is grateful to Mariko for her co-operation in helping her to complete her PUJ studies successfully and has promised her more holidays abroad – on Safari in Africa, the Amazon, and Egypt.

She has now been sent by the Employment Promotion Corporation to be an instructor in Oyama, some 3 hours journey from her home in Tokyo. This is an example of *Tanshin-funin* – the Japanese practice of transferring many employees to a work location far from their homes, often for several years at a time.

The effectiveness of the Equal Opportunity Law, passed in May 1985 and put into effect in April 1986, can be measured in part by the following statistics:

In 1985: 15,480,000 (= 35.9%) women were employed, compared to 27,640,000 males.

In 1994: 20,340,000 (= 38.8%) women were employed, compared to 32,020,000 males.

The comparison by type of industry for the percentage of women employed shows a remarkable decrease in manufacturing industry, but an increase in services.

	Secondary industry (manufacturing)	Tertiary industry (services)
1985	28.1%	30.0%
1994	23.1%	33.0%

As was noted in Chapter 8, most women resign on marriage or when giving birth to their first child. However, many of these later return to work. Nevertheless, it is still difficult for them to be employed as a normal employee due to the concept of lifetime employment. In this respect there is still discrimination against women. On the other hand, lifelong employment is also applied to benefit or protect a woman and her children, for example if her husband dies, by offering her employment in a suitable position. Japanese governmental organizations, for instance, often apply this approach and some such situations have occurred in the Japanese author's university.

Without order and hierarchy the Japanese are prone to collapse!

The above examples of changes in personnel and wage systems, opportunities for women, and even the taking of holidays in defiance of company rules are particularly significant in a Japan which traditionally has been a well-ordered and obedient nation.

For those intending to collaborate with the Japanese or indeed those aiming to use this book to compete with them commercially, it is difficult to overemphasize the need they have for structure. In the North Burma campaign in the Second World War, for example, the Japanese army lost only 142 troops that were captured by the British, compared to 17 166 killed, and most of those were unconscious or wounded at the time. In the case of most Western armies, surrender usually occurs when between one-quarter and one-third of the force is killed. Instead of this 3:1 or 4:1 ratio of captured to killed, the Japanese ratio in Burma was reversed and at an extraordinary 1:120.[1] However, in contrast to this total dedication to fighting to the death, according to the orders they had received, the situation became quite different once captured. At that point they saw themselves as dishonoured and no longer Japanese. They had received no orders as to what to do in the event of capture and the effect was dramatic:

Some men asked to be killed, 'but if your customs do not permit this, I will be a model prisoner'. They were better than model prisoners. Old Army hands and long-time extreme nationalists located ammunition dumps, carefully explained the dispositions of Japanese forces, wrote our propaganda and flew with our bombing pilots to guide them to military targets. It was as if they had turned over a new page; what was written on the new page was the opposite of what was written on the old, but they spoke the lines with the same faithfulness.[2]

One consequence of this need for order and structure is that Japanese companies bring many more people to meetings than one would find in the West. This is partly because they like doing things professionally and having all those with the necessary expertise present and partly because they want to keep everyone in their organization fully informed and involved. You will find that your Japanese hosts will have taken enormous trouble to prepare their questions, negotiating position, and so on, in advance; any foreign visitor, host, or negotiator who does not arrive similarly prepared should not be surprised if they do not succeed in achieving their objectives.

One British managing director of a large company commented 'In negotiating a major capital purchase from Japan and in the various stages of installation and commissioning, I was impressed by how professional the Japanese were. No meeting would close without drafting and typing out minutes which both parties signed there and then.'

Remember that the Japanese only respect professionalism and strength.

A military approach to industry

One of the misconceptions about Japan is the common belief that there is such a wide cultural distance from the West that there are few lessons from their success which are transferable. This is largely nonsense. One of the striking similarities in the West to the Japanese approach in industry is itself an outstanding example of professionalism, with a long history of triumphs – the British armed forces. As Ronald Dore comments in his book *British factory – Japanese factory*.

Hitachi's form of organisation is by no means foreign to Britain. It is very much the pattern of the British army or civil service. Japan's peculiarity lies in the fact that a type of organisation which in most Western countries is adapted for the army or civil service is adapted in Japan to industry.[3]

The British author mentioned this comparison to Michael Howard, at that time Secretary of State for Employment, when introduced to him at a conference in Cambridge in 1990, shortly before the Secretary of State went to Japan on a study mission. His immediate reaction was that of most people in the West – that 'we would not want to organize British industry like the army'. In that, with respect, he is wrong, but he was interested enough to request a copy of the author's 1985 Winston Churchill Fellowship Report, which he kindly acknowledged. The point made by Ronald Dore is a vitally important one. After listing various similarities between Hitachi and the British army, including 'primary identification with the corps rather than the trade', 'great importance attaches to seniority', and 'familism', he goes on to say

The reader will recall several other points at which the word 'bureaucracy' was used in earlier chapters of the book – apropos of the greater formalisation of training in Hitachi; the greater reliance on explicit written instructions and records; the formal classification of circulars and instructions of different levels of authority; the emphasis on formal qualifications; the structuring of careers and the management of promotion by a mixture of seniority and merit criteria; the existence of a system of personal ranks separate from, but related to, hierarchy of functional offices – and so on.[4]

Teamwork, together with superb training and discipline, is what has made the British Army so effective, it is what has made Japanese industry so effective, and its absence is what is causing much of the European and American industries to lose the commercial war against Japan. The Matsuya store

Fig. 11.3 A Matsuya store manager leading his staff from the front.

manager shown in Figure 11.3 is leading his staff from the front, in exactly the same way as British officers have so successfully led their troops over the centuries.

Too much bureaucracy in Japan

According to a study by Keidanren, (quoted by Akio Morita in his keynote speech referred to in the next paragraph) 40 per cent of Japanese businesses are subjected to administrative regulation. The price of non-regulated goods has come down as a result of the increasing value of the yen, but at the same time the cost of regulated goods has remained constant.

If the regulatory regime is to be relaxed, then many Japanese ideas must be changed radically. For example, when an accident happens, people blame the government, which in response introduces yet more administrative regulations. Akio Morita, President of Sony, has discussed this problem with President Clinton, as well as at a 1993 Germany–Japan economic symposium, at which he gave the keynote speech.[5] He admitted that the Germans have a similar view of Japan to that of the Americans. They are very frustrated by the trade imbalance between their two countries and argue that Japan's markets are not yet fully open. Both countries are becoming less and less tolerant of the

Japanese refrain of 'Be patient, we are endeavouring to open up our market. Please wait a little longer.' Morita argues that both Japan and Germany are bread manufacturers and they produce the same things. Why does a baker, he asks, have to buy bread from another baker?

The answer is probably that the Japanese 'baker' has become much stronger than the German 'baker'. There are now many Japanese 'bakers' and they are competing very successfully in North American and European markets at the expense of the native 'bakers' in those continents. But what is the truth of this allegation?

The story of Nidec – a world class company built on learning faster than the competition

In Chapters 4 and 5, for example, we looked at Nidec Corporation. Nidec and its group companies have, including overseas, 10 000 employees and manufacture small precision motors used in computer peripherals and business equipment. Shigenobu Nagamori, its Chairman, President, Chief Executive Officer, and founder, was one of the Japanese author's very first students when he started his final year project in 1966 in his poorly equipped laboratory. In his first class the topic of small AC motors used in tape-recorders was covered and the ten students were shown a model of the latest German model, which was, exceptionally, DC. Nagamori showed extraordinary interest in this German project.

The first assignment given to Nagamori was to translate a technical paper, published in German, on this type of motor. First thing the next morning, he was ready to discuss the paper; Shigenobu Nagamori had spent the entire night looking up words from a German dictionary so that he could translate the paper into Japanese. At that stage it was impossible to imagine that he would soon go on to overtake the predominant position held in the world market. For his final year project he was given training in the research and development department of a tape-recorder manufacturer. There he learned how to design conventional hysteresis motors and noticed the performance limitations of this type of machine.

He had worked for two companies for several years before he started Nidec, with the support of a fellow graduate who studied motor design as a student in the year behind him; he did not particularly distinguish himself as a student, but showed a brilliant talent in sales. Nagamori also recruited several mechanical engineers from his former university; they were well trained in workshop procedures and his most important policy was keeping to promised delivery dates.

Within a surprisingly short time, Nidec had caught up with a well-known German manufacturer and then went on to overtake it and become the world's number one company in that type of precision brushless DC motor.

The Japanese author recalls that, at the time he first showed his motor to Nagamori, the German supplier had the predominant market share in the USA.

In the Nidec brochure, in which Nidec's plants and facilities around the world are featured – including in Japan, the USA, China, Taiwan, Malaysia, Thailand, Singapore, and Germany – Mr Nagamori says

We at Nidec are a company of challengers. What do we do to gain our customers' satisfaction and confidence? We continue to challenge for a better solution to any problem that bears upon our customers' demands for satisfaction. This spirit has been our firm policy since we were founded. We started in business with nothing: no funds, and no facilities. However we had a big dream to establish a company which could develop, produce and sell products in the world market.

Nidec's 'Customer oriented' and 'Speed oriented' attitude has been working in our favour since our first days as a company. It's also an active principle in all our work, backed up by the 'can do' spirit of Nidec.

Japan is full of examples such as this. Does the West, therefore, have any real justification for continuing to complain so continually about 'unfair competition' from Japan? Is it not time, instead, that the West re-examined its whole approach to its lifelong learning processes?

Parallels with the matchlock gun and transistor

One thing in which the West has always been consistent is in the way in which it has repeatedly underestimated the Japanese – and continues to do so. There are interesting parallels between the current dispute between the West and Japan over trade imbalance and the introduction of the matchlock gun into Japan some four and a half centuries ago.

The record of the arrival of the gun with the Portuguese at Tanegashima Island (off the southern Japanese island of Kyushu) was described by a Buddhist priest writing in 1606 as follows:

At 6.00 pm on the evening of 25 August Tenbun 12 (1543), a large ship arrived at our village Nishiura Koura. Its country of origin was unknown. It had a crew of 100 and more, whose appearance was unlike ours and whose speech was not understood; they appeared quite mysterious to all who beheld them . . . They carried an object, some two or three feet in length. It was hollowed out, though needing to be sealed at the bottom. At its side was a small hole, a passage to conduct fire. Nothing was known that could be compared to it. A powerful powder was placed inside it and a lead ball was added . . . Taking the proper stance, by closing one eye, and firing through the hole, it was possible to strike a target immediately without a single miss. Lord Tokitaka looked at this and found it a most rare thing. In the beginning, its name was unknown and its usage was not detailed.

In fact only three of the crew of 100 were Portuguese and the rest Chinese. The Portuguese were hired by a Chinese international merchant named Wang.

Lord Tokitaka was then a 16 year old boy, but decided to buy two guns in return for a very large amount of gold; communicating in writing (the normal way in which educated Japanese in those days could converse with Chinese, since the spoken languages are so different), Lord Tokitaka said to the Portuguese through Wang's interpretation, 'I don't mean that I wish to possess this artefact, but I would like to learn about it.' He then let one of his men learn about how to produce gunpowder, while a swordsmith studied the manufacture of the gun. (It is thought that these guns had been manufactured somewhere in South East Asia, not in Europe.) A man from Negoroji Temple, in what is now Wakayama Prefecture, visited the island to ask Tokitaka to sell him one gun. Because of his enthusiasm, Lord Tokitaka gave him one and told him to devise a means of manufacturing gunpowder. Later, Matazō Tsubakiya, a merchant from Sakai, stopped over on the island on the way from trading in Ryuku (present-day Okinawa) and remained there for almost 2 years to learn everything possible about the gun. On returning to the port town of Sakai, Matazō began manufacturing guns. This arrival of the matchlock gun in Japan had significant effects since it happened during the Civil War Age, when the central control by the Muromachi Bakufu had become weak and local *daimyōs* were fighting each other to expand their territories and influence.

When the Portuguese returned to Japan in 1545, they found guns being manufactured in great quantities in Sakai, Wakayama, and Kyushu. A further 10 years later, they found that there were 30 000 guns in the Kokura clan's province.

This story is very similar, too, to the arrival of the transistor in Japan following its invention in the Bell Laboratory, as described on p. 180. Japan is now a silicon archipelago. From the mid-1970s the export of Japanese semiconductor devices to the USA expanded considerably and, as a result, a trade crisis developed between the two countries.

A major difference between the semiconductor and the gun was the effect on foreign trade. The Japanese matchlock guns were mainly produced for the domestic market and caused a drastic change in the history of Japan. Some classic guns were exported to the continent of Asia, but this was a relatively minor aspect. The important fact is that Japanese swordsmith technology at that time was sufficiently advanced to be adapted to the 'mass production' of the new Western weapon. This then led in turn to the isolation of Japan; because of the gun, the civil wars between the lords of the Muromachi Bakufu ended quickly and the final victory was won by Ieyasu, who founded the Tokugawa Bakufu (see p. 12). For his final battles he even produced cannons over 3 metres long. Ieyasu also constructed a large boat under the guidance of William Adams (1564–1620). After Ieyasu's death in 1616, however, his successor decided to ban the construction of large sea-faring boats to commence Japan's isolation.

During the 250 years of the Tokugawa era, the invention and improvement of tools were not allowed since it was considered that these were causes of social change and could lead to the collapse of the long-term peace in Japan. Instead, the skills of using conventional tools for producing fine artefacts advanced.

Come in through the narrow entrance and enjoy yourself

Another important influence from the West was Christianity. The port town of Sakai, near present-day Osaka, was like a town state and prosperous as a result of foreign trade during the eras of civil war. A merchant called Sen'no Rikyū (1522–1591), who was a genius, was successful in systematizing the Japanese art of the tea ceremony, unifying the Chinese religious philosophy of Zen with Christianity.

'Come in through the narrow entrance! The large entrance will lead to your collapse.' This is the first message of the tea ceremony.

When the tea ceremony is performed, the guest enters a small cottage through its *nijiri-guchi* or 2 foot square entrance. A samurai warrior, historically, could not pass through the *nijiri* entrance unless he took off his two swords and left them with his servant. Inside the cottage or a space separated from the secular world, social status is not an issue between the host and the guest. Instead, they must be broad minded, like the universe, in order to enjoy the relaxation of the tea ceremony.

Japan, too, must at times leave behind its swords of commercial warfare – the tools for and dedication to industrial victory. It must find ways of allowing its people the just fruits of their labours by increasing the time they can spend on hobbies and leisure. In that way they can enter through the *nijiri* and join the other nations around the world who put more emphasis on relaxation.

Some historical influences of the tea ceremony

When the battles between many *daimyōs* (lords) in the last stages of the Muromachi Bakufu were ended by the victory of Oda Nobunaga (1534–1582), peace returned to the country. Sen'no Rikyū (1522–1591) became influential as a tea connoisseur, as well as being a very successful merchant. Tea drinking became the highest form of pastime among the *daimyōs*. Rikyū was the mastermind of Toyotomi Hideyoshi (1537–1598), the successor to Nobunaga, as a tea master.

Eventually, however, Hideyoshi refused the narrow gate and gave Rikyū the order to commit *seppuku* (harakiri). Seven years later Hideyoshi died and a further 2 years after that in 1600 his successor was completely overcome in battle by Ieyasu and Hideyoshi's blood-line ended in 1614.

Tokugawa Ieyasu played an important role in bringing back Rikyū's successors to maintain the art of the tea ceremony. However, he was careful to learn the lessons from Hideyoshi and arranged things such that a tea master did not gain too much influence over the *daimyōs*.

In the Tokugawa era, tea was also enjoyed by the merchants. Social interaction between high-ranking samurai and rich merchants through the tea ceremony occurred towards the end of the civil wars and the beginning of the Edo period. When the merchants were placed at the bottom of the social order during the Edo period as part of the firm, war-free, feudal policy, rich merchants developed their own ways of enjoying tea amongst themselves. High-ranking samurai and the ruling family also developed their own ways, sometimes enjoying tea in the surrounding of magnificent gardens like Rikugi-en (in Tokyo) or the Katsura Detached Palace in Kyoto. The famous revenge by 47 Ako samurai on Lord Kira (who avenged the order for their master Lord Asano Naganori to commit *seppuku* in 1700 by killing the instigator of his death, Lord Kira, 2 years later and in their turn were ordered to commit *seppuku* – a classic Japanese legend of loyalty) took place on the snowy morning after a major tea ceremony at his palace.

Tea is a comprehensive art. For the apparently simple act of taking tea from a bowl, each aspect of the art, technique, and even religious philosophy used has its meaning: lacquered tea instruments, pottery, ironwork, paintings, calligraphy, and architecture, as well as the beauty of the garden. Interestingly, the concept of the narrow entrance is thought to have been taken from the teachings of the Portuguese missionaries.

As from some 15 years before the start of the Tokugawa Bakufu, Christianity was banned by the rulers of Japan and a large number of Roman Catholics were cruelly persecuted or even executed. However, the philosophy of people's equality in front of God has continued to live in Japan, concealing its explicity in a style of Zen in the tea ceremony.

From the tea ceremony to modern technology

The lords in the Edo era were patrons of skilled craftsmen, including tea ceremony utensil producers. This helped the rise in the production of various implements supported by the development of the merchant class. For example, samurai who were not required to go to the battlefield lived their spiritual life according to the principles of Bushido, which were formed in the Edo period, but spent some of their money on fine decoration for their swords and on drug containers they wore around their waists.

The greatest master of art (at the beginning of the Edo era) with an enormous spiritual influence on the craftsmen and artists who followed him was Hon'ami Kōetsu (1558–1637), who was also known as a sword craftsman and a connoisseur. He was granted large premises near Kyoto by Ieyasu and gathered his relatives, acquaintances, and craftsmen to manage the Kōetsu

Utopia. However, although Kōetsu was an excellent sword sharpener and a connoisseur, he is much better known for his foremost expertise in calligraphy, painting, ceramic art, and lacquerware.

There are some very exciting possibilities in exploring the relationship between the influence of traditional craftsmanship and Japanese successes in modern technology after the Meiji restoration. If we take account of Kōetsu's achievement in developing a modern style inspired by the classical art of the Heian period, we must examine a longer time span to see an overview of some further reasons for Japan's success. The root of classical art can be traced back to the Orient via the Silk Road, and modern science and engineering in Japan can be traced back to the West via British and American paths.

This subject is too large to deal with in a short chapter, but some key points need to be noted. It should be noted, for example, that special techniques were not open secrets amongst craftsmen, and they were very keen to 'steal' each other's techniques. The idea that the master is proud of his disciple's superiority is thought to have developed in Japanese society when the samurai ended and, in their place, the spirit of Bushido survived in modern organizations which were then mostly run by former lower-class, but diligent, samurai.

The spiritual environment or climate that could produce fine art may have contributed to the rapid progress of fine industries in modern Japan. For example, *raden* or mother-of-pearl lacquerware came from China via the Korean Peninsular, but it was in Japan that this technique was developed into a marvellously fine form of artwork. Korea, although it has had spectacular economic growth, has not yet been successful in the manufacture of fine dies, which are a key part in the production of precision stepping motors.

Okumura says in his book *From matchlock gun to the black ship*

Towards the end of the Tokugawa Bakufu and the beginning the Meiji era, competent people were produced in various areas. The technical area is no exception. There were many engineers who had struggled to accomplish the introduction of technology from the West. Under them, numerous craftsmen devoted themselves to this purpose. The broadness and depths of these people, the environments that produced them, the roles of clan schools in producing élites and those of the *terakoya* schools for education of the commoners, are all areas worthy of further examination. Furthermore, the root of social energy that yielded these capable people must be investigated further. The enthusiasm of the scholars who dedicated their whole lives to reading Dutch and English books to comprehend Western technology was by no means normal. The people's energy compressed during the 250 year isolation must have erupted through the outlet called *yōgaku* or Western Studies.[6]

It should be noted here that the Japanese tradition of apprenticeship established during the Tokugawa period did not vanish with the samurai class. As with the spirit of Bushido, its influence continued long after the Shoguns and samurai ended their rule in 1868. Apprenticeships continued until the mid-1950s; the national tradition of fine art thus maintained must have been a firm basis on which modern technology grew. In other words, without the craftsmanship of the Edo period, Japan's industrial modernization would not have been as successful as it actually was.

Another point is that such apprenticeships were certified only at skill levels and did not extend to higher academic levels such as degrees. Hence, the social status of craftsmen was not and is not high. Instead it could be left to the highly educated graduate élite to effect Japan's conversion quite easily to the latest scientific approaches. In this respect the 1958 Vocational Training Law may have been very effective. In contrast, Britain's approach to technology has always been based on the concept of craftsmanship (including the word 'engineer', for example, implying a lower level activity than the European 'ingenieur', which implies the ingenuity arising naturally from the well educated) and has always had great difficulty in attaining any form of technological leadership. Indeed, it is clear that British industry is now increasingly looking to the Japanese for salvation.

It is very interesting to examine the effect of banning invention throughout the two centuries of Japan's isolation, compared with Japan's rapid progress after her borders were reopened in 1854. Perhaps the long tradition in Japan of concentrating on fine art technology centred around the tea ceremony could be a firm basis for precision engineering in Japan, just as swordsmith technology was adapted to the manufacture of guns.

Looking at the UK from a Japanese perspective

Since we started this book by seeing how the West helped Japan to industrialize and modernize in the last century, it is interesting to hear how a former Japanese ambassador to the UK, Hiroshi Kitamura, sees the UK. In a lecture entitled 'European Trends Seen From the UK'[7] he made the following key points.

1. Forty-three per cent of Japanese investment in the European Union's 12 countries has been in the UK. The Japanese have built 280 factories, providing jobs for 70 000 people. Betweeen 70 and 80 per cent of the cars and high-tech products from these factories are being exported to Europe.
2. The reasons for such a high investment in Britain are the language, the City, and the high quality of labour available at low wages; in particular in the mining areas of Wales and Newcastle, there is a spiritual heritage of industriousness. There are many Oxbridge graduates in the senior layers of management, who are excellent as individuals.
3. One weakness, however, is inadequacy in the middle layers of management's practical communicating skills between management and workers, adjusting objectives in the production areas and in training the workers.
4. There is a need in the UK for polytechnic colleges like Japan's Kōsen.

5. What the British really appreciate in the Japanese is their management–labour relationship, rather than her production technology or management know-how. In Japanese-owned firms in the UK, not a single day has been lost through strikes.

6. The Anglo-Japanese link is not just a matter for these two countries. Rather it has wider meaning, since Japan's massive investment in the UK is aimed not only at the British market, but more at a Europe which is reinforcing its unification. Japan expects Britain will guide the European market on how to trade openly. The present Anglo-Japanese relationship is unlike former Anglo-Japanese alliances, which were only for limited (usually militarily strategic) purposes; rather it is much more broadly economic and political.

7. When the Iraquis withdrew from Kuwait, there was the possibility of booby traps in the Japanese embassy and envoys' houses. It was the British army that investigated this and confirmed they were safe. Even though poison gas masks were necessary for the Japanese there, they could not be exported from Japan because of regulations which treated this type of mask as a weapon. Instead the Japanese borrowed masks from the British army.

8. What he most envies is the way in which young Oxford/Cambridge graduates can be candidates in general elections by depositing a sum of £1000. In Japan political reform is proceeding, but it is too complicated. When seen from abroad, its direction is unclear. Its image is one which begs the question: 'What are the Japanese doing?' The Japanese have thus far been confident that businessmen and bureaucrats can carry the nation irrespective of poor politics. Until now there has been no perception that politics could ruin Japan's economy. However, in the future there is such a possibility. Once the image that Japan is politically unstable prevails abroad, cracks will penetrate into the Japanese overseas economy, no matter how good Japanese products are. (A Japanese idiom says that once a crack penetrates, things begin to decay.)

The Japanese are becoming disillusioned with politicians

Nothing better illustrates the disillusionment of the Japanese with their politicians than the election of two independent and anti-establishment candidates in April 1995 as Governors of Tokyo and Osaka, the two largest and most important metropolitan areas in Japan. One was a former comedian and the other a former television personality. Both soundly beat the candidates of the major parties.

Yukio Aoshima, a former Upper House member and TV personality did not even bother to campaign, spending most of his time at home. He easily beat

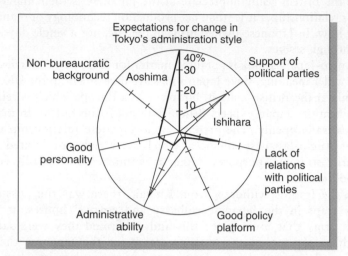

Fig. 11.4 Voters reasons for supporting Aoshima or Ishihara. *Source: Asahi Evening News*, 10 April 1995, p. 1.

his main rival, Nobuo Ishihara, a former Deputy Chief Cabinet Secretary (the nation's top bureaucratic post) who was supported by five parties, including the Liberal Democratic Party, the Social Democratic Party of Japan, and Komei. In Osaka, Knock Yokoyama, best known as a television personality and comedian, although he had won four 6 year terms as an Upper House member since 1968, used a noodle shop which he used to patronize – which is now closed – as his office. He hired no campaign staff; instead his family members and volunteers took turns with the office work. He used a bicycle to ride around Osaka to campaign – a routine which left him grimy, prompting him to soak in a public bath with some of his constituents in the evenings. Like Yukio Aoshima in Tokyo, he won a landslide victory, in his case against Takuya Hirano, a former Vice-Minister of the Science and Technology Agency, who was also supported by five major parties.

Figure 11.4 shows the reasons given by the voters for supporting Aoshima or Ishihara. Clearly there will be further political changes in Japan in the years to come. How these will affect Japan's competitiveness in the world remain to be seen.

The real competition to Japan comes from South East Asia

As Table 11.1 shows, Japan's economy has fared extremely well over recent decades in comparison with Western economies.

However, this is not where Japan's real competition now lies. The 'Dynamic

Table 11.1. Asian countries catching up on the G7

	Growth rates %				
	1970–1990	1991	1992	1993	1994
G7	2.7	0.7	1.6	1.3	2.8
America	2.6	–1.2	2.1	2.6	3.1
Japan	4.1	4.0	1.3	1.0	3.3
Britain	2.2	–2.2	–0.6	1.8	2.9
Dynamic Asians	8.0	7.5	5.7	6.4	6.9
South Korea	8.2	8.4	4.7	6.0	6.5
Taiwan	8.4	7.2	6.1	6.5	7.0
Hong Kong	7.2	4.2	5.0	5.5	6.0
Singapore	8.4	6.7	5.8	6.8	7.0

Source: OECD

Asians', otherwise known as the Tiger Economies, are now growing at a rate twice as fast as Japan. China is growing even faster, particularly in the area bordering Hong Kong and Macau; in this area economic growth is of the order of 25 per cent per annum.

In March 1995 the Governor of Hong Kong, Chris Patten, told the Fortune Global Forum in Singapore that, with just 6 million people, Hong Kong accounted for 26 per cent of China's economy and was richer per head than Britain, Canada, and Australia.

What does Japan face, therefore, over the next few decades in terms of competition from a newly invigorated China of 1200 million people, let alone from the Tiger Economies?

Japan has yet to come to terms with information technology

The Internet, the network connecting tens of millions of computers around the world, is a good example of the difficulties Japan faces in the field of information technology. The 1995 figures of the Internet Society showed that Japan had just 96 632 host computers connected to the Internet, compared to 241 191 in Britain, 207 717 in Germany, and over 2 million in America.

The Japanese Government has made efforts to encourage use of the Internet including holding a national e-mail day. Yet, when in 1994 the Telecommunications Minister unveiled plans for an 'info-communications infrastructure', it soon became obvious that he did not even know what an electronic mailbox is!

Table 11.2 Correlation of GNP to Internet hosts, 1995

Iceland	1.67
USA	2.79
Sweden	3.80
UK	5.93
Germany	10.03
France	15.30
Slovenia	35.37
Japan	43.38
Ecuador	44.92
Iran	22 500
Saudi Arabia	104 000

Source: *Daily Telegraph*, 11 April 1995, p. 14.

One difficulty facing the Japanese in this area is the fact that 90 per cent of communications over the network are in English, while it is difficult to use Japanese on it. Another problem is that fewer than one in ten offices in Japan are computerized, while at home the computers generally used by the Japanese are dedicated word processors and games consoles which cannot be connected to the Internet.

Therefore, in many ways, the Japanese are not as computer literate as many might assume. There are also cultural issues involved; for example, Murota Masaki, head of NTT Data in London, says 'Japanese companies are very hierarchical. The free exchange of opinion that e-mail encourages conflicts with that.'

The correlation of GNP to Internet hosts is shown in Table 11.2 and shows how surprisingly low Japan scores.

One of the areas of work in which the British author is involved is in the development of Personal Development Planner software such as that shown in Figure 11.5. The advantages of such software is that in many ways it emulates the Japanese learning processes, directly linking learning experiences to competencies, for example, and acting as a corporate skills database. Given the Japanese weaknesses in software and the West's strengths in this area, could this type of approach at last give other nations some comparative advantage in the learning process?

Another very significant use of software in the West is the use of groupware, particularly Lotus Notes. It is likely that such software, with enormous implications for sharing knowledge and learning, will not be much used in Japan. On the other hand, there is equally evidence that the West does not have the learning processes in place to make the best use of groupware. There is much potential there for both Japan

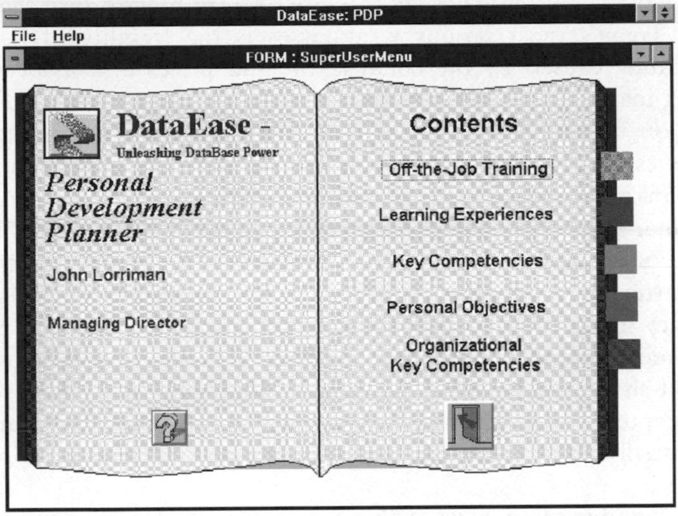

Fig. 11.5 Sample of Personal Development Plan software developed by the British author.

and the West to learn from each other in this area, to their mutual advantage.

Banzai – '10 000 years'!

On the other hand, one of Japan's great strengths is that her people, her companies and her governments take a long-term view. It is no coincidence that the traditional cry is 'Banzai' – meaning '10 000 years'. In the West a long-term view by a company is between 2 and 5 years; in Japan it is for between 15 and 250 years.

But Japan does have some fundamental weaknesses!

Let us conclude by giving some hope to Japan's competitors. The over-reliance on systems and structures is ultimately a major weakness. When the seasons change in the spring and autumn, for example, the Japanese all wear the new season's clothes on the same first day, whatever the weather.

In Britain people use their initiative in a way that would be unthinkable in Japan and that is why the British armed forces, using all the similar traditions to Japanese industry in other respects, were able to achieve the seemingly impossible in recovering the Falkland Islands from the Argentinians in 1982, a feat which would almost certainly have been beyond the Japanese.

The tragedy for Western industry is that they have allowed Japan to win in many ways by default; it is not yet too late to learn how to turn the tide!

One of Japan's most serious weaknesses is the fragility of its banking system, mainly caused by the collapse of land prices and associated non-performing loans.

In addition, the recession in Japan post-1990 has been very different from the previous ones after the end of the Second World War; not only manufacturers, but also banks, the stock exchange and real-estate agents have been having a difficult time. To overcome this recession, Japan needs to change its industrial structure. For example, sub-contractor companies – normally wholly depend-ent on a particular sub-contracting company for the designs and specifications of what they manufacture – are having to become independent in producing their own designs and tapping new markets. Reliable, low-cost production is going off-shore and Japanese industry is 'hollowing-out'. However, as we saw in Chapter 9, the Japanese are a much more innovative nation than they are usually given credit for, and they are seeking new ways to display their talents.

And yet Japan in many ways is also a tired nation. At the beginning of this chapter we described how both authors travelled in June 1994 to a lifelong learning conference on the outskirts of Tokyo. On the train travelling there, the British author found himself sitting next to a teenage uniformed Japanese schoolgirl in the middle of a weekday afternoon. Her eyes slowly shut, her head started nodding, and eventually she fell asleep on his left shoulder! On his right-hand side sat a typical Japanese 'salaryman' in his suit, holding his briefcase. His eyes too started to shut, his head nodded, and he dozed on the author's right shoulder. At the conference he quoted this as symbolic of the exhaustion many Japanese suffer from throughout their lives. Thus, the typical Japanese 'salaryman' is tired with his daily business combat, high school pupils are exhausted from cramming for university entrance exams, and university students are lethargic. One of the challenges facing Japan, therefore, is to raise the quality of life in ways other than those they have so far adopted. As Figure 11.6 shows the Japanese are increasingly looking for spiritual fulfilment instead of material wealth.

But there can be no complacency in the West!

In the *Daily Telegraph* newspaper on the 13 April 1995, there was an article by John Casey, a Fellow of Gonville and Caius College, Cambridge University. He finished it by writing ironically

So there you have it: a regimented society which subordinates the individual to the group, and sets little value on self expression; an educational system overwhelmingly based on rote-learning; a people who still cherish a sense of their own uniqueness. The

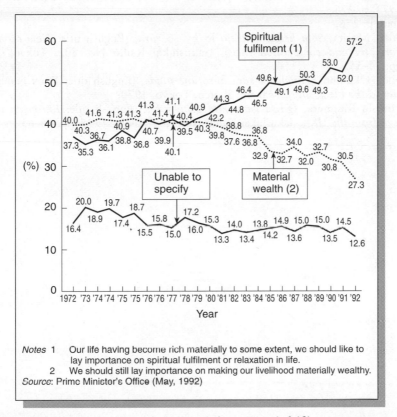

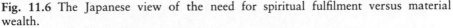

Fig. 11.6 The Japanese view of the need for spiritual fulfilment versus material wealth.

result is a prosperous, peaceful people, with no underclass and no vandalism. They must surely have gone wrong somewhere.

Other nations, particularly in the West, can justifiably criticize many aspects of Japan. But, as John Casey's last sentence humorously illustrates, the ultimate message is that Japan continues to have the edge in many of the areas which really matter – and particularly in the three winning margins of management, training, and education.

References

1 Ruth Benedict, *The chrysanthemum and the sword*, Charles E. Tuttle Company, Rutland, Vermont 1954, p. 38.
2 Ibid. p. 41.

3 Ronald Dore, *British factory – Japanese factory*, University of California Press, 1973, p. 275.
4 Ibid. p. 276.
5 Akio Morita, *Shin keizai chitsujo to kyōsō rūru*, (English title: *New economic harmony and competition rules*), Gakushikai Kaihō No. 802, Tokyo, 1994, pp. 44–55.
6 Shōji Okumura, *Hinawajū kara kurofune made*, (English title: *From matchlock gun to the black ship*), Iwanami Shoten, Tokyo, 1970.
7 Hiroshi Kitamura, *Igirisu kara mita ōshū jōsei*, (English title: *European trends seen from the UK*), Gakushikai Kaihō No. 807, Tokyo, 1995, pp. 48–63.

INDEX

Abe, Shintarō 34
Adams, William 13, 226
adapting 1, 2, 178, 183
Aeon Group 7
ageism 102
Agricultural College, Sapporo 40, 175
Air Conditioning Services Ltd 73, 166
Akihito, Emperor 11, 31
Alcan 83
   British 81
Alcan Aluminium 81
Alexander, Lamer 54
amakudari 155
American automobile industry 185
American Western Electric 35
Aoki, Ihei 214
Aoshima, Yukio 217, 231, 232
appraisals 198–200
apprentices 93–4, 140
apprenticeship 135–6, 140, 229
Asakawa, Dr Shigeru 111
Asahara, Shōkō 211
AT&T 35, 98
Aum sect 211, 213
Australia 233
Ayrton, William 25, 26–7

Bakufu 12, 15, 226, 227
Balz, Erwin 28
banzai 235
Barings Bank 211
Battle of Tsushima 2
Becker, Boris 81
Bell Laboratory 226
Bienkowska, Christina 50
Blake, Ted 89
bottom-up 92, 100
British army 222, 231
British Chamber of Commerce,
   Japan 185

buchō 161
Buddhism 11
Burton, William K. 27
Bush, George 185
Bushido 14, 16–19, 228, 229

Canada 233
Capron, Brigadier-General Horace 24
career development 115, 152–69, 195
   198, 200
Casey, John 236–7
Chrysler 6
Civil War Age 13, 226
Clark, Rodney 42, 166
Clark, Rosy 50
Clark, William Smith 24
Clinton, President 223
colonialism 102–3
commercial battles 206
Conder, Josiah 27
'conferences' 109–10, 112, 154,
   195, 205
Confucian(ism) 11, 16–17, 49
crammer 41, 58

Dai-ichi Kangyo Bank 6
daimyō 12, 13, 15, 226, 227, 228
Daiwa Bank 212
Deming, W. Edwards 24, 33, 85
   Prize 118, 133
Denki Rōren (Japanese Federation of
   Electrical Machine Workers Unions)
   55–6, 96, 99, 120, 156–9, 161–3
distance learning 121
Doi, Takako 167
Dore, Ronald 222
Douglas, Commander Archibald 28
Dyer, Henry 1, 25–6, 36

earthquake (Kobe) 211, 212